FUN PASSOVER ACTIVITY BOOK

Puzzles and Games for 9-13 Year Old Boys & Girls

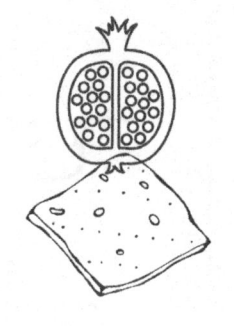

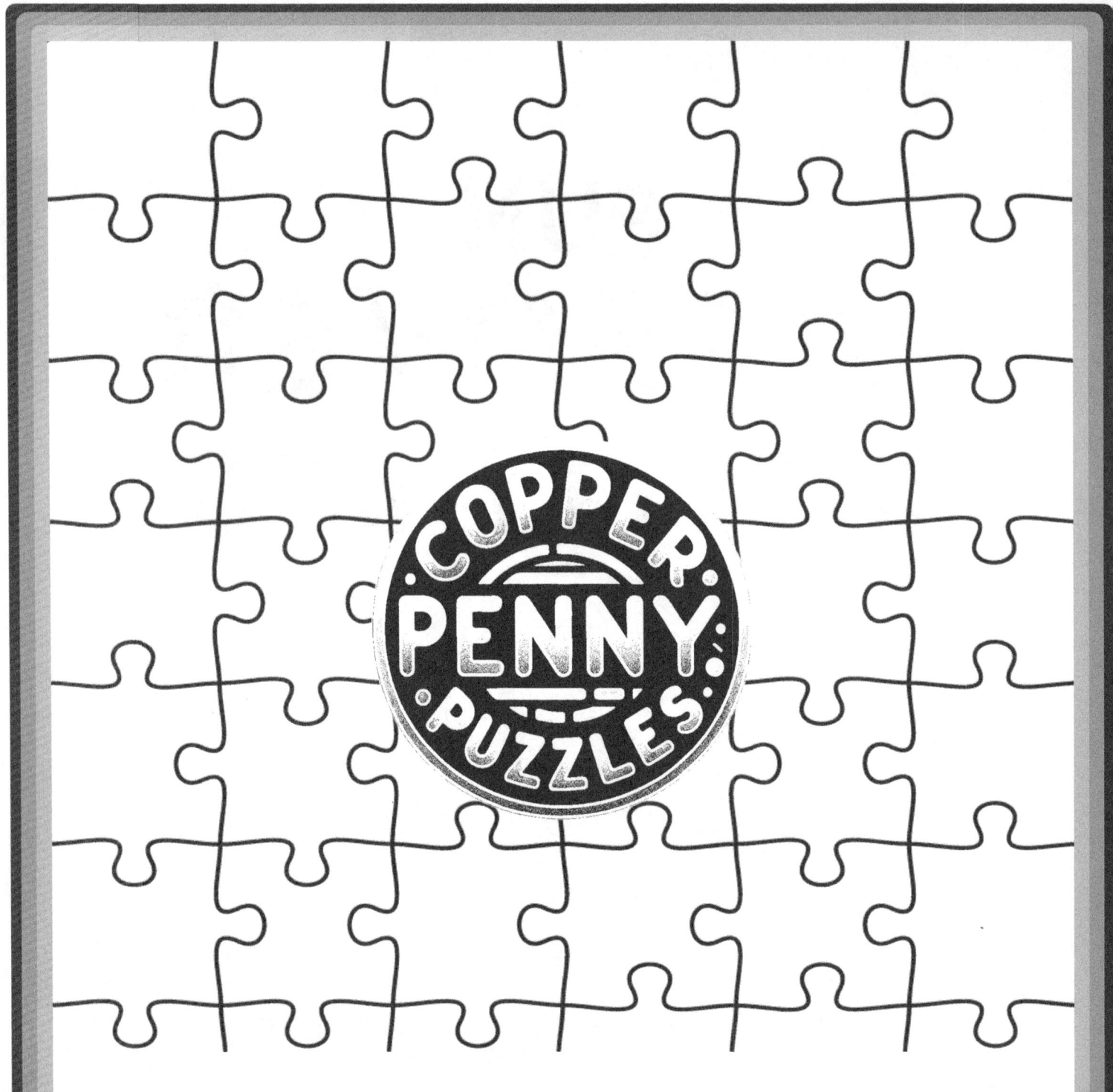

©2024CopperPennyPuzzles™. All rights reserved. No part of this book may be reproduced, stored in a retrieval system, or transmitted in any form or by any means, mechanical or electronic, including photocopying, recording and scanning, without permission in writing from the publisher. Unauthorized reproduction of any part of this publication is an infringement of copyright.

The designs, activities and information included in this book are for general purposes only. We try to keep the contents as accurate and up-to-date as possible, but there are no representations or warranties, express or implied, about the completeness, accuracy, suitability or availability of the information, graphics, and content contained within this book.

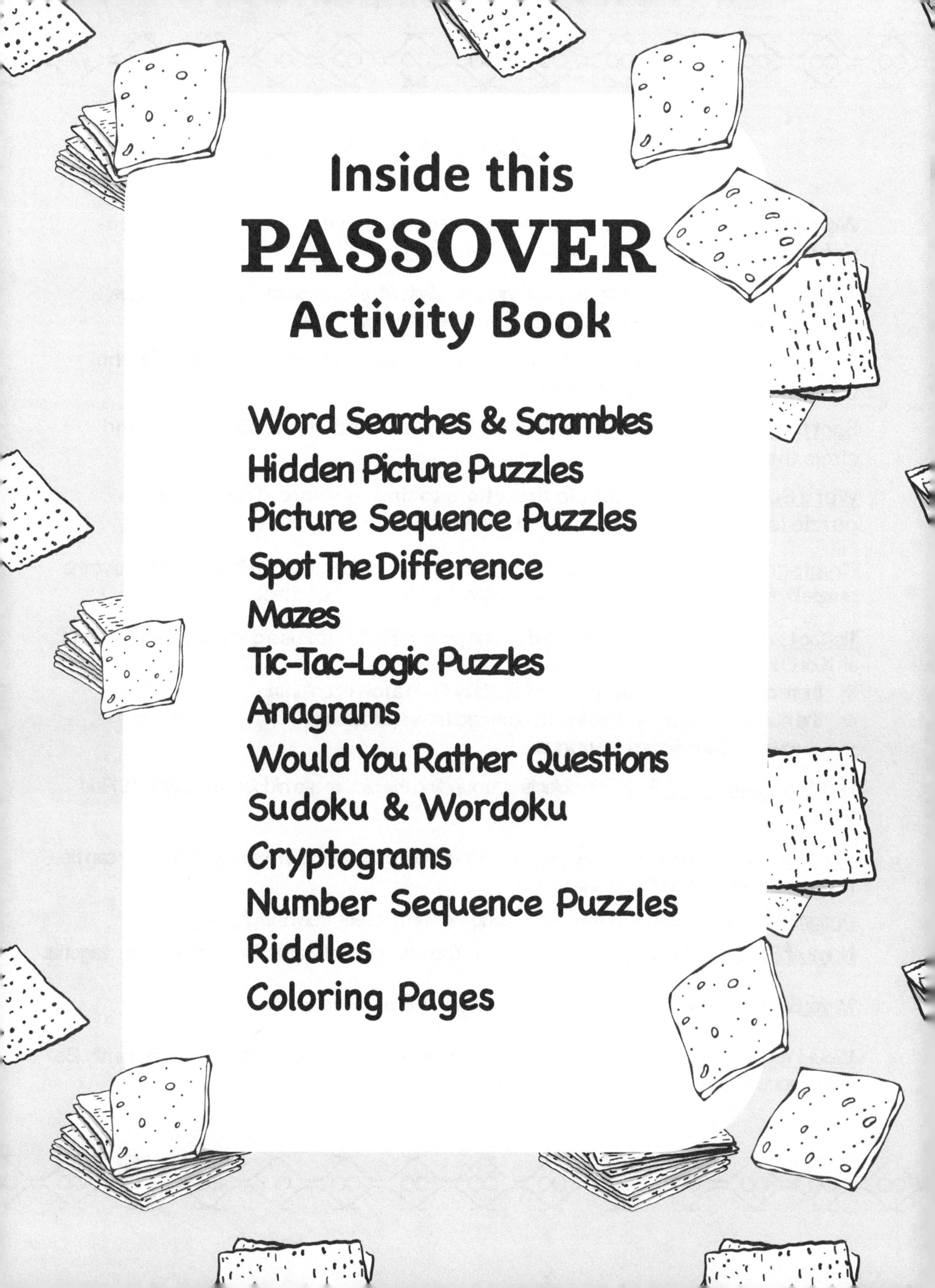

Inside this
PASSOVER
Activity Book

Word Searches & Scrambles
Hidden Picture Puzzles
Picture Sequence Puzzles
Spot The Difference
Mazes
Tic-Tac-Logic Puzzles
Anagrams
Would You Rather Questions
Sudoku & Wordoku
Cryptograms
Number Sequence Puzzles
Riddles
Coloring Pages

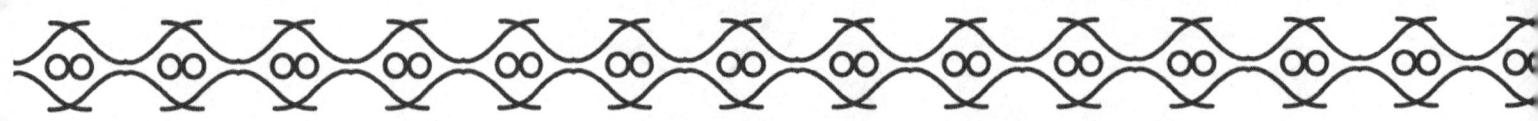

How To Solve The Puzzles

Word Search: Find words from the list by searching up-and-down, left-to-right and on the diagonal. Then circle them.

Sudoku: Each row, column, and square must be filled with the numbers 1-9 or with images one time each. Don't repeat any numbers or images in the row or column.

Wordoku: Each row, column and square must be filled with the letters of the given six letter word. No repeating.

Spot the difference: Compare the two images to find all the differences and circle them.

Word Scramble: Unscramble the letters to find the word. The title of the puzzle is a clue for the words that are scrambled.

Cryptograms: Codes where each letter of a phrase is substituted with a different letter. Solve the puzzle by figuring out what letter belongs in each spot on the alphabet table.

Tic-Tac-Logic: Like tic-tac-toe but played by one person. Each puzzle is a grid with Xs and Os. Puy an X or O in the remaining squares so that:
- there are no more than two consecutive Xs or Os in a row or column
- the number of Xs and Os are the same in each row and column
- all rows and all columns are unique.

Hidden Picture Puzzles: The objects surrounding the picture are hidden in the picture. Find them!

Picture Sequence Puzzles: Find the pictures of three identical objects in a straight line. They can be horizontal, vertical or on the diagonal.

Anagrams: Make at least one other word, using the same letters, from the given word.

Number Sequence: Find the string of numbers. They can be backwards, forward or on the diagonal.

Maze: Start at the entry point (arrow) and work your way to the exit (arrow)..

Would You Rather: Answer the questions by yourself or make it a game with friends and family. Be outrageous if you want. The object is to have fun!

Passover

```
C A R J B Q F V H H O L Y D A Y S
D I A N X O E Z D A Z Y A D H H K
J L E W T K P N L I J K N J S B E
Y S T S N V M L E G K I J E E C N
C D A F A L I G H T S A L L T S H
A E R L N X E O Q H S A C E I C O
Y L O I E O M D T T I A L W L R E
Z I M B V K M P U W F A A M E V N
Z V E E O I Y M E T C W J T A Q I
D E M R C G S R U I I R P C R S T
A R M A E H B B L O D V X P S B S
B A O T N E P B V H A K R U I R E
W N C I H C I G C P D M I E M V L
W C V O E B F A I I H O H O S W A
B E A N H N S Y T I N U M M O C P
Y B R R F E C K W B L B C D N Q A
O S X A P L V F T I Q T S L U I D
```

BIBLICAL   COMMEMORATE   COMMUNITY
COVENANT   DELIVERANCE   EGYPT
ELIJAH   HEBREW   HOLY DAYS
ISRAELITES   LIBERATION   LIGHTS
PALESTINE   PESACH   SERVITUDE

Solution on page 71

Seder Plate On The Table

Find One Word Word Search
Word To Find: CANDLE

N	C	L	E	A	E	D	A	N	A	N	N
E	L	C	L	E	N	C	N	N	E	A	A
E	L	L	C	L	A	A	A	D	A	C	D
L	L	D	D	A	N	C	D	A	D	L	N
D	L	D	A	N	N	L	E	L	C	A	D
A	A	D	E	A	A	D	E	N	D	N	L
N	C	D	N	L	A	C	L	N	C	N	L
A	A	E	N	N	A	L	N	E	L	L	L
C	C	D	D	C	L	N	N	L	L	N	D
C	C	L	D	L	E	A	A	A	N	N	C
E	N	D	A	L	E	C	A	L	L	E	C
N	L	L	D	N	C	A	D	C	E	C	D

Solution on page 75

Would you rather...

be stuck in car traffic for an hour or sit on a plane on the runway for an hour?

have the ability to fly like a bird or the ability to become invisible?

be able to teleport through space or land on the moon?

have super strength or a photographic memory?

have crazy itchy poison ivy or a burning red sunburn?

Find The Strings Of Numbers #1
They can be horizontal, vertical, on the diagonal and backwards, too!

0	5	2	4	9	9	9	3	0	4	0	1
9	0	9	4	3	6	6	3	0	3	6	5
7	6	5	7	1	4	4	5	0	3	2	3
1	1	3	5	6	9	4	4	8	5	9	1
4	1	9	0	7	9	9	0	7	6	2	3
3	6	1	9	1	8	6	8	6	6	4	1
8	3	1	8	2	0	4	5	0	5	3	2
8	5	0	9	4	5	4	3	7	5	3	9
3	1	6	3	2	3	0	8	8	3	0	0
6	2	6	6	8	3	4	6	1	6	2	5
0	9	7	0	3	4	2	6	6	2	8	3
2	6	6	6	8	3	0	6	5	6	8	0
5	1	7	5	5	1	7	8	0	5	4	8
9	0	2	9	8	0	8	7	6	8	2	6

- ☐ 6668
- ☐ 5663
- ☐ 0281
- ☐ 036
- ☐ 330
- ☐ 7199
- ☐ 557843
- ☐ 0656
- ☐ 434406

Solution on page 78

Cryptograms

Puzzle #1

A	B	C	D	E	F	G	H	I	J	K	L	M	N	O	P	Q	R	S	T	U	V	W	X	Y	Z
												I													

_ _ _
O C W

_ I
N E

_ _ I _
J C N E

_ _ _ I _
K N A C J

_ _ _ I _ _ _ _
Z N U U M X M K J

_ _ _ _
U X Q R

_ _ _
V P P

_ _ _ _ _
Q J C M X

_ _ _ I _ _
K N A C J E

Puzzle #2

A	B	C	D	E	F	G	H	I	J	K	L	M	N	O	P	Q	R	S	T	U	V	W	X	Y	Z
								B																	

B _ _ _ _ _ _
I L S K Y K A

B _ _ _
I L B Z

10 Solution on page 84

The History

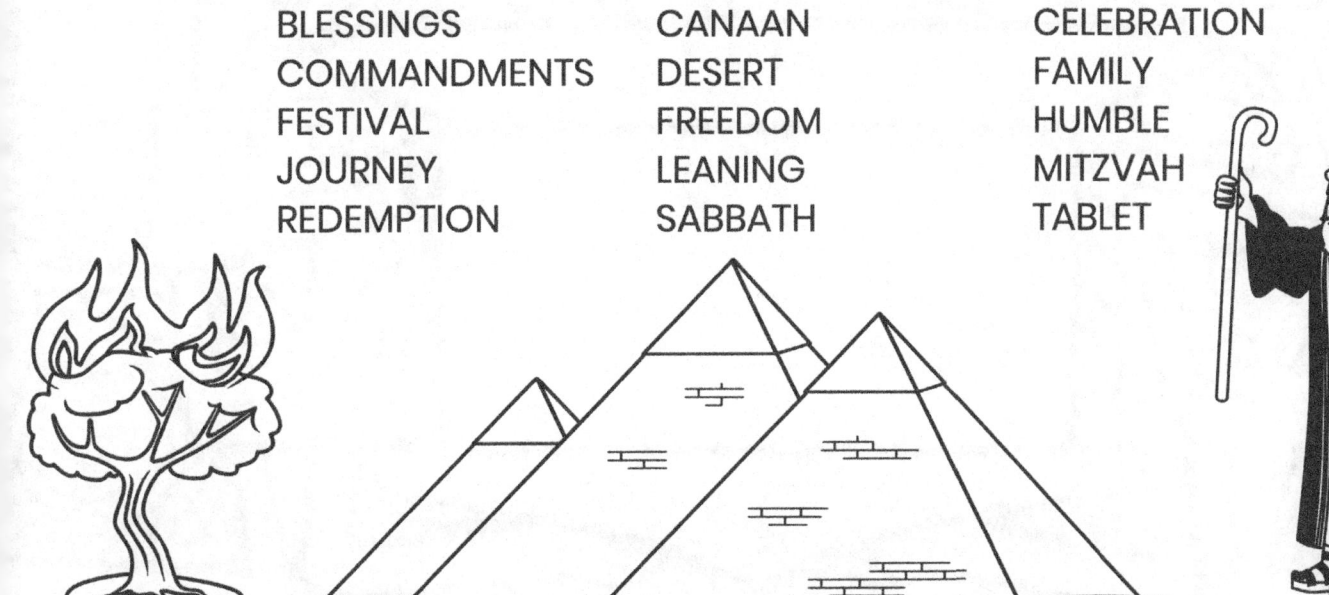

```
Y E X C C Y M B G M L G H M C A D
S F C I M P F X Q D Z U S X P E B
O N U E E Z M E O Q M P K L F P T
N X S J L K C G S B M J U H H V V
O W G N O E C P L T F U A B T R D
I V N P J H B E C F I V P F S Y B
T N I G D T I R A G Z V R D E H O
P O S H W A R M A T G E A N Y I B
M Z S T Y E I E I T E N R L C I J
E L E A X L M M S D I U I A S T F
D T L B Y I H J O E O O B N N U T
E N B B R F M M Q J D F N A A A E
R Y B A U Z M H L T D S P I K E G
K D V S C O M M A N D M E N T S L
L T Q T A B L E T K H J U L A M A
X K D C V O F N A A N A C U T C I
O O G I P M Y J F J L S I C Q M Q
```

BLESSINGS
COMMANDMENTS
FESTIVAL
JOURNEY
REDEMPTION
CANAAN
DESERT
FREEDOM
LEANING
SABBATH
CELEBRATION
FAMILY
HUMBLE
MITZVAH
TABLET

Solution on page 71

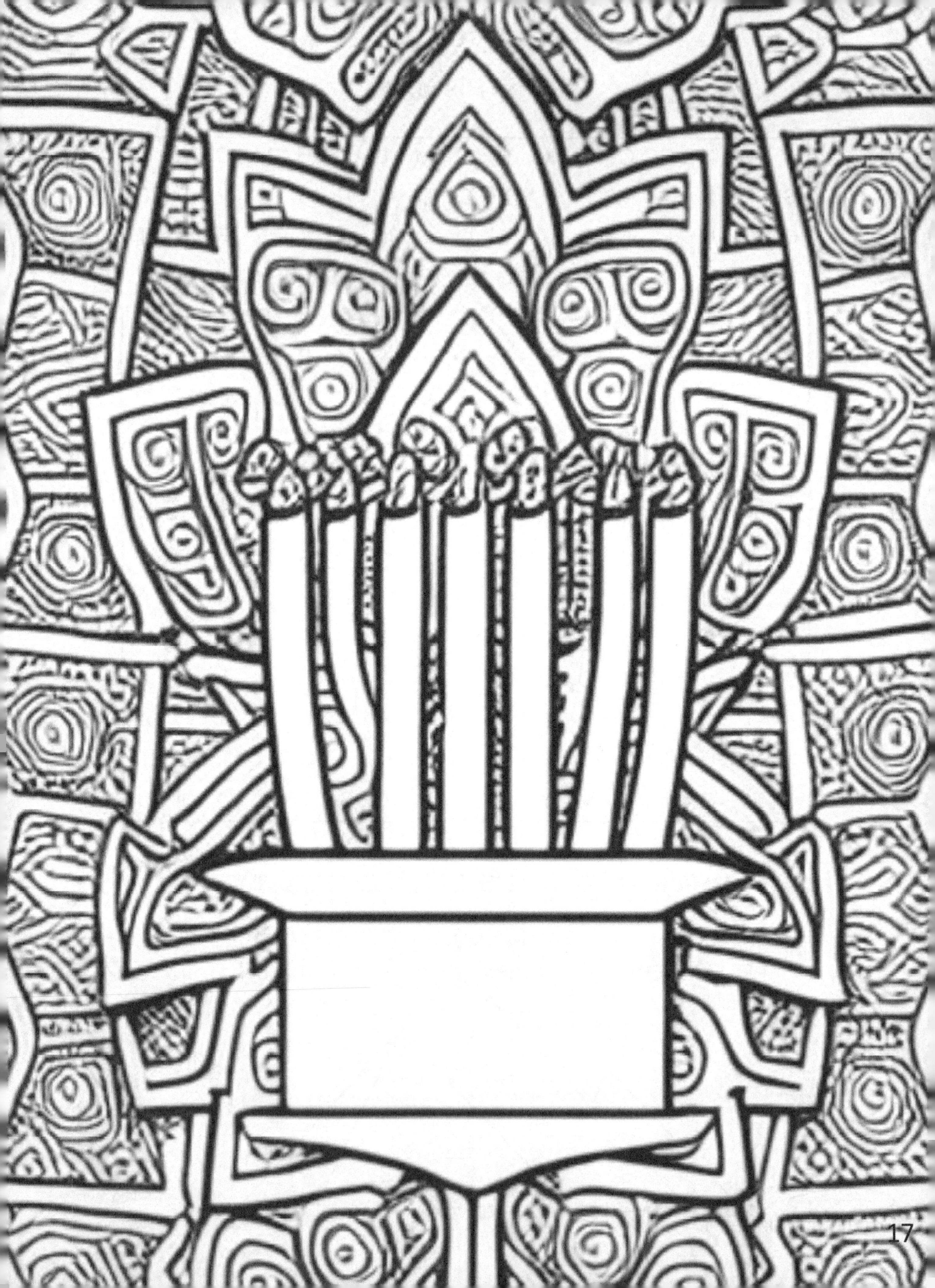

Find One Word Word Search
Word To Find: **CUSTOM**

S	U	C	O	U	M	O	M	O	S	C	U
C	M	U	M	S	M	O	T	S	M	S	O
S	M	O	M	T	U	M	M	C	U	C	M
M	O	C	O	O	U	O	T	U	U	T	C
M	T	U	O	M	C	T	C	S	U	T	T
M	S	S	C	C	S	C	O	C	S	C	O
O	U	U	M	O	T	S	S	C	M	T	O
U	C	T	M	T	C	S	M	S	T	S	U
S	O	S	C	O	O	T	T	O	S	U	M
C	T	S	O	C	U	C	O	S	S	C	M
M	O	O	M	O	C	T	C	O	U	O	T
S	C	T	S	U	T	S	O	O	M	U	M

Solution on page 75

Macaroons For Dessert

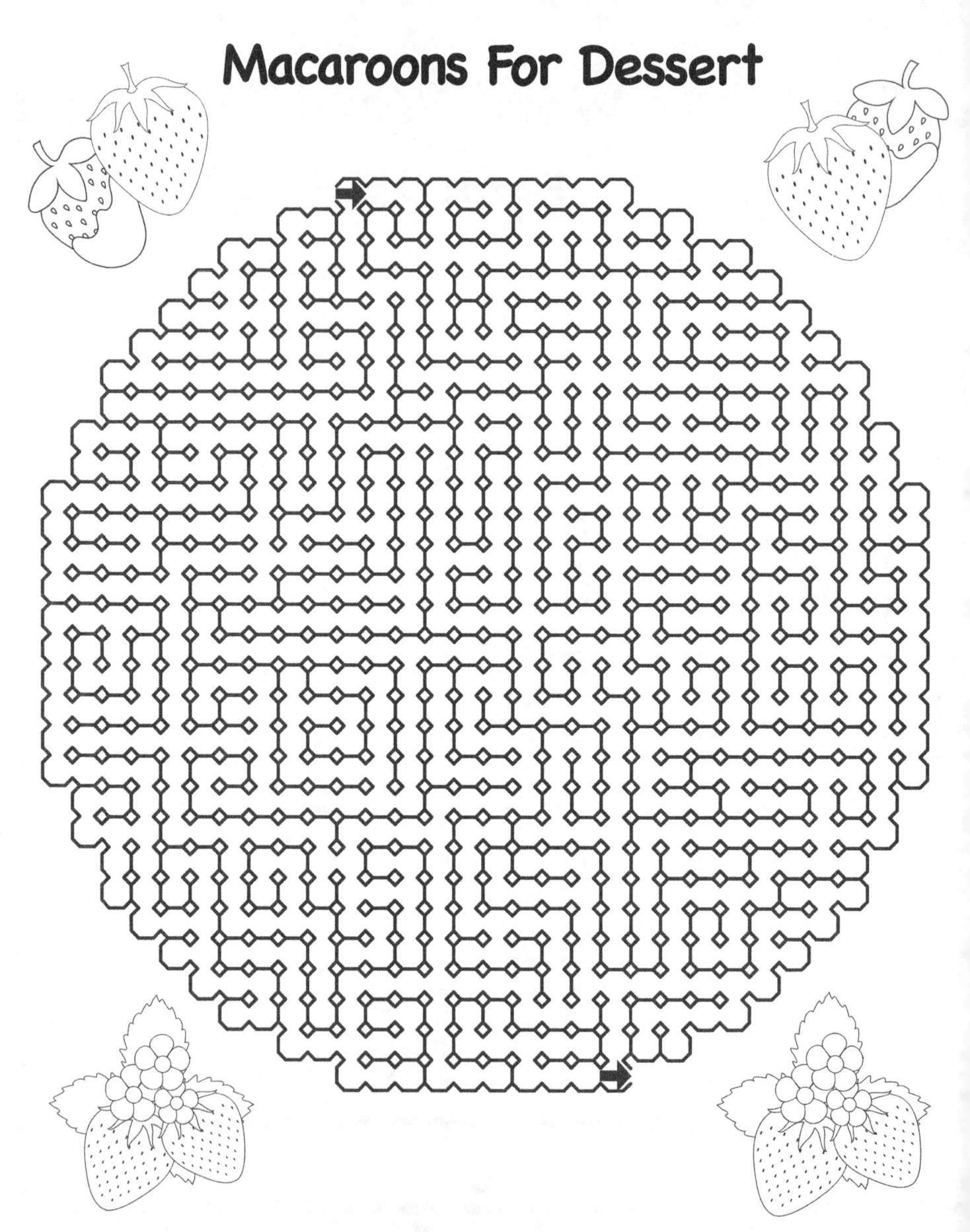

Exodus

```
U F Q K C L J R W L E A R S I I J
U C E G Y P T D Z Z J A B V G E N
C M A R U E T K S B U D L G L L S
Y U R P S K F F S T D Q A K K K L
O C O K A K I S I S R E U E F W X
E P P C N K H D I R T L T R B B E
M I S H C U E E D A S Z I L V E T
I L A T T J U M R U N T R F N Y D
T G I I N L B B G S A B C P P D
G R D A F E E A M F T H S O H A P
N I H F Y L J R J Y M C M S R G B
I M E G E L O U V I P N M V I N K
R A B C C N D H V Z K Q O F G N Q
P G R X T A N F A Y T M F V Z V D
S E E Q I K G N X T Z E Z M V X O
B L W C X T O R A H M U Y A A A B
W K A L S E J Q X C F J K U K Y H
```

CELEBRATE	DIASPORA	EGYPT
FAITH	FIRST BORN	HEBREW
ISRAEL	JUDAICA	KIDDUSH
NISSAN	PILGRIMAGE	RITUAL
SANCTIFY	SPRINGTIME	TORAH

Solution on page 71

Seder Plate
Picture Sequence Puzzle

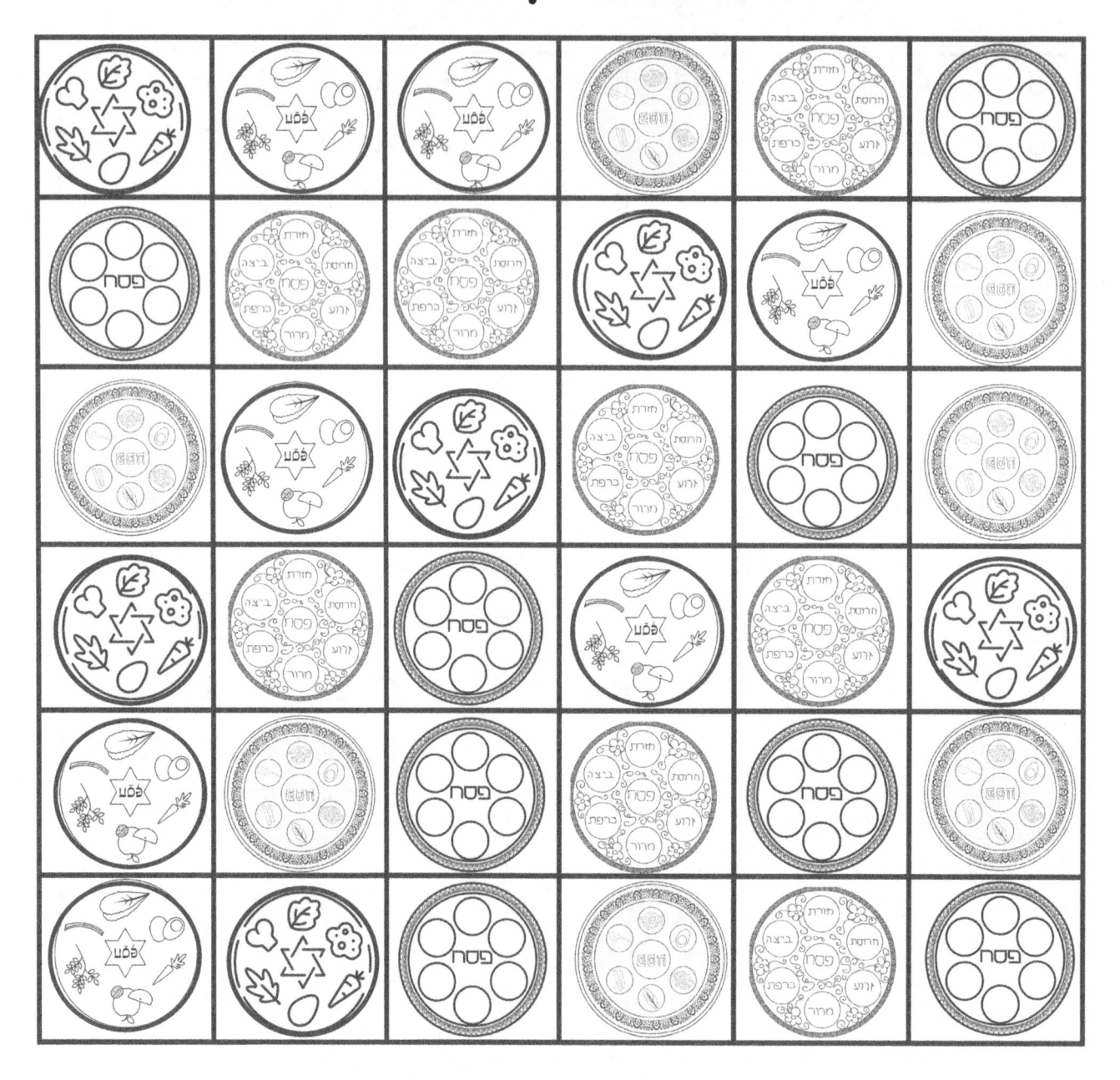

Find the pictures of *Three Identical Seder Plates* in a straight line?

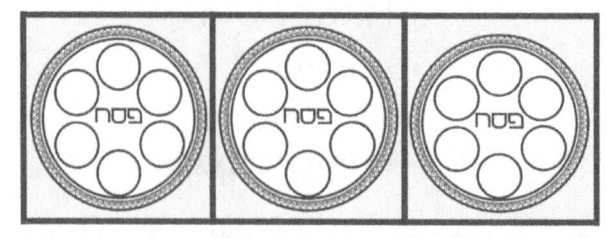

The three *Seder Plates* must be next to each other but the line of them can be horizontal, vertical or on the diagonal.

Solution on page 78

Cryptograms

Puzzle #3

A	B	C	D	E	F	G	H	I	J	K	L	M	N	O	P	Q	R	S	T	U	V	W	X	Y	Z
																						D			

__ __ __ __ __ __ __ D   __ __ __ D
T F H S X J N W   Z L M W

Puzzle #4

A	B	C	D	E	F	G	H	I	J	K	L	M	N	O	P	Q	R	S	T	U	V	W	X	Y	Z
															L										

L __ __   __ __   __ __ __ L __ __   __ __
R Z P   A E   C Z I C R Z   Y I

HAPPY PASSOVER

Solution on page 84   17

Riddles

How do you make seven even?

What comes once in a minute, twice in a moment but never in a thousand years?

What do you call a bear with no teeth?

Which is faster hot or cold?

Why did the nose feel sad?

What does an evil hen lay?

Solution on page 80

What's Hidden?

```
S Q W R E M W S R H A L A K H A N
K S N A U V G N Y S H K G D U T S
O S D U U P C F S H A S Z Z J S U
C T U B N U F A Z T V F S X Y A T
J G M U V F K B X I Z I I D V C U
B L E S S I N G S N T O N R R R I
U F K R E W A R D T I Z J P E I C
R H L G W M F T L M M T R D E F N
J M H W Q U R P Y W G A E F A I R
L P R G J E Y M N L H M U F J C L
T D M I S C Q Q Y T P G I X P E X
H I H S T E G U F T N K B W R N J
W B E J E E T L I I O G O Q E Y L
O D P A A W E O K M V C F K S X C
F V N F L W N P E K V P O G E N O
M N O Q T B A N T V J R X P N M E
V S O U W N Q K P C B Q U L T A Z
```

AFIKOMEN   BLESSINGS   BROKEN
DESSERT   HALAKHA   MATZO
MITZVAH   NAPKIN   PRESENT
REDEMPTION   REWARD   SACRIFICE
STEAL   TWELFTH   TZAFUN

Solution on page 72

The Holiday Table
Find The 18 Hidden Objects

Solution on page 77

Going To Grandma's (Bubbe's) for Seder
Find The 18 Hidden Objects

Solution on page 77

21

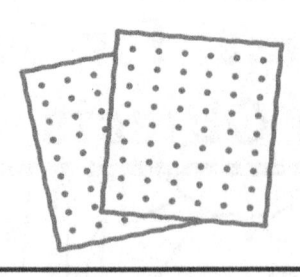

Matzah

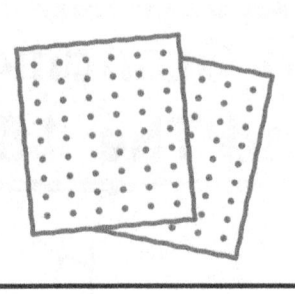

```
W C Z S D S M F S Z V Y E Q F X X
B B C G Y M P T Q J G K N T O C I
A E A T A O R E A I C O K D I S Z
R G E M F U W N L E I B A M T P G
L Z G T C H J A E T H R V W M P N
E Y Z O I X A E C E U W U K S I Q
Y V T I K R E I L O T D R P J M X
M C E I U T L O L D A H R E U P T
W I M F R F G F O E B E G E T E Z
F G A Z F J C U R D K D V I I A Y
W W H A G F G B N C R N J R E E W
V A C C G H T D A Y Y V Z J D W U
N I X D S A T R G G E L U F J L B
X K V S L O C K R U S E W Y G U H
X H A F U M A F O N I A R G Y R K
E A C Y R T Y U N L E A V E N E D
M J M Y U A Q P T P B B H U Q E K
```

AFFLICTION	BARLEY	CHAMETZ
CRACKER	DOUGH	EIGHTEEN
FLATBREAD	FLOUR	GRAIN
OAT	RYE	SPELT
UNLEAVENED	WATER	WHEAT

Solution on page 71

Around The Table Maze

Solution on page 73

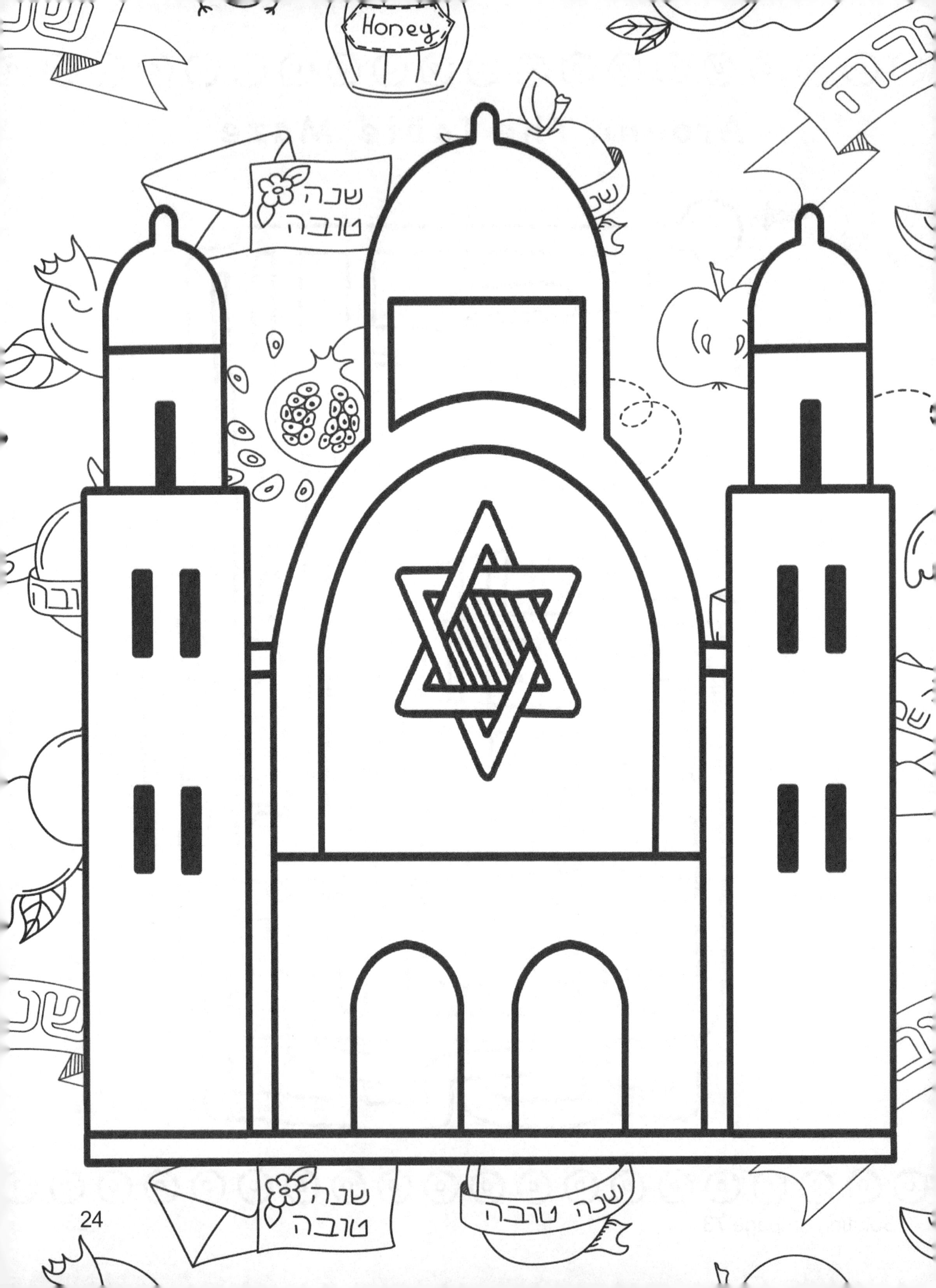
Honey
שנה טובה
שנה טובה
שנה טובה

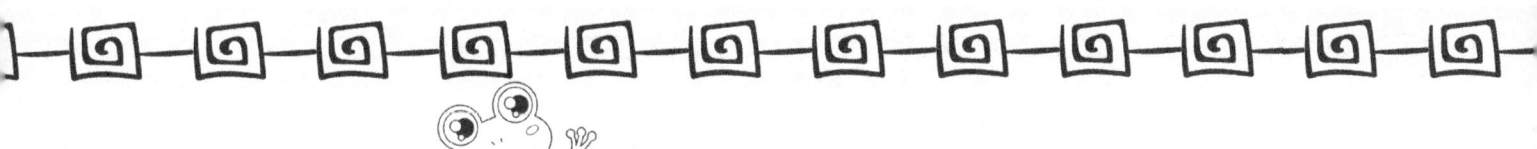

The Plagues

```
C E Z Y T C P E S T I L E N C E P
D E K S S S E Y O J Z G D V T X
Z B Y G V S E B P F W U G Y P G Y
D U O J T B H K G I T B D Y S V I
G R J S L O A C L N S L G E Y S L
F A E L A C I L B I B E I R V S Z
V L U Q B Z L Q W S A L S T P E S
Q T Z V D G N I R E F F U S N N H
W M N R O B T S R I F F C A H K L
K R B A O E V V U O L G I J E R O
O O M T L K J M H R I W P C F A C
P N T B B Z O Y J C Z I K R D U
V W T Z O H U S Q H T L L G T W S
G Q L Y K I Z E S X I I G C J D T
C I T W A K L S Z P O E F U Y T S
I F U J U O K S Z L N M G S Z K G
C L G S B V N K N C Q S B T A E G
```

AFFLICTION   BIBLICAL   BLOOD
BOILS   DARKNESS   EGYPT
FIRSTBORN   FLIES   FROGS
HAIL   LICE   LOCUSTS
MOSES   PESTILENCE   SUFFERING

Solution on page 72

25

PASSOVER WORDOKU PUZZLE 1

U	D	Y	N	A	
			U	Y	
Y	U		E		A
E	A			U	Y
D	Y	U		E	
N		A		D	

Word Used in Puzzle: DAYENU

PASSOVER WORDOKU PUZZLE 2

T	A	I		O	
		N	I	A	T
	I	N	T	N	
		O	N	I	A
	N			T	I
	O	T	A		

Word Used in Puzzle: NATION

Find One Word Word Search
Word To Find: <u>FAMILY</u>

I	A	Y	M	Y	F	F	M	I	A	F	Y
F	L	Y	F	L	M	I	Y	I	L	M	L
L	M	Y	Y	M	A	M	I	M	A	M	L
L	F	L	M	L	I	F	M	M	A	I	M
M	M	M	Y	M	I	L	M	I	A	A	M
A	F	L	M	L	M	M	A	L	A	A	A
I	F	M	M	M	I	F	A	A	F	Y	M
L	L	F	F	L	I	L	Y	F	A	F	F
F	M	A	I	F	L	Y	L	M	A	Y	I
A	A	A	L	A	M	Y	A	M	L	F	A
A	L	I	A	M	M	Y	F	Y	F	L	I
F	L	Y	I	I	M	L	M	Y	A	A	L

Solution on page 75

Would you rather . . .

be without the internet or without your phone for a week?

be able to talk to animals or speak every language fluently?

eat blindfolded or while holding your nose?

be able to read people's minds or be able to make them do what you want with a snap of your fingers?

have a bullseye appear on your forehead when you tell a lie or have your nose grow an inch?

Solution on page 65

Find One Word Word Search

Word To Find: **KOSHER**

```
R S R S S K S R O O S E
H H K H H R O R H R K R
E R S S S S R S K S H H
R H O E O R R H R O R O
S O S S S E E R O H H R
S E E H R E S H O O E E
E R K E E R O E S E R R
S E S O E O S K R O O O
K R K H K S K R E K K K
O S H O O S H O S S S S
K E S O H H O S R H O O
R R R S S O O R K S K R
```

Solution on page 76

29

Riddles

What gets wetter the more it dries?

Why was the math book sad?

How do trees get on the internet?

Where do books hide when they're scared?

When you drop a yellow hat in the Red Sea what does it become?

Why don't eggs tell jokes?

Solution on page 80

SEDER WORD SCRAMBLE

HADAGGAH

POHARAH

CTEHMAZ

KDUSDIH

CNLADE

CORHSEAT

SSMOE

DYNAEU

PAECSH

RRMAO

EAJLIH

AOKEIFMN

Solution on page 73

31

Find One Word Word Search
Word To Find: **FAMINE**

```
E I M N F E I N M F A F
E N N M F M A I F F A F
E M N E F I F E M E E F
E F M F M E N M F A I E
N M F M N E E A F M F M
N I N F E N M I M E M F
E A E M E I F E E N I M
N F M F N E M I N N M I
M N I E E E N M I I N F
N F A A M I M M I E E I
E F N I N M A E I I A N
E M F F F A F I A N F N
```

Star Of David Maze

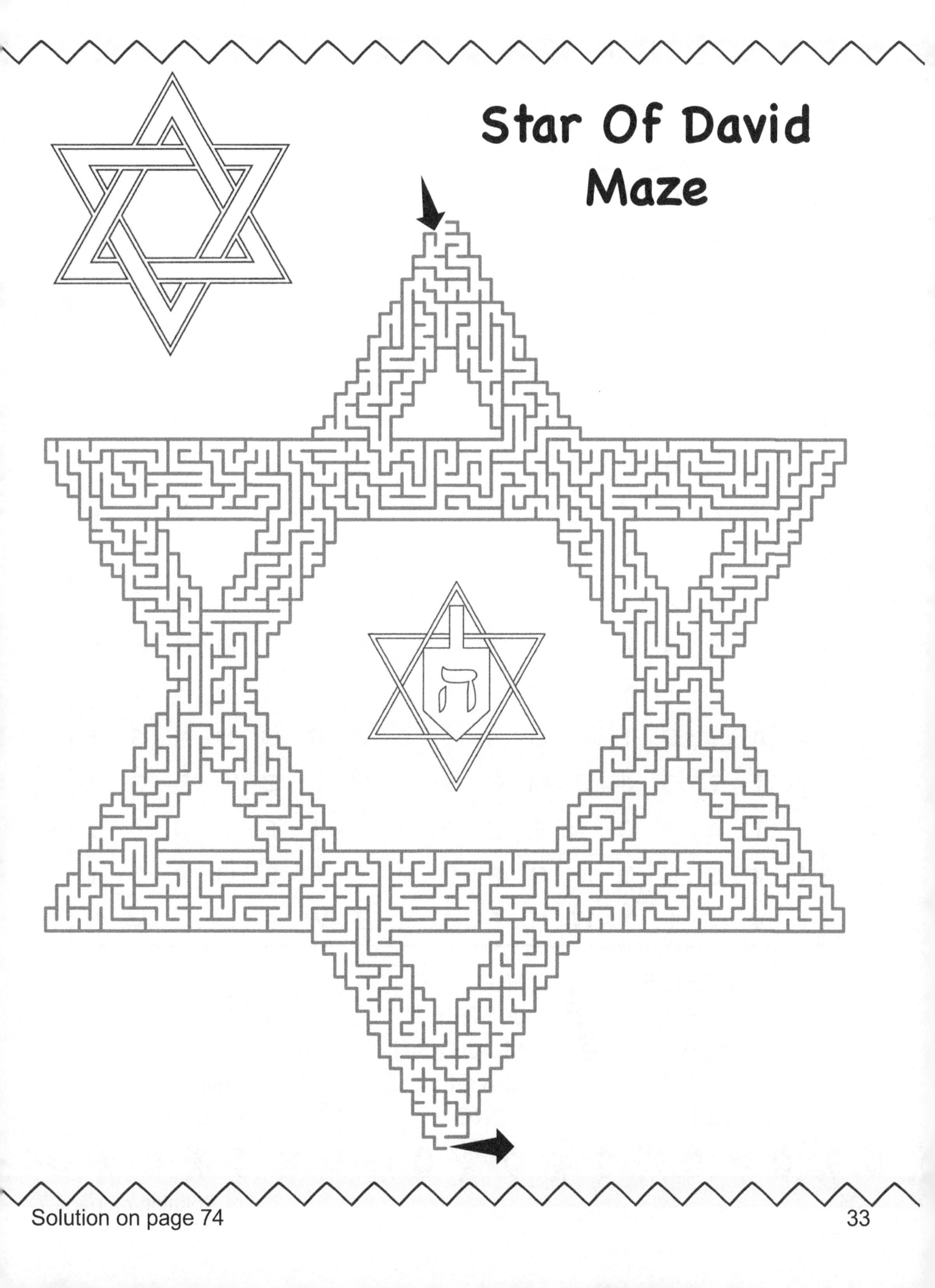

Solution on page 74

Dayenu

```
G I A N I S T N U O M Y M B D O D
E F Y R E V A L S L R R E E Y V C
C S V H R T N F E Y G A H O S G S
M I D Y T N E I C I F F U S S O K
U I E E I X W B I X H P C D E G Y
G Y R F E G X K T H G A G J N Y L
G S Z A X R H D S B U W X N E F K
N S Z T C K F H U A O Q K P S I B
Z H A U N L Z O J J N Z L B O T R
F A A A X E E S A G E D M T L C I
O B B N Z B T S A E E K S Q C N K
B B F F N F Q V I P S G B O N A A
X A T O I A O B T Z G R Q S N S I
Y T T G J G M O Y J M G C W D G X
K T A Y C T E Z G R A T E F U L V
I X S N Q Y O P P R E S S O R S I
L V V L X W H E J K Z W B D D M N
```

CLOSENESS ENOUGH   GIFTS
GRATEFUL   JUSTICE   MANNA
MIRACLES   MOUNT SINAI OPPRESSORS
SANCTIFY   SEA OF REEDS SHABBAT
SLAVERY   SONG   SUFFICIENT

34   Solution on page 72

Find The Strings Of Numbers #2
They can be horizontal, vertical, on the diagonal and backwards, too!

```
5 2 3 5 3 4 3 7 6 4 2 1
0 1 1 5 2 0 4 5 3 4 9 5
9 3 8 6 9 4 0 8 2 1 5 5
1 4 6 5 2 6 8 2 7 4 9 4
9 9 6 2 4 1 1 0 4 1 3 2
4 8 3 5 6 3 3 8 9 0 7 8
8 3 1 3 2 1 5 8 7 5 3 9
0 7 7 2 1 3 1 7 1 9 7 4
2 3 4 0 6 0 5 5 2 4 5 5
5 3 8 9 7 9 2 8 9 8 2 4
2 8 5 5 4 4 5 8 7 0 0 5
7 8 3 1 7 9 9 1 6 4 4 5
5 1 8 6 2 1 1 7 7 5 1 7
1 0 2 9 5 1 9 0 5 2 3 1
```

- ☐ 011426
- ☐ 310
- ☐ 6953
- ☐ 97138
- ☐ 524809
- ☐ 336538
- ☐ 494
- ☐ 188
- ☐ 195

Solution on page 78

Spot The 11 Differences Between Puzzles A & B
Puzzle A

36

Solution on page 79

Spot The 11 Differences Between Puzzles A & B
Puzzle B

Solution on page 79

37

STICK FIGURE SUDOKU

Fact: Matzah has holes to keep it from rising. The matzah dough can't be worked for more than 18 minutes because the natural process of fermentation, or leavening, will happen.

Solution on page 78

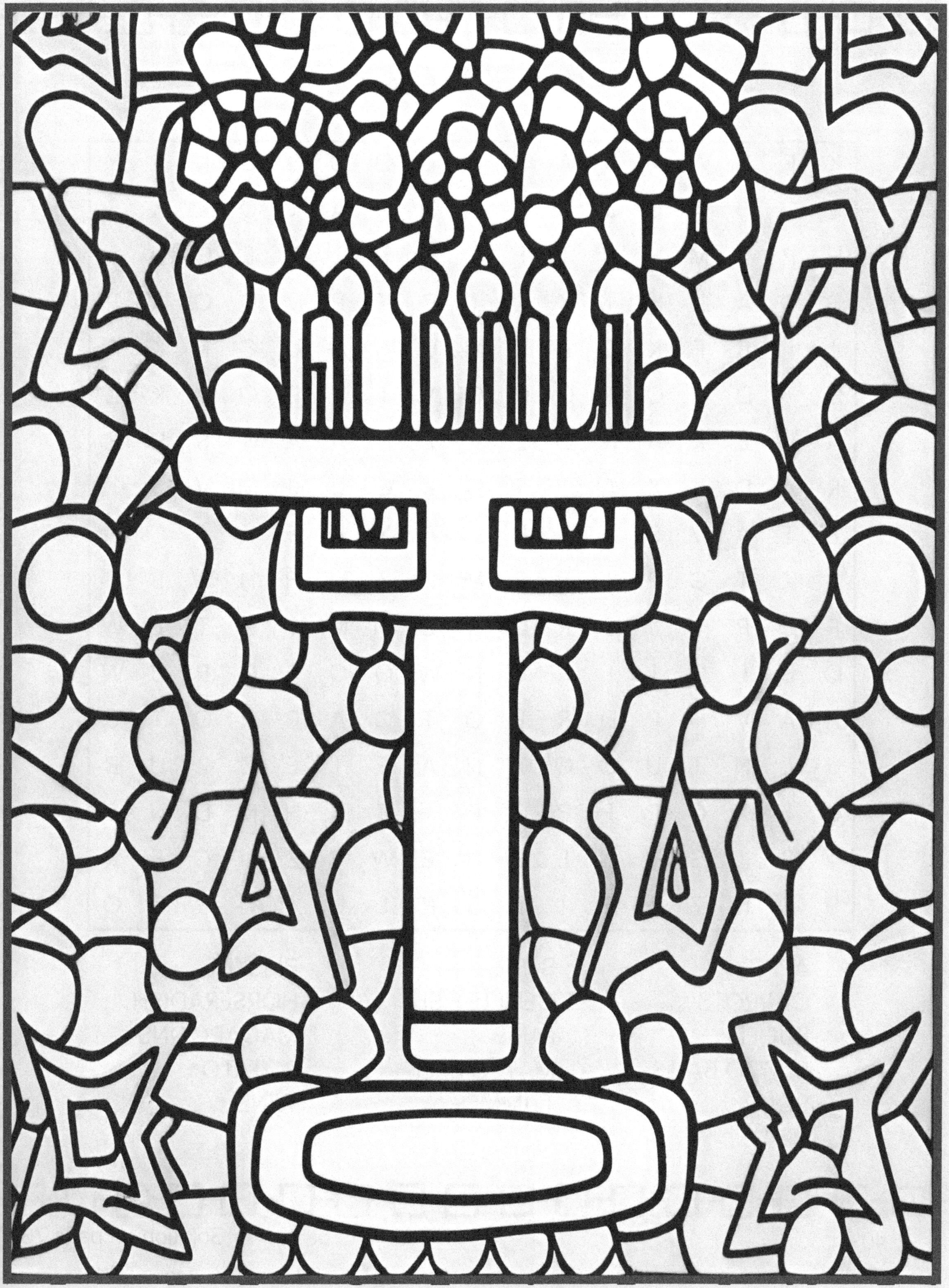

Passover Food

```
K F G W Y R W K U E O O S U K S Y
I O D A B J J S P O T A T O K X S
H P S M H S I F E T L I F E G N T
S Q A K H I X L I R K P M D O W P
I L B F K Q P U M U W A U O K K A
D T D V Q P O G G Y T U R O D K Z
A M E K A N G E F Z H A A W S B E
R A D K X A L T O E C U J M V S X
E T A M S L L B L A X K P K A T N
S Z T C P I R D M Z Z M H H W E B
R O P L J E R C S E M M I Z T E W
O B L D I L R B N W Q O S Q R B W
H A V H P D R E Q T C A R R O T S
J L N T U C Q X N A E I E Z Z U B
Q L X C P F B C P I E B H M D N E
V S I S V C E P H E W V Z U C F K
B S N Z I S I V S P L U I H P Q O
```

APPLE   BEETS   BRISKET
CARROTS   GEFILTE FISH   HORSERADISH
KUGEL   LAMB   MACAROONS
MATZO BALLS   MATZO BREI   POTATO
SOUP   TZIMMES   WINE

Matzah Maze

Solution on page 74

PASSOVER WORDOKU PUZZLE 3

		E	A	V	L
	A	L	E	E	
	E	N			
L	V	E	N		E
E	L		E	N	
	E		L		V

Word Used in Puzzle: LEAVEN

✗✗✗✗✗✗✗✗✗✗✗✗✗✗✗✗✗✗

PASSOVER WORDOKU PUZZLE 4

M	H		A	A	Z
		A	M	H	
A	T				H
H		Z	T		A
T		M			A
Z		H	A		M

Word Used in Puzzle: MATZAH

42   Solution on page 81

Cryptograms

Puzzle #5

A	B	C	D	E	F	G	H	I	J	K	L	M	N	O	P	Q	R	S	T	U	V	W	X	Y	Z
									H															J	

_ _ _ _   _ _ _   _ _ _ _ J _ H
R T G   Z H   F K V X P J

Puzzle #6

A	B	C	D	E	F	G	H	I	J	K	L	M	N	O	P	Q	R	S	T	U	V	W	X	Y	Z
					A																				

_ _ _ _ _   _ A _ _ A _ _
I Z Q D X S   F T N I F G M

Solution on page 84

43

Find One Word Word Search

Word To Find: PLAGUE

G	L	E	P	L	L	P	U	U	G	P	E
L	U	G	E	A	A	P	E	E	P	L	L
G	E	P	U	E	U	P	G	U	L	P	A
A	L	G	U	P	P	L	G	A	E	A	P
E	G	G	L	U	L	A	P	P	G	P	G
P	A	E	U	L	P	G	L	U	U	A	U
A	E	L	E	G	U	E	E	E	U	L	L
G	A	L	G	L	U	L	E	E	G	P	A
E	G	E	L	G	P	G	L	E	P	G	L
U	G	L	A	A	E	E	U	U	P	A	G
L	L	L	L	U	U	U	G	A	A	L	A
L	P	G	A	A	L	L	A	G	U	E	E

Build Your Own Seder Plate

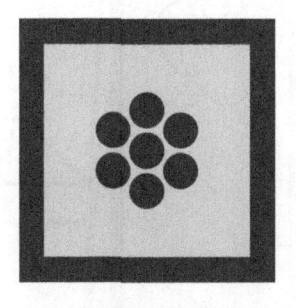

The Kitchen Is Ready
Find The 18 Hidden Objects

46

Solution on page 77

Looking For The Afikomen
Find The 18 Objects Hidden In The Picture

Solution on page 77

47

The Seder Plate

```
A K U U R T S Q Z J W H N I J Q
R S B R E H R E T T I B Y M K Q U
T S V D N C U S S G X G A J A O I
I F J J N S R E F O Z C L P K E H
C Y G I H S C P L O R A N G E R O
H L T L Z T Y T X B S A B D Q H R
O N Q I N M I W W T A P H L N F S
K U E F U Y C C X U Y T B C L J E
E T P H L R K Q Y P A R E U J J R
S S T Q E P F P S M O T H G M O A
E P R Y L X K L F R S V C S E N D
G A S H A N K L A K A R P A S V I
G R Y P L Y O M C S E V I L O W S
H S O P O S L O B M Y S U P W Z H
K L Q R W H X M L C I V R Z E X W
O E I R Y T C S Z Q V M M D L H U
R Y E Z E I W V Z G L W W M Q U O
```

ARTICHOKES   BITTER HERBS   CHAROSET
EGG   FRUIT   HORSERADISH
KARPAS   MAROR   NUTS
OLIVES   ORANGE   PARSLEY
SHANK   SYMBOLS   VEGETABLE

48   Solution on page 72

Picture Puzzle
Find Three Identical APPLES In A Row

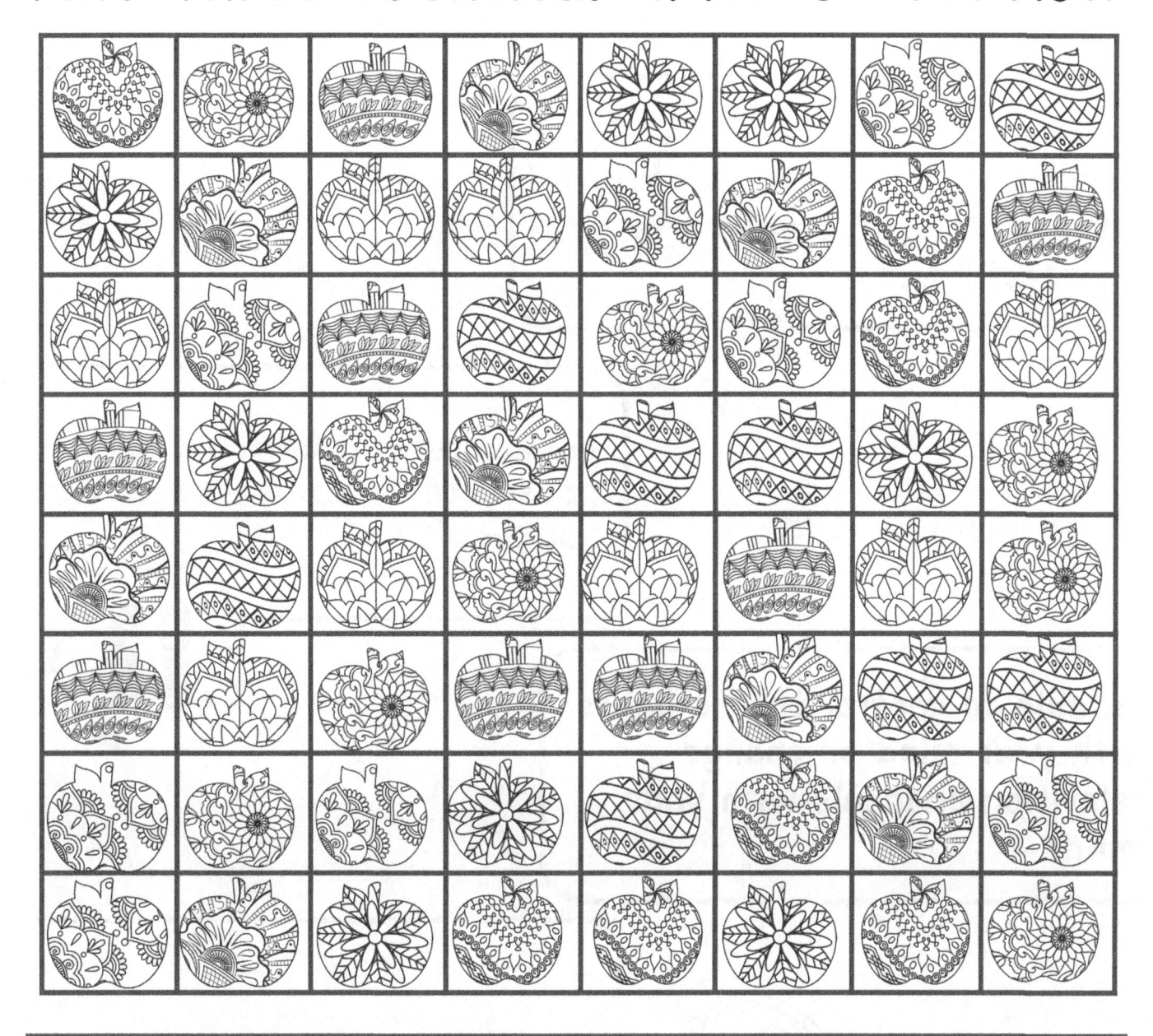

Can you find the **THREE IDENTICAL APPLES** in a row?

The three APPLES must be next to each other and the line of them can be horizontal, vertical or on the diagonal.

Solution on page 78

49

Would you rather...

go into the past and meet your ancestors or go into the future and meet your great-great-grandchildren?

have a rewind button or a pause button to use whenever you want?

be able to control traffic lights with your mind or change television channels with your mind?

have x-ray vision or super hearing?

be able to take back anything you say or hear every conversation around you?

Solution on page 67

PASSOVER WORDOKU PUZZLE 5

		R	E	I	A
I	E	A	S	R	P
				A	S
			I	E	R
	A	I	R		E
		P	A	S	

Word Used in Puzzle: PRAISE

PASSOVER WORDOKU PUZZLE 6

	P	S		E	H
			S	C	
	H	C		S	
A	S		E	H	
		E	H		
S			C		

Word Used in Puzzle: PESACH

Solution on page 82

51

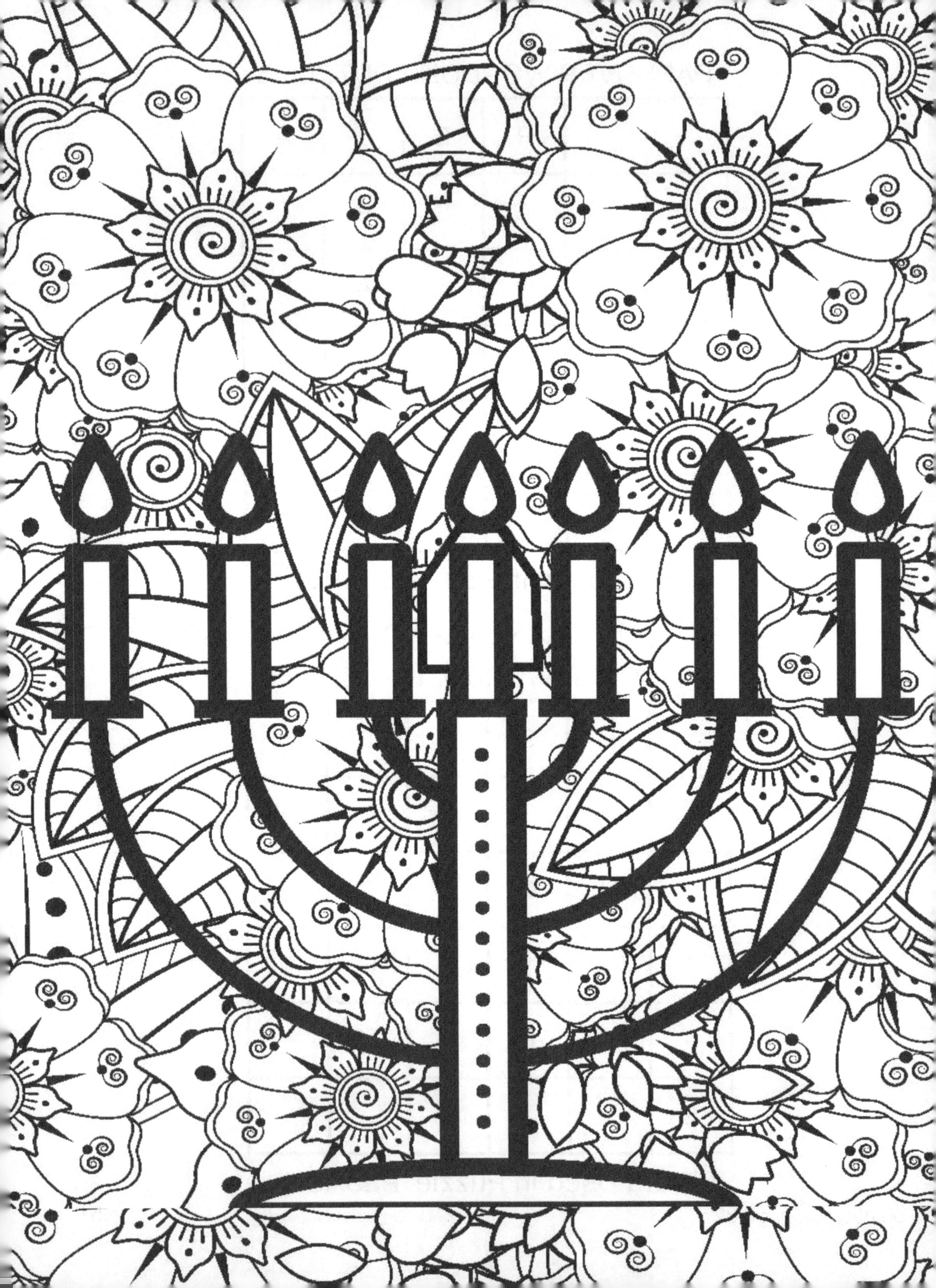

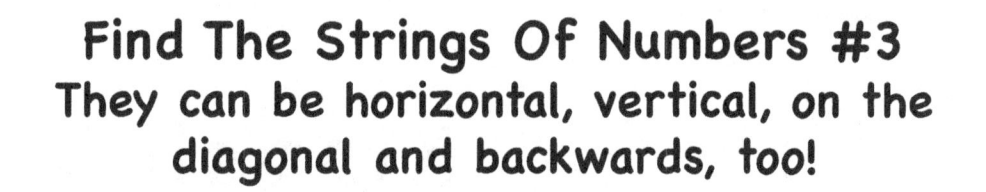

Find The Strings Of Numbers #3
They can be horizontal, vertical, on the diagonal and backwards, too!

0	4	9	8	6	2	9	6	3	1	7	4
8	5	1	8	4	6	8	8	7	8	8	3
9	3	0	5	2	2	7	7	7	8	0	0
6	8	2	5	1	9	0	1	2	8	6	1
4	1	6	0	2	6	4	6	4	4	4	0
6	2	3	4	0	0	1	5	6	6	4	4
3	8	8	2	3	3	5	9	8	0	0	7
5	8	9	3	5	6	2	4	6	3	0	0
3	0	0	5	1	2	7	5	3	4	4	7
0	0	9	4	9	7	4	7	1	3	0	2
1	4	6	0	7	9	3	7	7	3	5	8
8	6	8	4	2	4	1	8	0	4	1	3
9	3	5	5	2	1	7	1	8	7	0	0
3	1	0	8	6	0	2	1	0	6	3	2

- ☐ 821091
- ☐ 533288
- ☐ 005127
- ☐ 24603
- ☐ 1804
- ☐ 846887
- ☐ 53985
- ☐ 868
- ☐ 466510

Solution on page 78

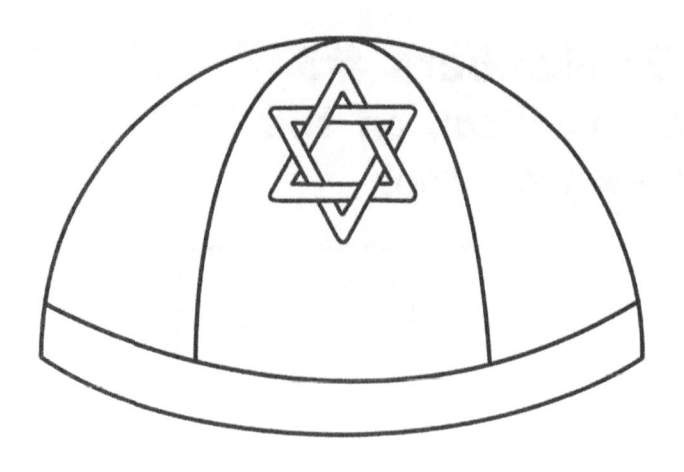

Kippah Maze From Top To Bottom

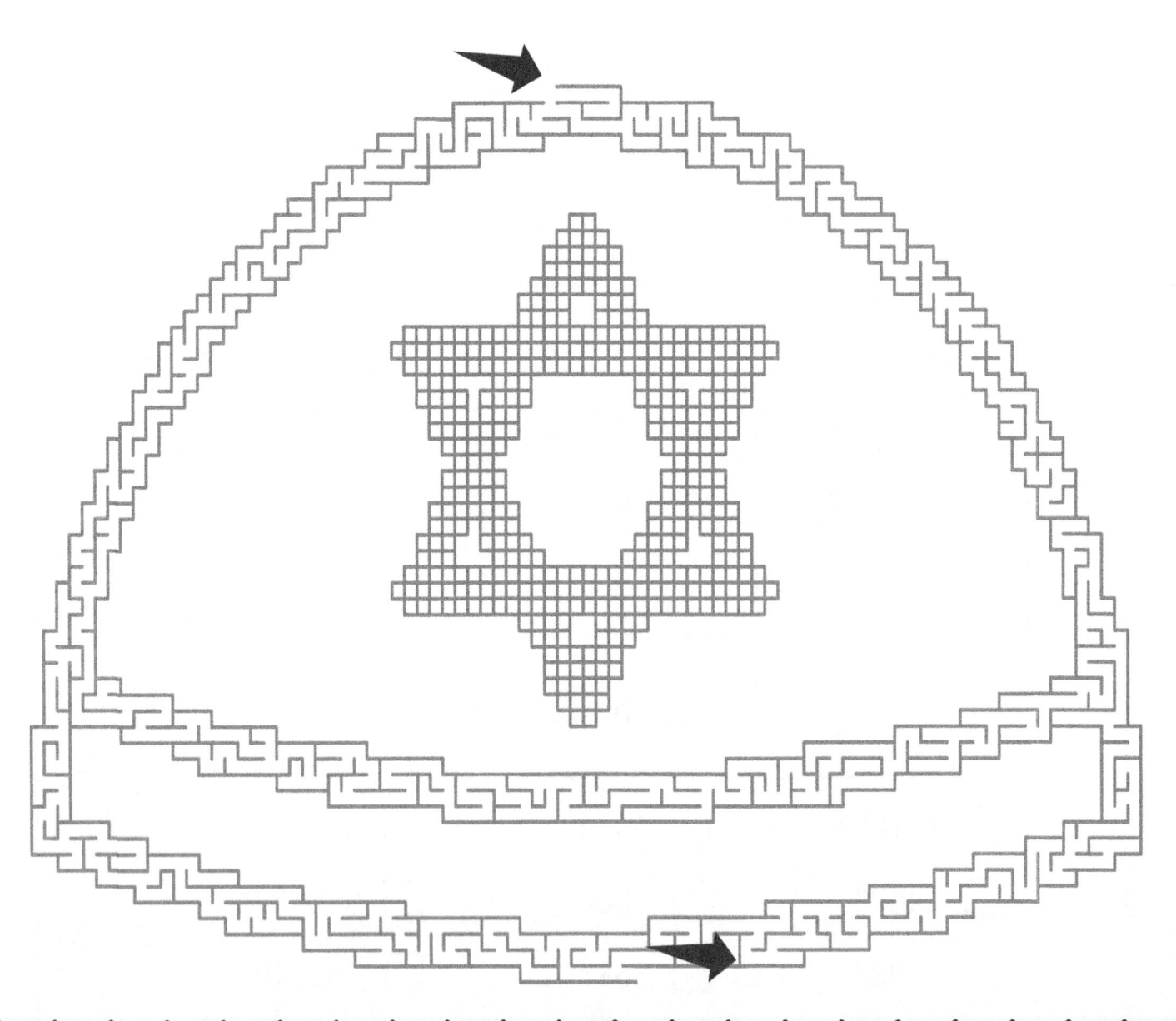

54

Solution on page 74

ANAGRAMS

MAKE AT LEAST ONE OTHER WORD FROM THE WORDS SHOWN BELOW. HERE'S AN EXAMPLE: APE -> PEA

ARE	->	- - -
ARM	->	- - -
URN	->	- - -
TEA	->	- - -
TAB	->	- - -
WHO	->	- - -
WON	->	- - -
NAP	->	- - -
BARE	->	- - - -
BEAK	->	- - - -
BEST	->	- - - -
BOSS	->	- - - -
CAFÉ	->	- - - -
CARE	->	- - - -
FLOW	->	- - - -
MEAT	->	- - - -
RING	->	- - - -
SINK	->	- - - -
POTS	->	- - - -
NIGHT	->	- - - - -

Solution on page 83

The Star

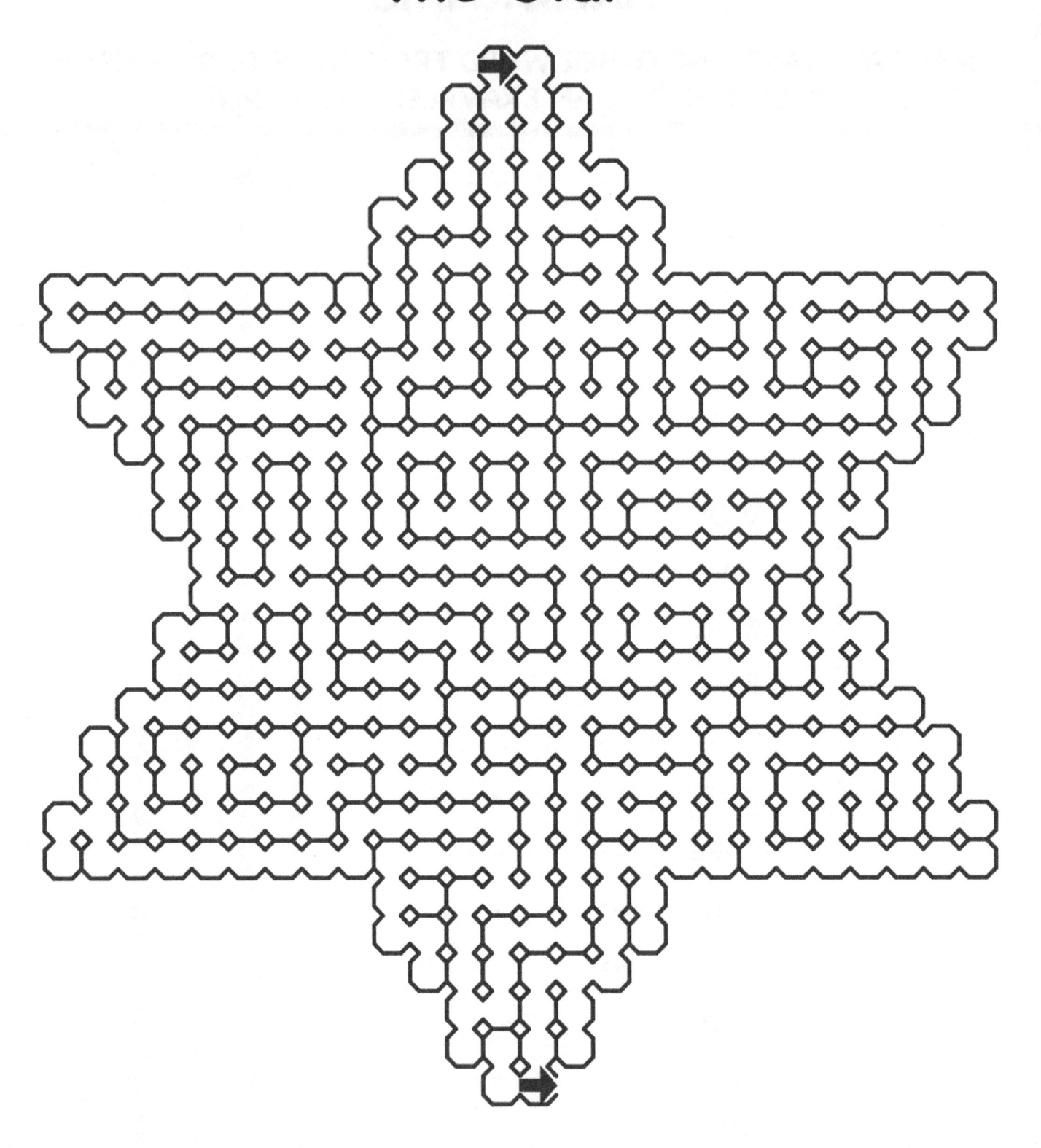

Something to think about: Was Moses the first person to download info onto a tablet from the cloud?

Tic-Tac-Logic

Tic-Tac-Logic #1

X		X		O	X
	X		O		X
O		O		X	
	O				O
O			X	O	
	O		X	X	

Tic-Tac-Logic #2

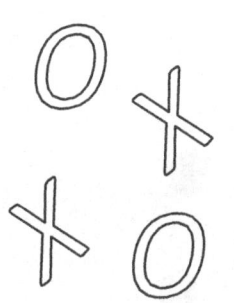

X	X			X	O
O		X		X	
		O		X	X
X		O		X	
		X			X
X			X	O	

Put an X or O in the open squares so that:
1. there aren't more than two consecutive Xs or Os in a row or column
2. the number of Xs is the same as the number of Os in each row and column
3. all rows and all columns are unique.

Tic-Tac-Logic #3

	O		O		X
	X	O		X	
X		O	X		X
	X			X	
		X	X		X
X		O			O

Tic-Tac-Logic #4

	X		X		X
X		O		X	O
	O		O		
O		X	O		X
	O	O			
O				O	O

Solution on page 84

57

58

Searching For Afikomen 3D Maze

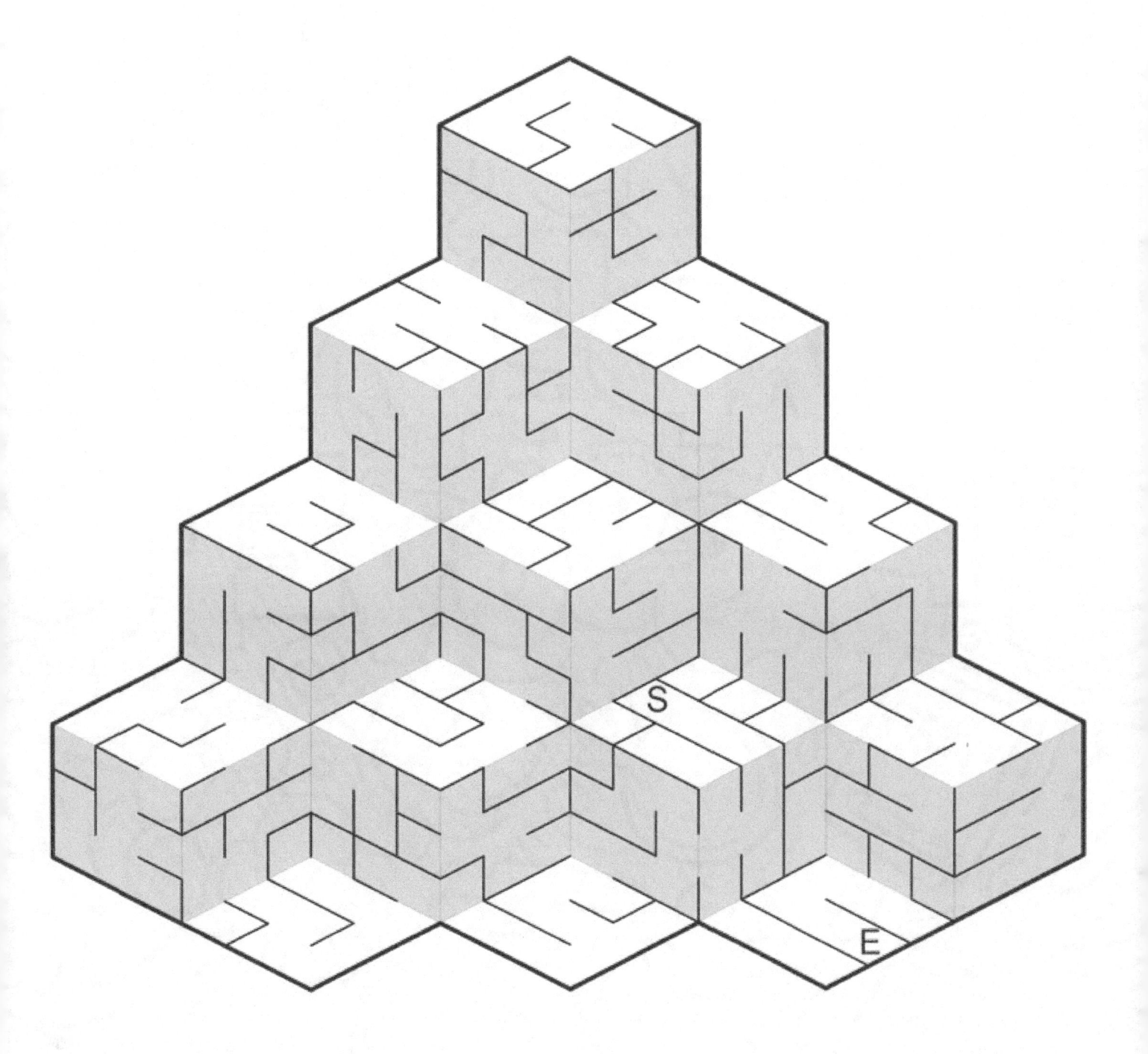

Solution on page 83

HAPPY PASSOVER

SHAPE SUDOKU

Spot The 10 Differences Between This Page And The Next Page (Puzzles A & B)

Puzzle A

62

Solution on page 79

Puzzle B # Spot The 10 Differences

Solution on page 79

63

Find One Word Word Search

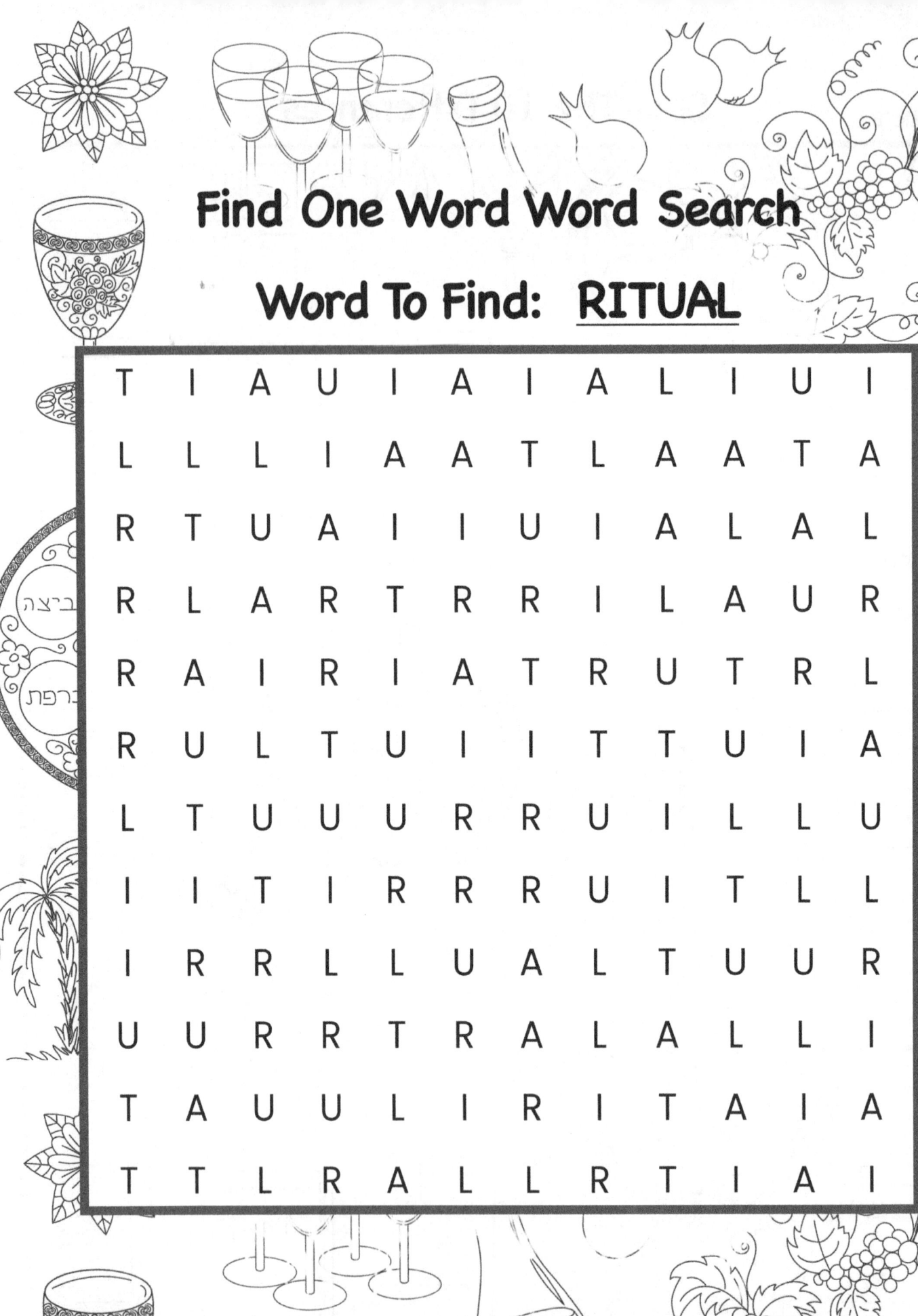

Word To Find: RITUAL

```
T I A U I A I A L I U I
L L L I A A T L A A T A
R T U A I I U I A L A L
R L A R T R R I L A U R
R A I R I A T R U T R L
R U L T U I I T T U I A
L T U U U R R U I L L U
I I T I R R R U I T L L
I R R L L U A L T U U R
U U R R T R A L A L L I
T A U U L I R I T A I A
T T L R A L L R T I A I
```

Haggadah

Q	P	B	J	F	S	K	I	W	D	C	G	Y	S	K	X	W
C	X	A	Z	B	L	U	V	U	C	I	K	L	Q	P	K	O
V	F	G	X	S	W	P	M	L	G	Y	A	C	T	L	Y	M
V	O	Q	R	B	E	L	R	M	A	U	X	M	L	B	T	M
O	U	I	D	L	A	F	A	A	T	F	O	P	O	D	B	Q
K	R	X	H	T	T	G	X	I	Y	P	Z	O	C	I	Z	P
Y	Z	X	N	D	G	R	R	M	V	E	K	C	N	K	P	T
Z	L	V	F	I	S	O	A	T	M	Q	R	L	B	F	B	E
J	H	Y	D	H	S	K	B	D	F	C	K	S	A	Z	Y	L
K	L	P	X	Q	U	E	S	T	I	O	N	S	C	Y	F	L
U	S	G	N	I	D	A	E	R	L	T	S	I	T	Q	O	I
Q	E	L	Y	Y	Y	C	N	O	J	E	I	G	B	A	K	N
A	I	G	R	A	T	I	T	U	D	E	L	O	N	N	Q	G
O	H	P	F	Y	R	F	E	H	Z	C	B	L	N	O	R	G
W	M	P	D	Y	R	O	T	S	H	Z	L	H	A	S	S	I
I	E	L	B	A	R	A	P	B	J	Q	L	M	M	H	D	S
W	T	O	I	F	K	Z	N	L	E	A	G	I	D	J	X	X

BOOK FOUR GRATITUDE
HALLEL MAGGID PARABLE
PRAYERS QUESTIONS READINGS
RITUALS SONGS STORY
TALMUD TELLING TRADITIONS

Solution on page 73

PASSOVER WORDOKU PUZZLE 7

A		R	K		
K	P	A	A		
		P	R	A	
R	K				P
		S			
P		K	S		R

Word Used in Puzzle: KARPAS

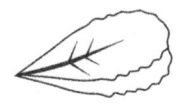

PASSOVER WORDOKU PUZZLE 8

		A		O	
		L	M		
A	S		O	L	
		M		A	H
		S			O
H	L	O	A		S

Word Used in Puzzle: SHALOM

Solution on page 82

Blessings and good wishes TO YOU and YOUR FAMILY ON Passover!

You Found The Afikomen

Find One Word Word Search

Word To Find: WANDER

```
N E E E D D W D A N R N
D R R E R R R E W A E R
D E E N D E D W E A D N
N N N E D N W D E W N A
N E N W R A N N N A A E
R A R W R N N N D R W D
R R R D R R R A N D W A
N R A D D N D N D R R W
R W D R A E R W R A E D
E E R E E R A D D A A A
E N E A E W R W W A W W
E E D R W W W R D R A R
```

Solution on page 76

69

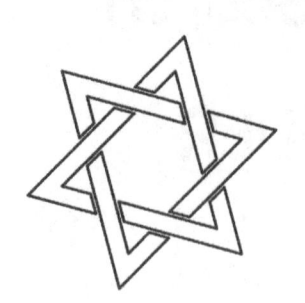

Solutions

Passover - Solution

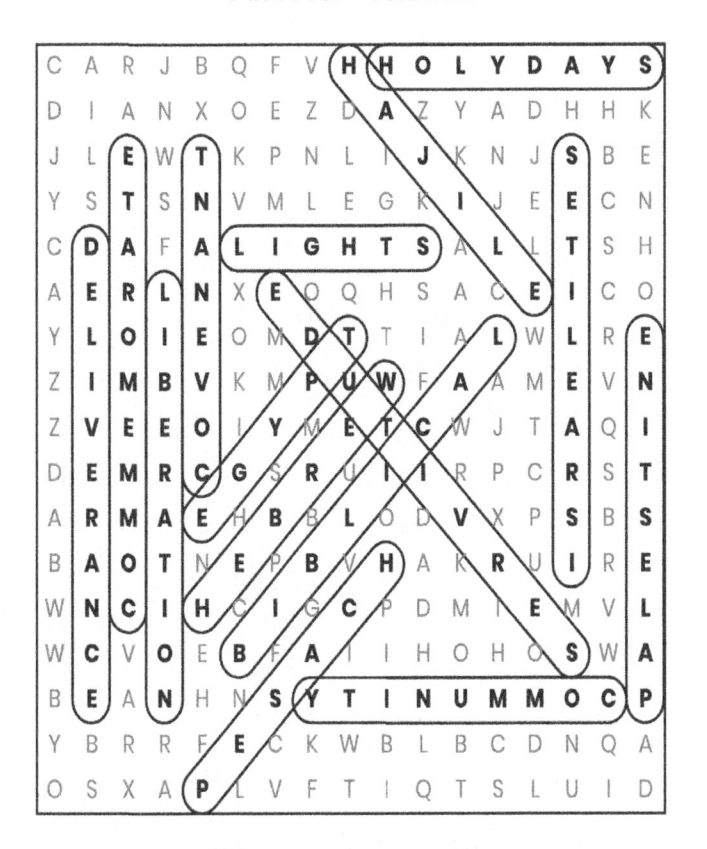

The History - Solution

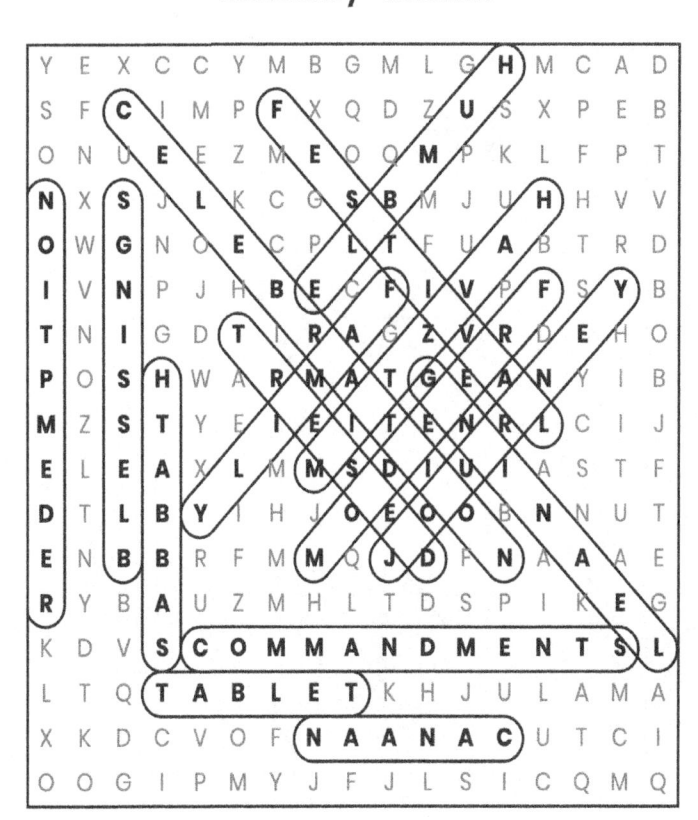

Exodus - Solution

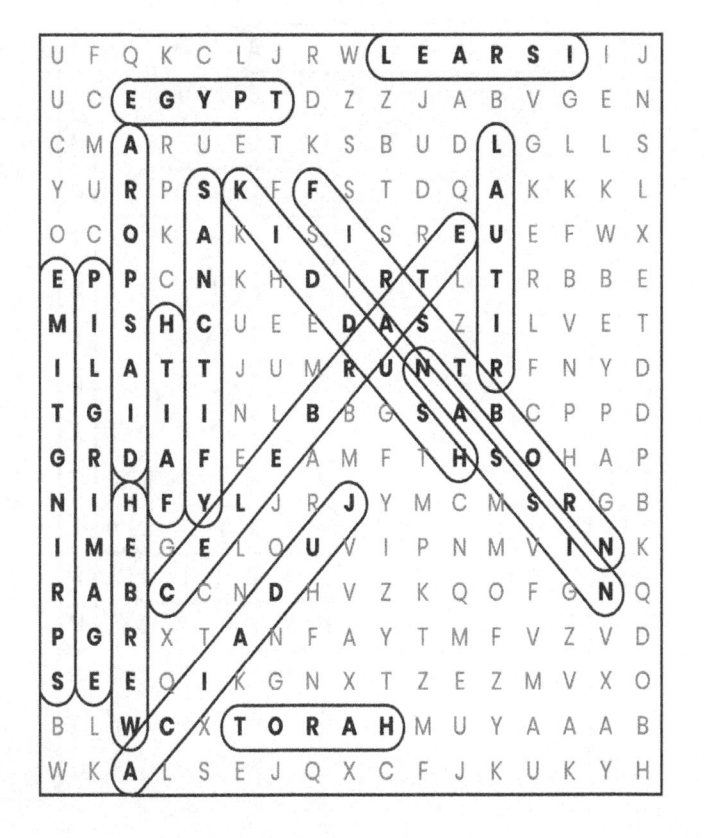

Matzah - Solution

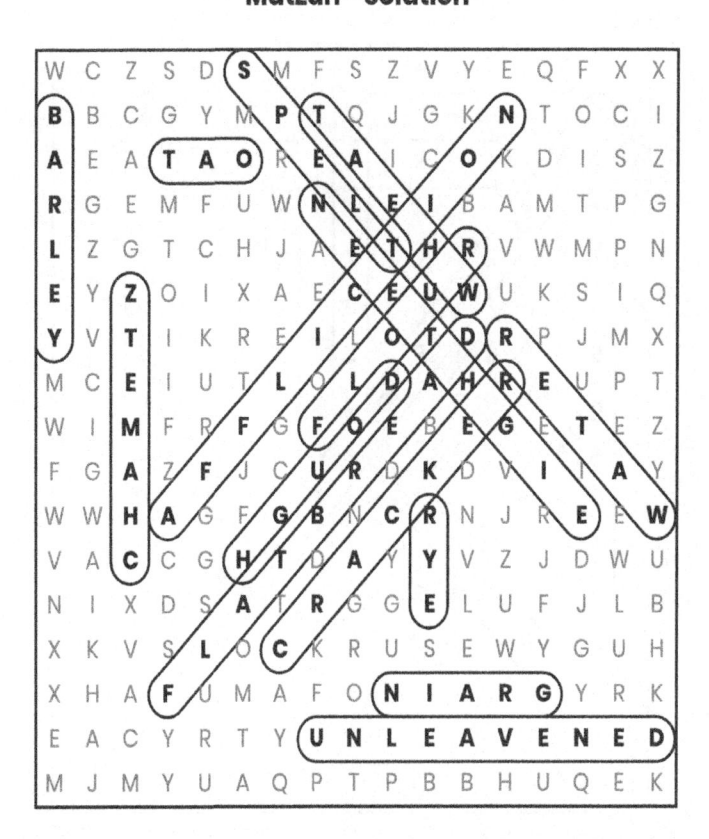

71

What's Hidden? - Solution

The Plagues - Solution

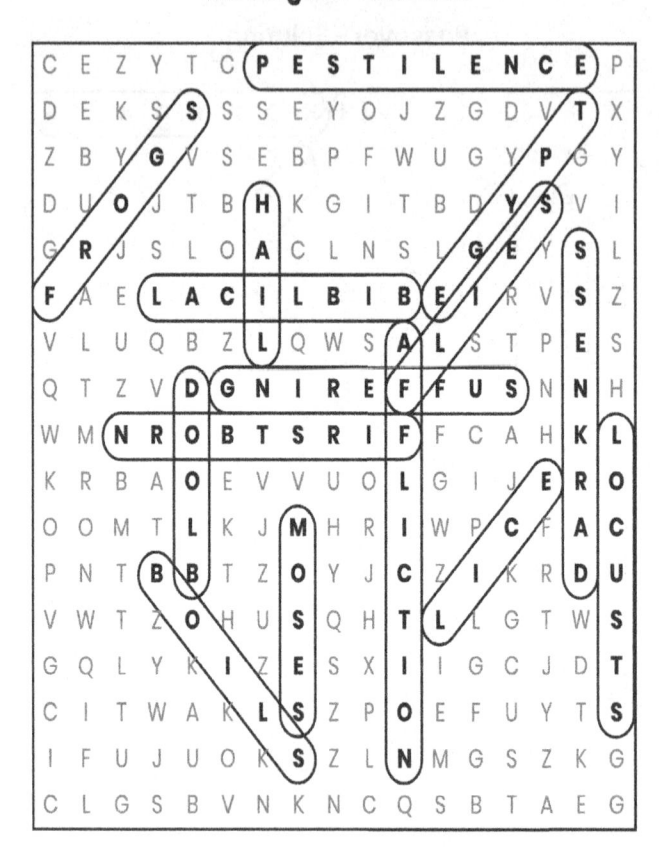

Dayenu - Solution

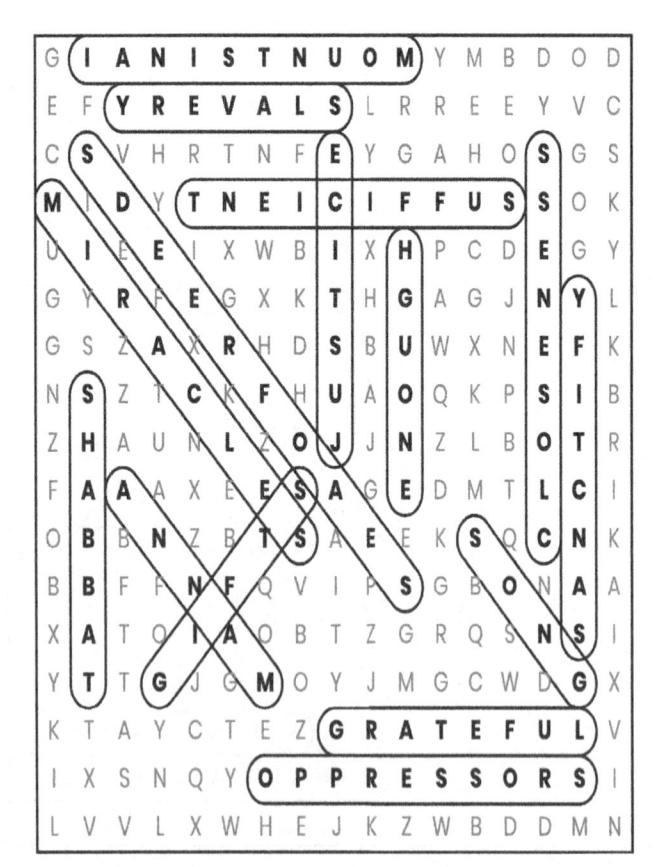

The Seder Plate - Solution

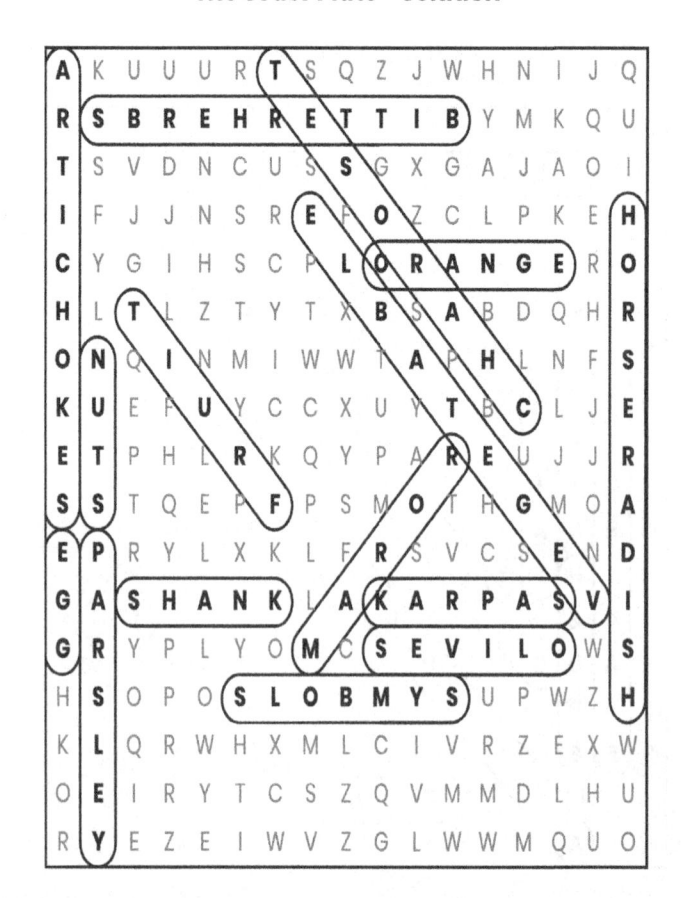

Passover Food - Solution

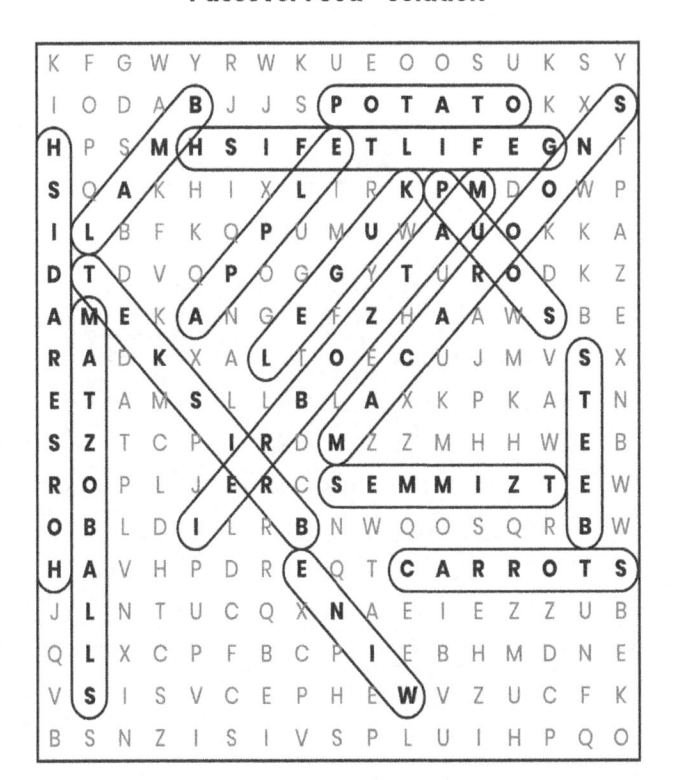

Haggadah - Solution

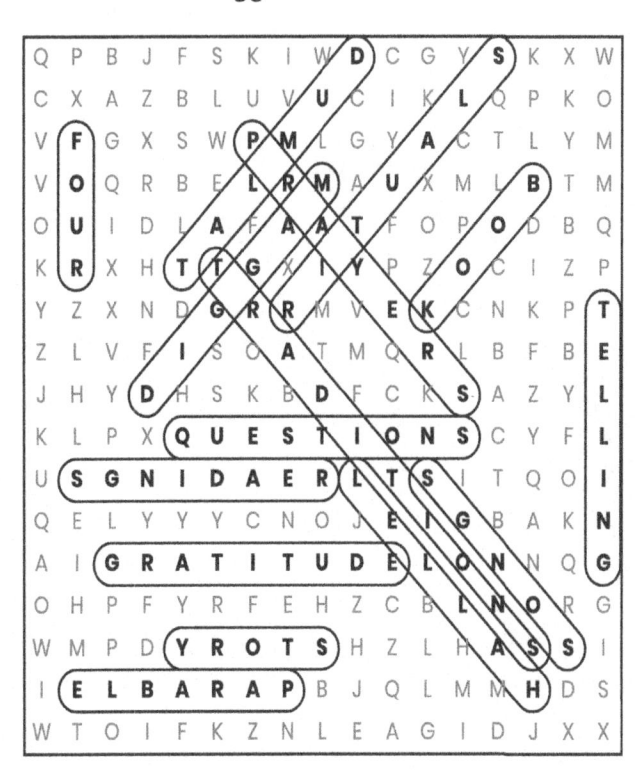

SEDER SCRAMBLE - Solution

HADAGGAH	HAGGADAH
POHARAH	PHARAOH
CTEHMAZ	CHAMETZ
KDUSDIH	KIDDUSH
CNLADE	CANDLE
CORHSEAT	CHAROSET
SSMOE	MOSES
DYNAEU	DAYENU
PAECSH	PESACH
RRMAO	MAROR
EAJLIH	ELIJAH
AOKEIFMN	AFIKOMEN

Around The Table

Maze Solutions

Kippah

Macaroons

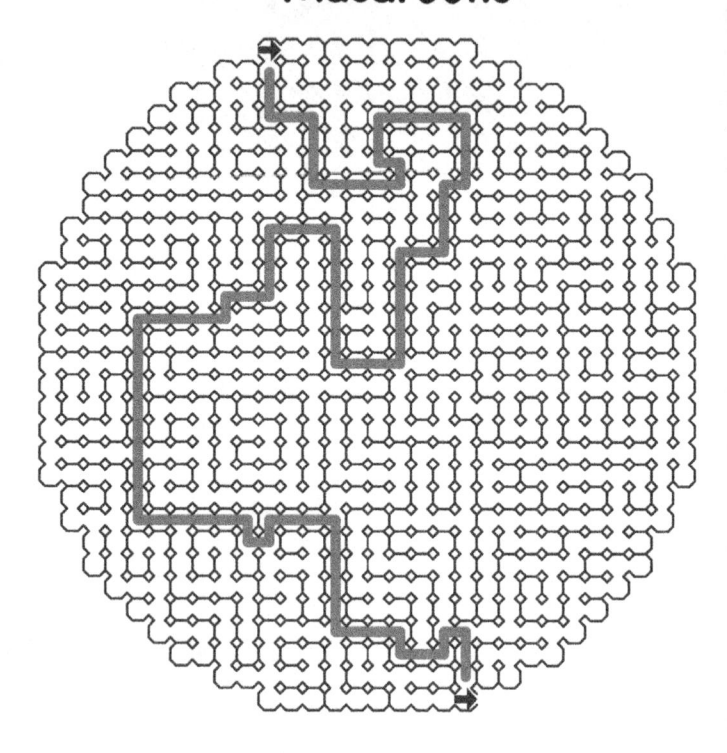

Matzah

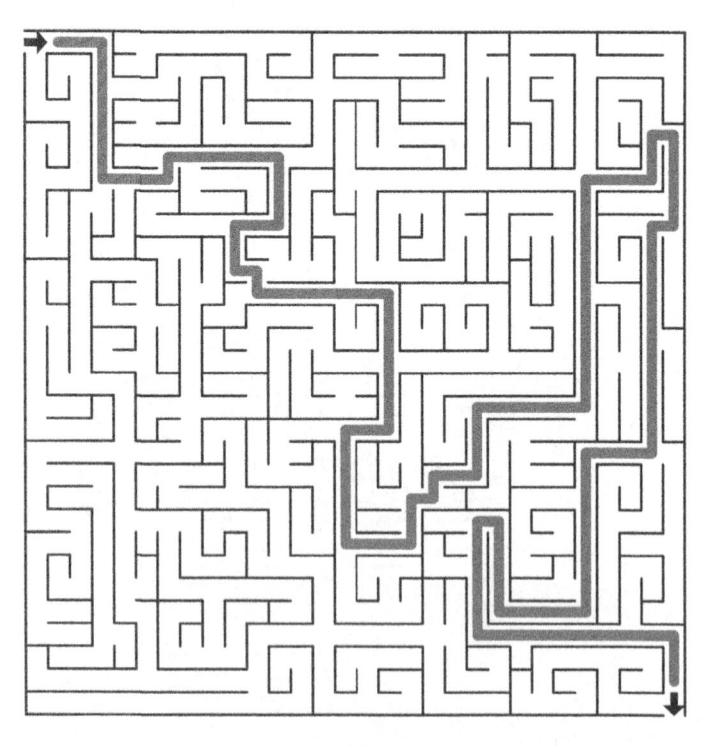

Star Of David

74

Candle word search.

N	C	L	E	A	E	D	A	N	A	N
E	L	C	L	E	N	C	N	N	E	A
E	L	L	C	L	A	A	A	D	A	C
L	L	D	D	A	N	C	D	A	D	N
D	L	D	A	N	N	E	L	C	A	D
A	A	D	E	A	A	D	E	N	D	L
N	C	D	N	L	A	C	L	N	C	L
A	A	E	N	N	A	L	N	E	L	L
C	C	D	D	C	L	N	N	L	L	N
C	C	L	D	L	E	A	A	A	N	C
E	N	D	A	L	E	C	A	L	L	E
N	L	L	D	N	C	A	D	C	E	D

Custom word search.

S	U	C	O	U	M	O	M	O	S	C
C	M	U	M	S	M	O	T	S	M	S
S	M	O	M	T	U	M	M	C	U	C
M	O	C	O	O	U	O	T	U	U	T
M	T	U	O	M	C	T	C	S	U	T
M	S	S	C	C	S	C	O	C	S	C
O	U	U	M	O	T	S	S	C	M	T
U	C	T	M	T	C	S	M	S	T	S
S	O	S	C	O	O	T	T	O	S	U
C	T	S	O	C	U	C	O	S	S	C
M	O	O	M	O	C	T	C	O	U	O
S	C	T	S	U	T	S	O	O	M	U

Family word search.

I	A	Y	M	Y	F	F	M	I	A	F
F	L	Y	F	L	M	I	Y	I	L	M
L	M	Y	Y	M	A	M	I	M	A	M
L	F	L	M	L	I	F	M	M	A	I
M	M	M	Y	M	I	L	M	I	A	A
A	F	L	M	L	M	M	A	L	A	A
I	F	M	M	M	I	F	A	A	F	Y
L	L	F	F	L	I	L	Y	F	A	F
F	M	A	I	F	L	Y	L	M	A	Y
A	A	A	L	A	M	Y	A	M	L	F
A	L	I	A	M	M	Y	F	Y	F	L
F	L	Y	I	I	M	L	M	Y	A	A

Famine word search.

E	I	M	N	F	E	I	N	M	F	A
E	N	N	M	F	M	A	I	F	F	A
E	M	N	E	F	I	F	E	M	E	E
E	F	M	F	M	E	N	M	F	A	I
N	M	F	M	N	E	E	A	F	M	F
N	I	N	F	E	N	M	I	M	E	M
E	A	E	M	E	I	F	E	E	N	I
N	F	M	F	N	E	M	I	N	N	M
M	N	I	E	F	E	N	M	I	I	N
N	F	A	A	M	I	M	M	I	E	E
E	F	N	I	N	M	A	E	I	I	A
E	M	F	F	F	A	F	I	A	N	F

75

Kosher word search.

R	S	R	S	S	K	S	R	O	O	S	E
H	H	K	H	H	R	O	R	H	R	K	R
E	R	S	S	S	S	R	S	K	S	H	H
R	H	O	E	O	R	R	H	R	O	R	O
S	O	S	S	S	E	E	O	H	H	R	
S	E	E	H	R	E	S	H	O	E	E	
E	R	K	E	E	R	O	F	S	E	R	R
S	E	S	O	E	O	S	K	R	O	O	O
K	R	K	H	K	S	K	R	E	K	K	K
O	S	H	O	O	S	H	O	S	S	S	S
K	E	S	O	H	H	O	S	R	H	O	O
R	R	R	S	S	O	O	R	K	S	K	R

Plague word search.

G	L	E	P	L	L	P	U	U	G	P	E
L	U	G	E	A	A	P	E	E	P	L	L
G	E	P	U	E	U	P	G	U	L	P	A
A	L	G	U	P	P	L	G	A	E	A	P
E	G	G	L	U	L	A	P	P	G	P	G
P	A	E	U	L	P	G	L	U	U	A	U
A	E	L	E	G	U	E	E	E	U	L	L
G	A	L	G	U	U	L	E	E	G	P	A
E	G	E	L	G	P	G	L	E	P	G	L
U	G	L	A	A	E	E	U	U	P	A	G
L	L	L	U	U	U	G	A	A	L	A	
L	P	G	A	A	L	L	A	G	U	E	E

Wander word search.

N	E	E	E	D	D	W	D	A	N	R	N
D	R	R	E	R	R	R	E	W	A	E	R
D	E	E	N	D	E	D	W	E	A	D	N
N	N	N	E	D	N	W	D	E	W	N	A
N	E	N	W	R	A	N	N	N	A	A	E
R	A	R	W	R	N	N	N	D	R	W	D
R	R	R	D	R	R	R	A	N	D	W	A
N	R	A	D	D	N	D	N	D	R	R	W
R	W	D	R	A	E	R	W	R	A	E	D
E	E	R	E	E	R	A	D	D	A	A	A
E	N	E	A	E	W	R	W	W	A	W	W
E	E	D	R	W	W	W	R	D	R	A	R

Ritual word search.

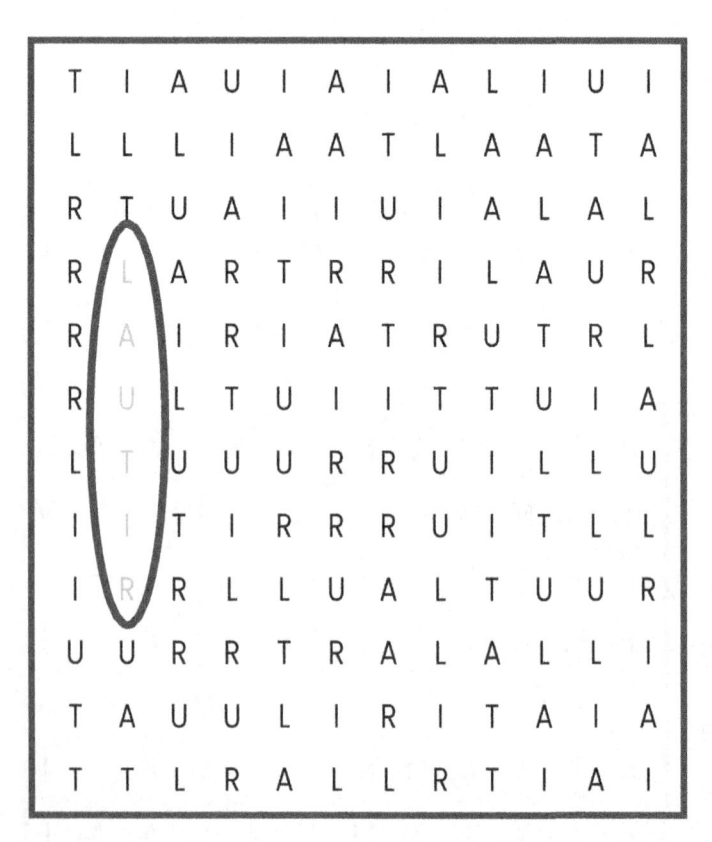

T	I	A	U	I	A	I	A	L	I	U	I
L	L	L	I	A	A	T	L	A	A	T	A
R	T	U	A	I	I	U	I	A	L	A	L
R	L	A	R	T	R	R	I	L	A	U	R
R	A	I	R	I	A	T	R	U	T	R	L
R	U	L	T	U	I	I	T	T	U	I	A
L	T	U	U	U	R	R	U	I	L	L	U
I	T	I	T	I	R	R	R	U	I	T	L	L
I	R	L	L	U	A	L	T	U	U	R	
U	U	R	R	T	R	A	L	A	L	L	I
T	A	U	U	L	I	R	I	T	A	I	A
T	T	L	R	A	L	L	R	T	I	A	I

76

Holiday Table

Going To Grandma's

Kitchen Is Ready

Looking For Afikomen

77

Stick Figure Sudoku

Find 3 Identical Seder Plates In A Row

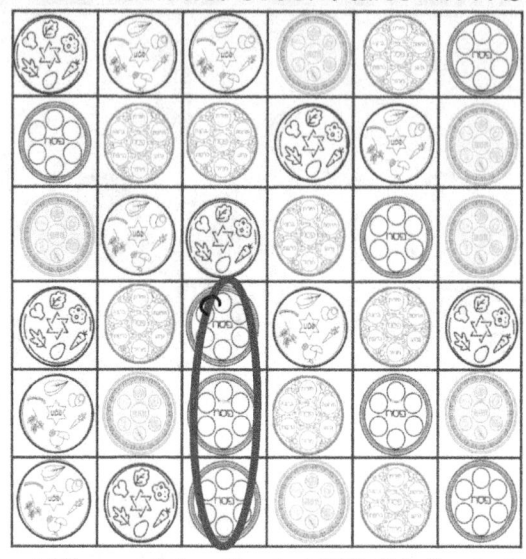

Find Three Identical APPLES In A Row

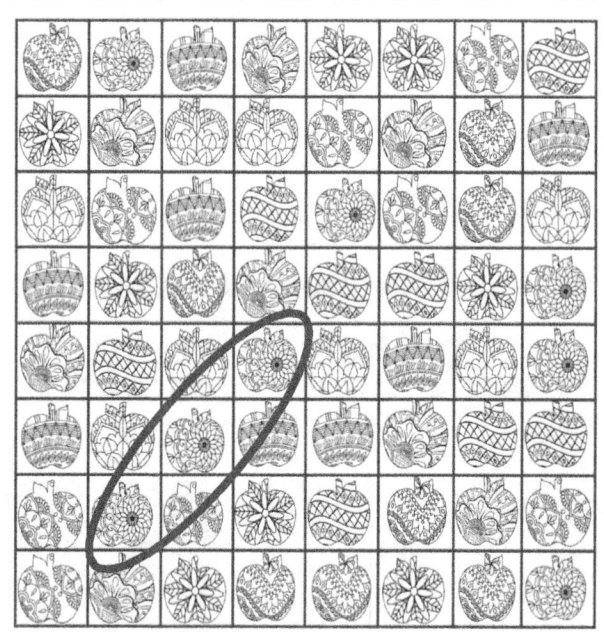

Number Sequence #1

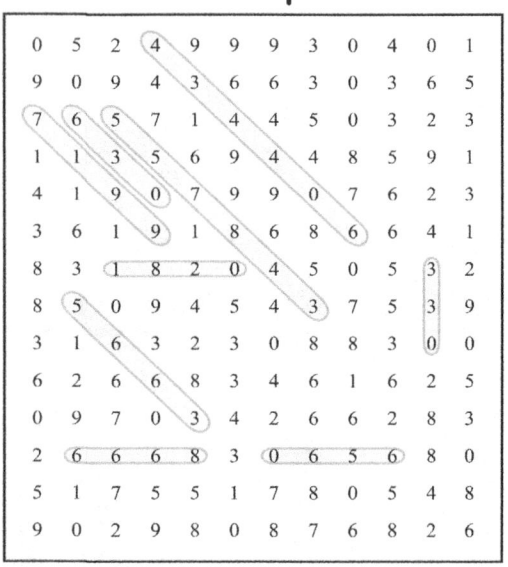

0	5	2	4	9	9	9	3	0	4	0	1
9	0	9	4	3	6	6	3	0	3	6	5
7	6	5	7	1	4	5	0	3	2	3	
1	1	3	5	6	9	4	8	5	9	1	
4	1	9	0	7	9	9	0	7	6	2	3
3	6	1	9	1	8	6	9	6	4	1	
8	3	1	8	2	0	4	5	0	5	3	2
8	5	0	9	4	5	4	3	7	5	3	9
3	1	6	3	2	3	0	8	3	0	0	
6	2	6	6	8	3	4	6	1	6	2	5
0	9	7	0	3	4	2	6	6	2	8	3
2	6	6	6	8	3	0	6	5	6	8	0
5	1	7	5	5	1	7	8	0	5	4	8
9	0	2	9	8	0	8	7	6	8	2	6

Number Sequence #2

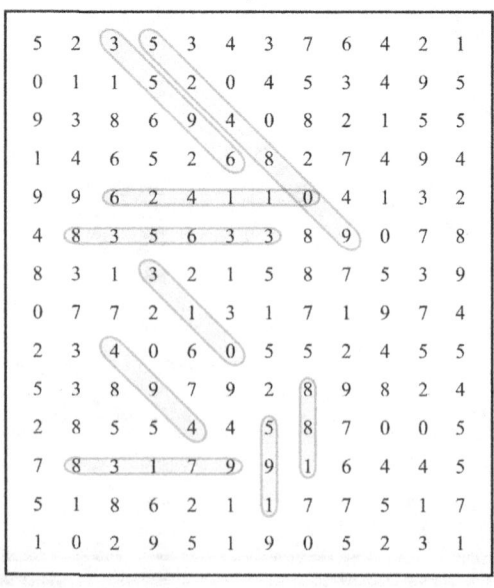

5	2	3	5	3	4	3	7	6	4	2	1
0	1	1	5	2	0	4	5	3	4	9	5
9	3	8	6	9	4	0	8	2	1	5	5
1	4	6	5	2	6	8	2	7	9	4	
9	9	6	2	4	1	1	0	4	1	3	2
4	8	3	5	6	3	3	8	9	0	7	8
8	3	1	3	2	1	5	8	7	5	3	9
0	7	7	2	1	3	1	7	1	9	7	4
2	3	4	0	6	0	5	5	2	4	5	5
5	3	8	9	7	9	2	8	9	8	2	4
2	8	5	5	4	4	5	8	7	0	0	5
7	8	3	1	7	9	9	1	6	4	4	5
5	1	8	6	2	1	7	7	5	1	7	
1	0	2	9	5	1	9	0	5	2	3	1

Number Sequence #3

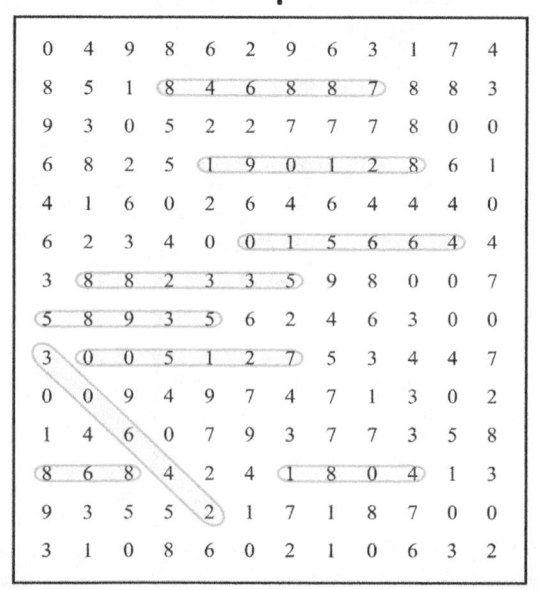

0	4	9	8	6	2	9	6	3	1	7	4
8	5	1	8	4	6	8	7	8	8	3	
9	3	0	5	2	2	7	7	8	0	0	
6	8	2	5	1	9	0	1	2	8	6	1
4	1	6	0	2	6	4	6	4	4	0	
6	2	3	4	0	0	1	5	6	6	4	4
3	8	8	2	3	3	5	9	8	0	0	7
5	8	9	3	5	6	2	4	6	3	0	0
3	0	0	5	1	2	7	5	3	4	4	7
0	0	9	4	9	7	4	7	1	3	0	2
1	4	6	0	7	9	4	7	7	3	5	2
8	6	8	4	2	4	1	8	0	4	1	3
9	3	5	5	2	1	7	1	8	7	0	0
3	1	0	8	6	0	2	1	0	6	3	2

78

Spot The 10 Differences Between This Page And The Next Page (Puzzles A & B)

Puzzle A

Puzzle B

Spot The 10 Differences

Spot The 11 Differences

Spot The 11 Differences

79

The Star

Seder Plate

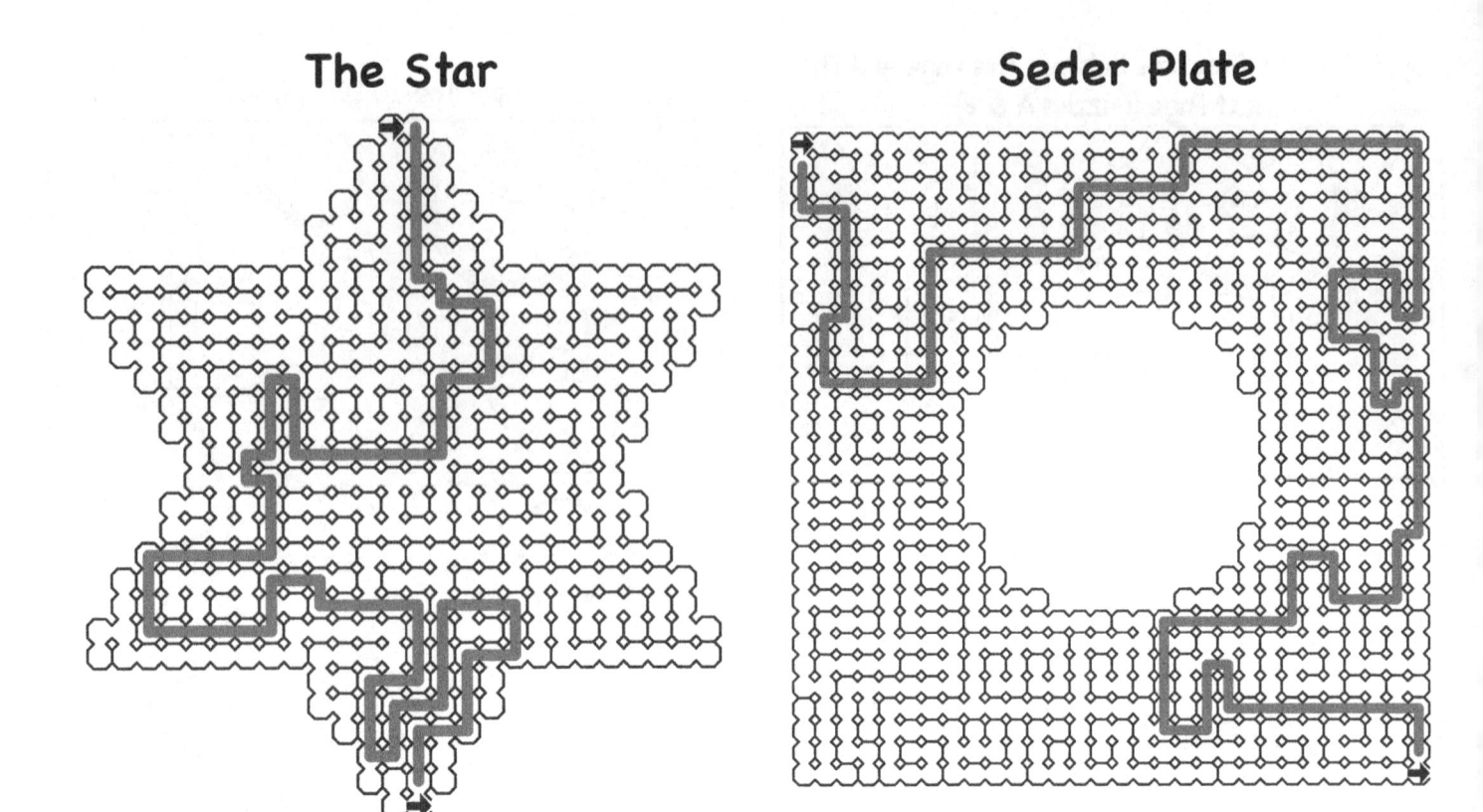

Riddles

1. What comes once in a minute, twice in a moment but never in a thousand years? The letter M.

2. What do you call a bear with no teeth? A gummy bear.

3. Which is faster, hot or cold? Hot, because you can catch a cold.

4. How do you make seven even? You take away the s.

5. What does an evil hen lay? Deviled eggs.

6. How do trees get on the internet? They log in.

7. Why did the nose feel sad? It was always getting picked on.

8. Where do books hide when they're scared? Under their covers.

9. Why was the math book sad? It had too many problems.

10. What gets wetter the more it dries? A towel.

11. Why don't eggs tell jokes? They'd crack each other up.

12. When you drop a yellow hat in the Red Sea what does it become? Wet.

PASSOVER WORDOKU PUZZLE 1

U	D	Y	N	A	E
A	N	E	U	Y	D
Y	U	D	E	N	A
E	A	N	D	U	Y
D	Y	U	A	E	N
N	E	A	Y	D	U

DAYENU

PASSOVER WORDOKU PUZZLE 2

T	A	I	N	O	N
O	N	N	I	A	T
A	I	N	T	N	O
N	T	O	N	I	A
N	N	A	O	T	I
I	O	T	A	N	N

NATION

PASSOVER WORDOKU PUZZLE 3

E	N	E	A	V	L
V	A	L	E	E	N
A	E	N	V	L	E
L	V	E	N	A	E
E	L	V	E	N	A
N	E	A	L	E	V

LEAVEN

PASSOVER WORDOKU PUZZLE 4

M	H	T	A	A	Z
A	Z	A	M	H	T
A	T	A	Z	M	H
H	M	Z	T	A	A
T	A	M	H	Z	A
Z	A	H	A	T	M

MATZAH

81

PASSOVER WORDOKU PUZZLE 5

P	S	R	E	I	A
I	E	A	S	R	P
R	I	E	P	A	S
A	P	S	I	E	R
S	A	I	R	P	E
E	R	P	A	S	I

PRAISE

PASSOVER WORDOKU PUZZLE 6

C	P	S	A	E	H
H	E	A	S	C	P
E	H	C	P	S	A
A	S	P	E	H	C
P	C	E	H	A	S
S	A	H	C	P	E

PESACH

PASSOVER WORDOKU PUZZLE 7

A	S	R	K	P	A
K	P	A	A	R	S
S	A	P	R	A	K
R	K	A	A	S	P
A	R	S	P	K	A
P	A	K	S	A	R

KARPAS

PASSOVER WORDOKU PUZZLE 8

S	M	A	H	O	L
O	H	L	M	S	A
A	S	H	O	L	M
L	O	M	S	A	H
M	A	S	L	H	O
H	L	O	A	M	S

SHALOM

82

Shape Sudoku

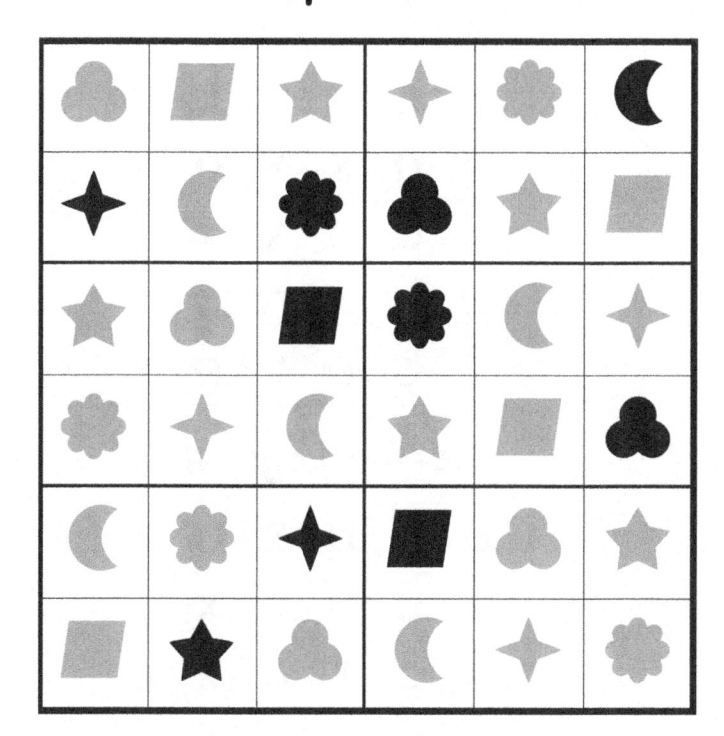

Searching for Afikomen

Anagrams

ARE	->	EAR
ARM	->	RAM
URN	->	RUN
TEA	->	EAT
TAB	->	BAT
WHO	->	HOW
WON	->	NOW
NAP	->	PAN
BARE	->	BEAR
BEAK	->	BAKE
BEST	->	BETS
BOSS	->	SOBS
CAFÉ	->	FACE
CARE	->	RACE
FLOW	->	WOLF
MEAT	->	TEAM
RING	->	GRIN
SINK	->	SKIN
POTS	->	STOP
NIGHT	->	THING

There can be other anagrams, too.

Tic-Tac-Logic #1

X	O	X	O	O	X
O	X	X	O	O	X
O	X	O	X	X	O
X	O	X	O	X	O
O	X	O	X	O	X
X	O	O	X	X	O

Tic-Tac-Logic #2

X	X	O	O	X	O
O	X	X	O	X	O
O	O	X	X	O	X
X	O	O	X	X	O
O	X	X	O	O	X
X	O	O	X	O	X

Tic-Tac-Logic #3

O	O	X	O	X	X
X	X	O	O	X	O
X	O	O	X	O	X
O	X	X	O	X	O
O	O	X	X	O	X
X	X	O	X	O	O

Tic-Tac-Logic #4

O	X	O	X	O	X
X	O	O	X	X	O
X	O	X	O	X	O
O	X	X	O	O	X
X	O	O	X	O	X
O	X	X	O	X	O

Cryptograms

1. WHY IS THIS NIGHT DIFFERENT FROM ALL OTHER NIGHTS
2. BURNING BUSH
3. PROMISED LAND
4. LET MY PEOPLE GO
5. CUP OF ELIJAH
6. ENOUGH ALREADY

Found The Afikomen

OTHER BOOKS FROM COPPER PENNY PUZZLES

ROAD TRIP FUN
TRAVEL ACTIVITY BOOK
for 6 to 9 year olds
Boredom Buster Puzzles
Games & Coloring Activities
for Curious Kids

https://amzn.to/38A18b6

ROAD TRIP
AGES 9-12 YEARS OLD
FUN TRAVEL ACTIVITY BOOK
adventure is just ahead

https://amzn.to/3twP1mL

ROAD TRIP FUN
Puzzles, Games & Coloring Activities
for 3 to 5 year olds

https://amzn.to/3Qk5UdD

ICE HOCKEY Activity Book for Kids 9 – 12
Word Search, Word Scrambles
Hidden Picture Puzzles
Mazes, Cryptograms & More
for Girls and Boys

https://amzn.to/48w7L8r

SEARCH AND FIND EMBARRASSING MOMENTS
HIDDEN PICTURE PUZZLES
Over 150 Objects to Find

https://amzn.to/3WXFC4q

SOCCER ACTIVITY BOOK for KIDS 9-12
FUTBOL FOOTBALL
Fun Word Search Puzzles,
Mazes, Cryptograms, Crosswords
& More for Girls and Boys

https://amzn.to/3D4gnDM

CUTE CREEPY KAWAII MONSTERS
SEARCH FOR HIDDEN FOOD
SEARCH AND FIND THE HIDDEN OBJECTS
PUZZLE AND COLORING BOOK

https://amzn.to/3fQTcG0

SOCCER ACTIVITY BOOK
6-8 year old girls & boys

https://amzn.to/3roypzv

SEARCH AND FIND CREEPY HORROR PARTY
HIDDEN PICTURE PUZZLE & COLORING BOOK
Freaky and Frightening
Zombies, Witches & Ghouls

https://amzn.to/3G0QI2w

Table of Contents

1. Ruby Citrus-Berry Fusion
2. Beetroot Citrus Smoothie 
3. Beetroot-Berry Power Smoothie 
4. Detox Smoothie 
5. Cocoa Beet Shake 
6. Buttermilk Berry Delight 
7. Blueberry Oat Smoothie 
8. Berry Blast Smoothie Bowl 
9. Red Energy Smoothie 
10. Berry Bell Pepper Fusion 
11. Watermelon Bliss Smoothie 
12. Fall Pumpkin Smoothie 
13. Sunshine Carrot Juice 
14. Citrus Carrot Boost 
15. Golden Smoothie 
16. Apricot Sunrise Smoothie 
17. Melon Avocado Mint Smoothie 
18. Green Orchard Smoothie 
19. Green Ginger Glow Smoothie 
20. Crisp Morning Smoothie 
21. Pear Spinach Smoothie 
22. Grape Splash Pineapple Bliss 
23. Green Garden Smoothie 
24. Cucumber Buttermilk Smoothie

Table of Contents

25 Moroccan Avocado Smoothie

26 Creamy Avocado Bowl

27 Orange Blossom Cinnamon Lassi

28 Banana Lassi

29 Banana-Date Dream Smoothie

30 Almond Smoothie

31 Nutty Sesame Delight Smoothie

32 Nutty Fig Smoothie

33 Pomegranate Juice

34 Watermelon Mint Lemonade

35 Watermelon Hydration Boost

36 Zesty Ginger Lemonade

37 Refreshing Lemon Trio

38 Pineapple Lemonade

39 Homemade Ginger Ale

40 Citrus Cinnamon Infusion

41 Grapefruit Thyme Sparkler

42 Cherry Basil Sparkler

43 Tropical Grapefruit Refreshment

44 Strawberry Rose Milkshake

45 Dragon Fruit Smoothie

46 Sunset Mango-Strawberry Smoothie

47 Frozen Colorful Smoothie

48 Peanut Butter and Oatmeal Smoothie

49 Minty Chocolate Smoothie

50 Café Mocha Power Smoothie

Ruby Citrus-Berry Fusion

| EASY | SERVES: 4 LARGE CUPS | PREP TIME: 10 MINUTES |

INGREDIENTS

360ml (1 1/2 cups) pomegranate juice
300ml (1 1/2 cups) fresh orange juice
300g (10.5 oz) raspberries, fresh or frozen
1 teaspoon grated fresh ginger
Natural sweetener (honey, maple syrup, or any favorite)
Ice cubes for serving (optional)

BENEFITS

Pomegranates are a fruit that is low in calories and fat, but high in fiber, vitamins, and minerals. They contain antioxidants and polyphenolic compounds, such as punicalagins, anthocyanins, and hydrolyzable tannins, which help protect your cells from free radical damage and may help prevent chronic inflammation associated with disease. Pomegranates have also been observed to have anticancer effects and may slow tumor growth and spread and reduce inflammation, although more research is needed to learn more about these effects.

STEPS

1. In a food processor, combine pomegranate juice, orange juice, and raspberries. Blend on high speed until the mixture is completely smooth and the raspberries are fully incorporated

2. Add the fresh ginger and sweetener to the blender. Continue blending for another minute, ensuring all the ingredients are thoroughly mixed.

3. If you prefer a silky-smooth texture, pass the smoothie through a strainer to remove any seeds or pulp. Serve immediately.

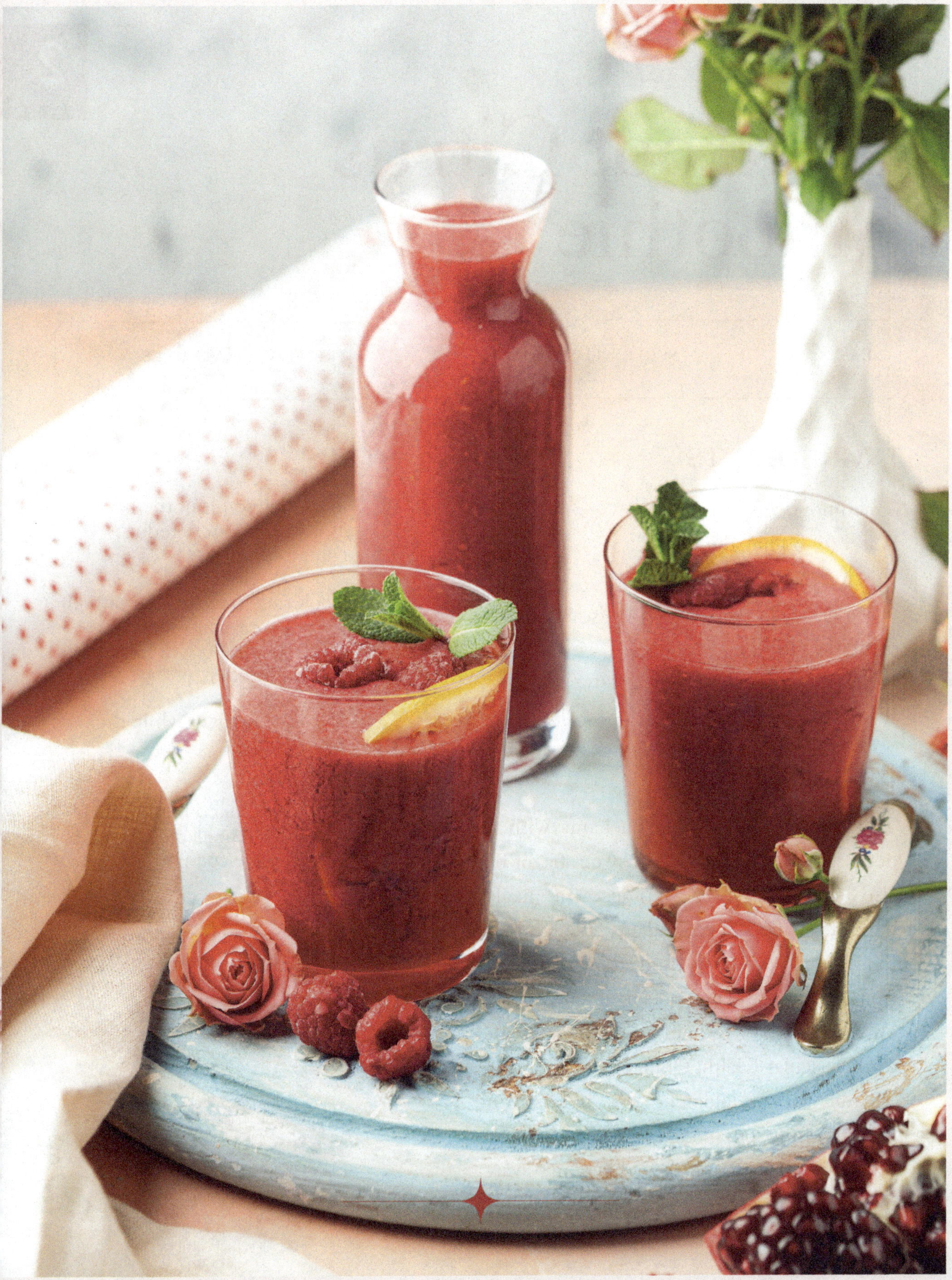

Beetroot Citrus Smoothie

| EASY | SERVES: 4 LARGE CUPS | PREP TIME: 10 MINUTES |

INGREDIENTS

3 medium beets
Water for boiling the beets
5 oranges
Natural sweetener (honey, maple syrup, or any favorite)
1 tablespoon orange blossom water
Ice for serving (optional)

BENEFITS

This beet juice not only enchants with its deep ruby hue and naturally sweet flavor but also serves as a powerhouse of health benefits. Rich in antioxidants, beets aid in fighting inflammation and protecting cells from damage. The presence of nitrates improves blood flow, enhancing stamina and cardiovascular health. Oranges, bursting with Vitamin C, complement this by boosting immune function and skin health, while the subtle hint of orange blossom water introduces a uniquely Moroccan aromatic pleasure.

STEPS

1. Trim both ends of the beets and score them to reduce cooking time.

2. Cook the beets in a pot of boiling water on medium-high heat for about 25 minutes, or until they are fork-tender.

3. Juice the oranges while the beets are cooking.

4. Cool the cooked beets in cold water, then peel and cube them once they're completely cool.

5. Combine the cubed beets, sweetener, orange blossom water, and fresh orange juice in a blender. Blend until smooth. Serve immediately

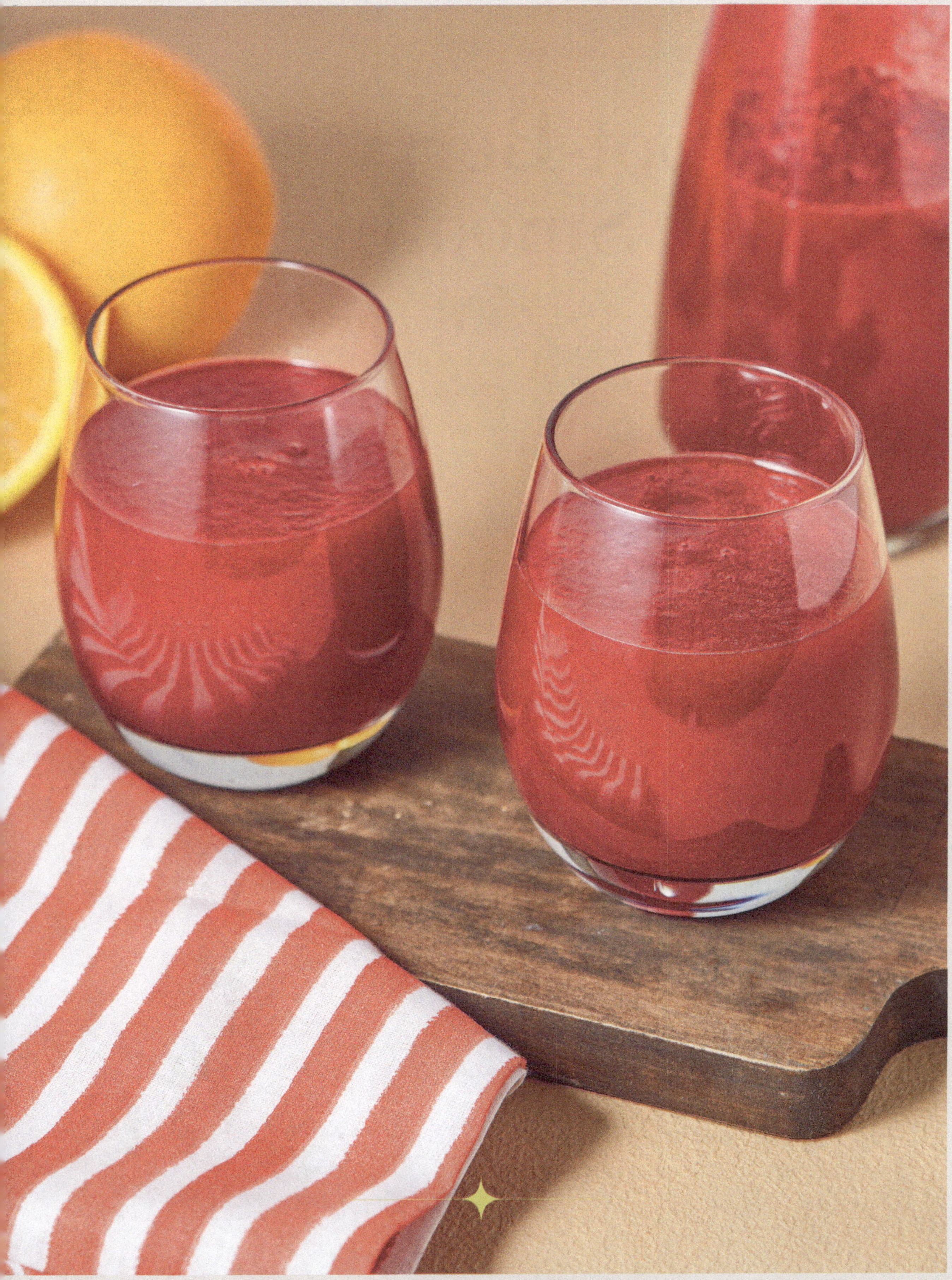

Beetroot-Berry Power Smoothie

| EASY | SERVES: 3 CUPS | PREP TIME: 15 MINUTES |

INGREDIENTS

1/2 large beetroot

25 strawberries, frozen

1/2 medium banana, frozen

2 medjool dates, pitted

125ml (1/2 cup) milk

BENEFITS

The beet smoothie is a vibrant blend of natural sweetness and earthy flavors, creating a nutrient-packed drink that's both delicious and healthful. Frozen strawberries and banana offer a naturally sweet base, rich in vitamins and fiber, while the beetroot adds a beautiful color, antioxidants, and a subtle earthiness that's surprisingly refreshing. Medjool dates provide additional sweetness and a boost of energy, along with essential minerals. This smoothie is not just a pleasure for the palate but also a boon for heart health, digestion, and energy levels.

STEPS

1. Peel the raw beetroot and chop into medium-sized pieces.

2. In a blender, place the beetroot pieces, frozen strawberries, frozen banana, dates, milk, and cocoa powder. Blend the mixture until smooth. Serve immediately!

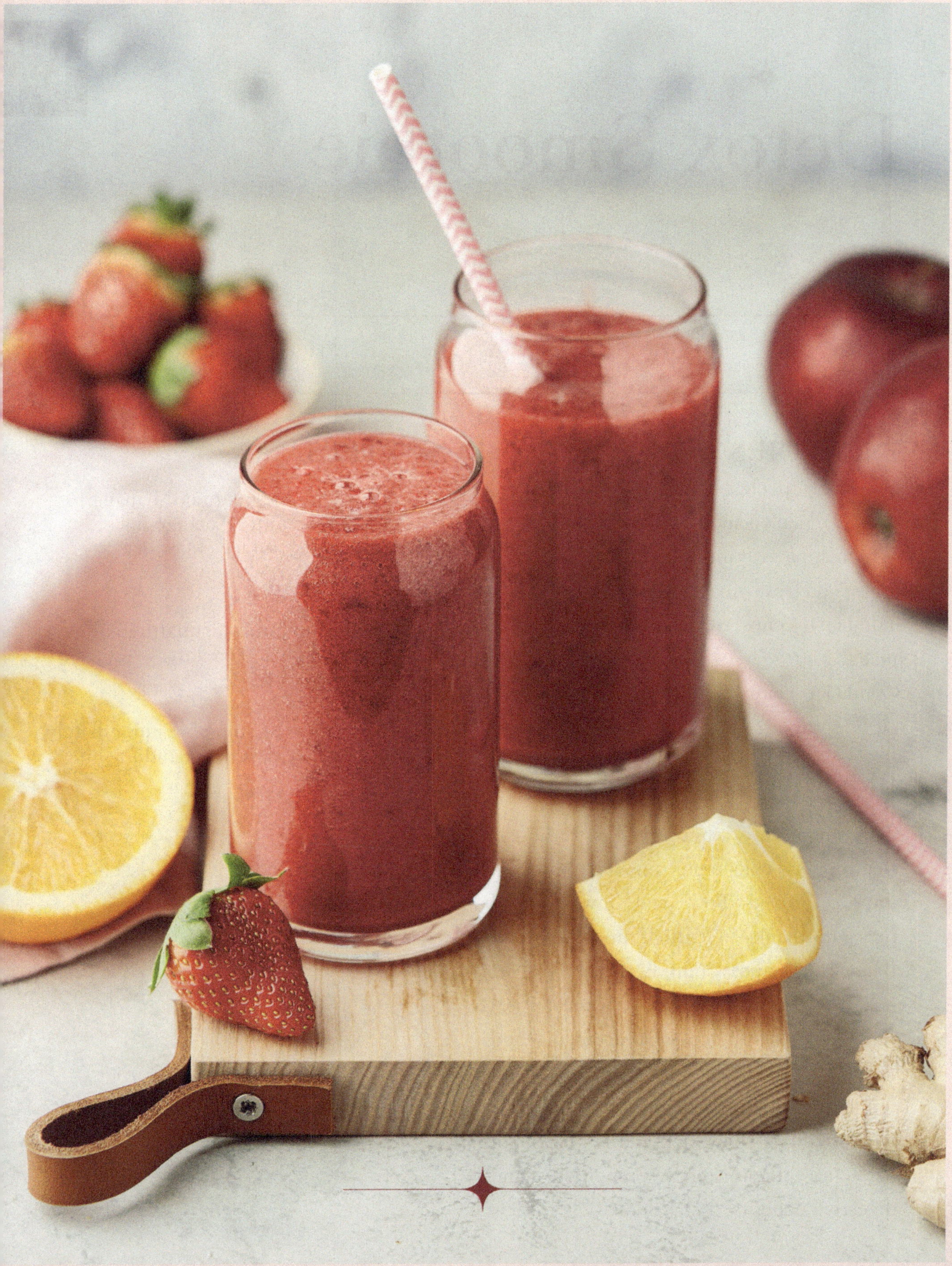

Detox Smoothie

| EASY | SERVES: 2 CUPS | PREP TIME: 10 MINUTES |

INGREDIENTS

2 beetroots, peeled and cut into small cubes
1 banana, peeled and cut into chunks
1 green apple, cut into chunks
1 teaspoon fresh ginger, peeled and grated
300ml (1 1/4 cups) freshly squeezed orange juice
300ml (1 1/4 cups) water
6 ice cubes

BENEFITS

This smoothie is a nutritional powerhouse. Beetroot is celebrated for its ability to improve blood flow and lower blood pressure, thanks to its high nitrate content. Bananas offer potassium, essential for heart health and muscle function, while apples provide a rich source of antioxidants and dietary fiber, promoting gut health and reducing the risk of chronic diseases. Ginger adds a spicy kick and is known for its anti-inflammatory properties and digestive benefits.

STEPS

1. Combine beetroots, banana, apple, ginger, orange juice, water, and ice cubes in a blender.

2. Blend until the mixture is smooth and creamy.

3. Serve the smoothie immediately for the best flavor and freshness.

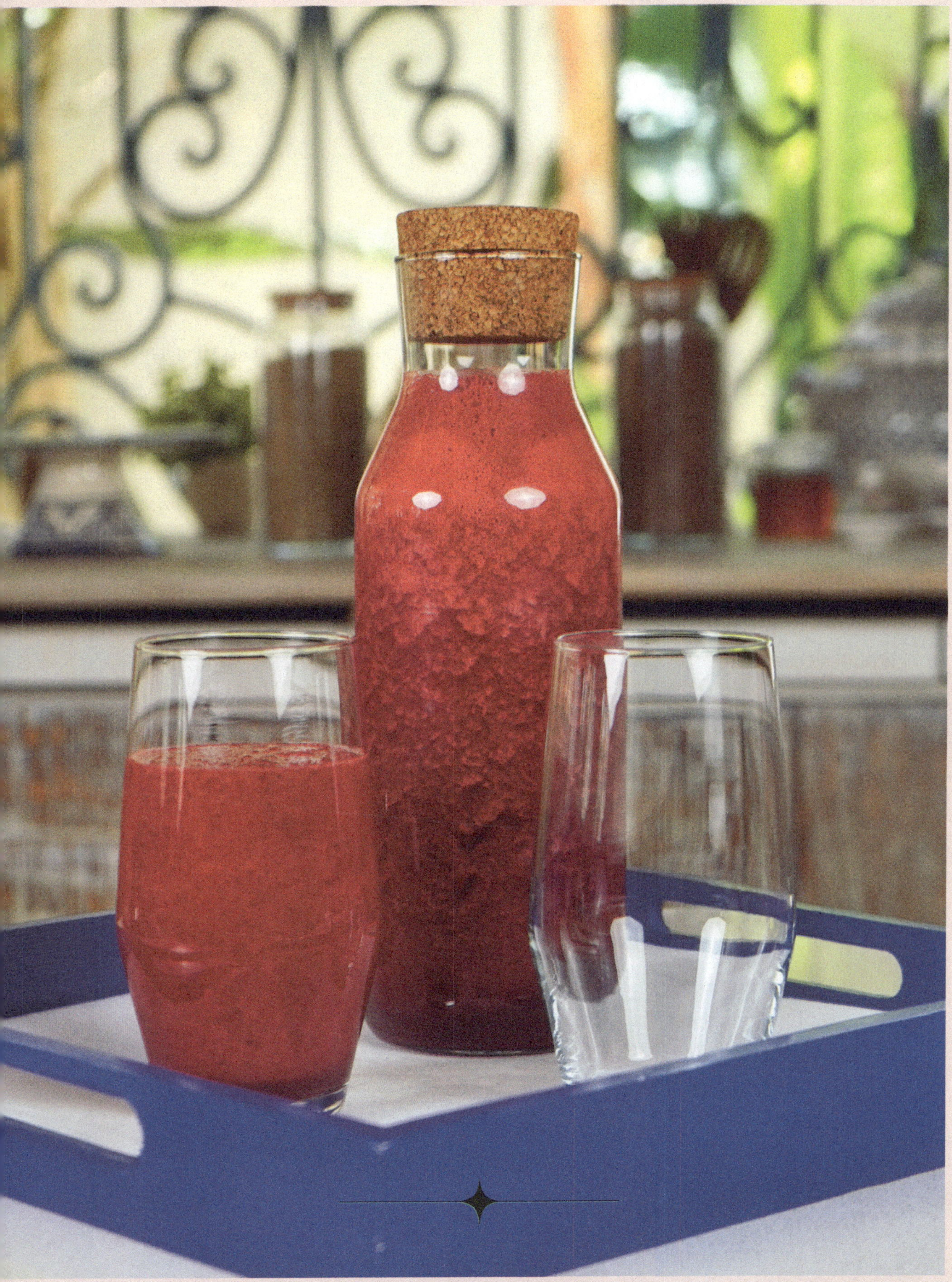

Cocoa Beet Shake

| EASY | SERVES: 1 LARGE CUP | PREP TIME: 15 MINUTES |

INGREDIENTS

5 strawberries, hulled and frozen
1/2 medium banana, peeled, sliced, and frozen
1/2 large beetroot
2 Medjool dates, pitted
120ml (1/2 cup) milk
1 tablespoon unsweetened cocoa powder

BENEFITS

This smoothie is a nutritional powerhouse. The beetroot provides dietary fiber, vitamins, and minerals, such as potassium and iron, supporting blood flow and cardiovascular health. Frozen strawberries and banana not only add natural sweetness and creaminess but also supply vitamin C and potassium, enhancing immune function and energy levels. The addition of cocoa powder introduces antioxidants known as flavonoids, which have been linked to improved heart health and cognitive function.

STEPS

1. Peel and chop the beetroot into smaller pieces for easier blending.

2. In a blender, combine the chopped beets, frozen strawberries, frozen banana, pitted Medjool dates, milk, and cocoa powder.

3. Blend all the ingredients until the mixture is smooth. If the smoothie is too thick, add a little more milk to adjust the consistency. Serve immediately!

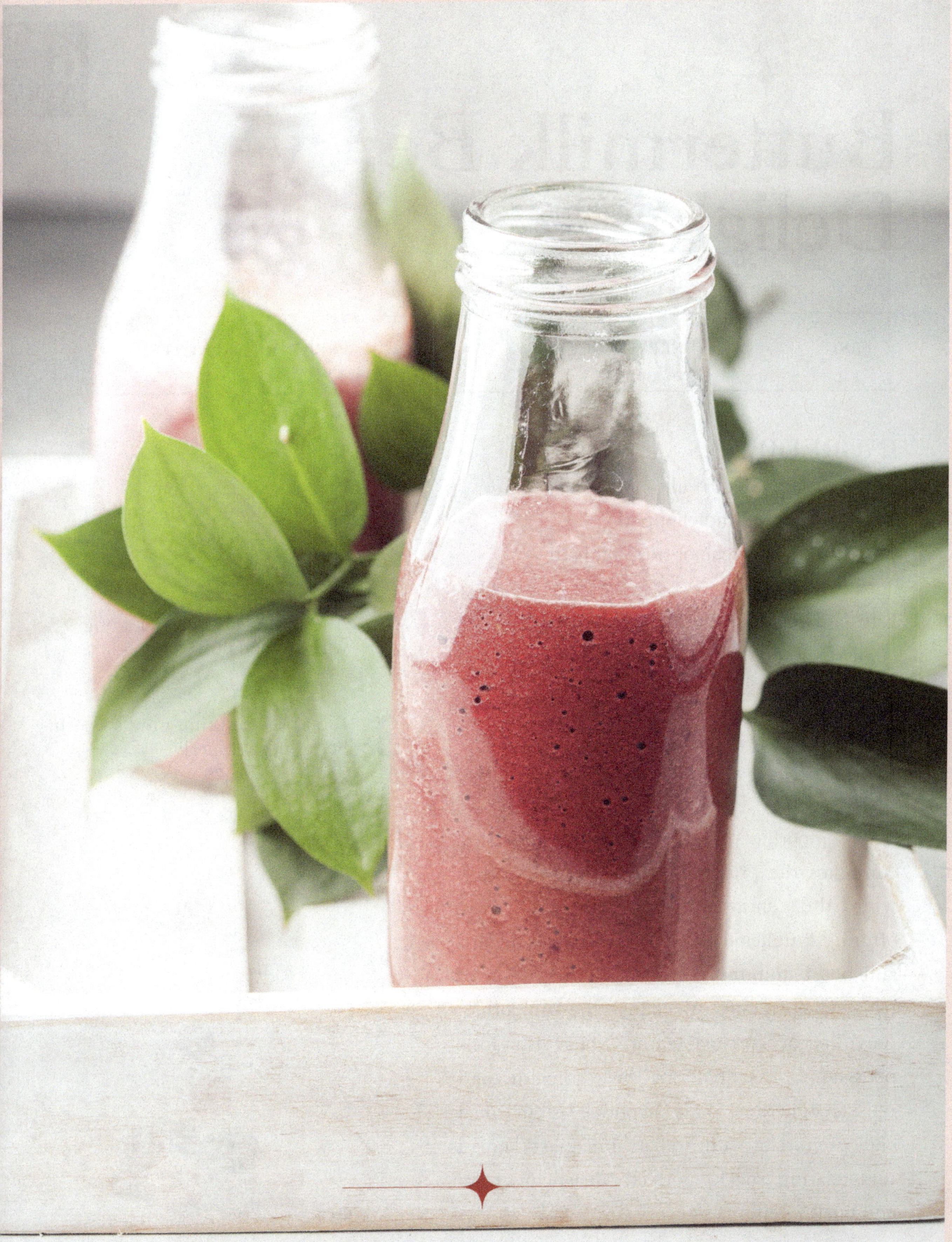

Buttermilk Berry Delight

EASY   SERVES: 2 CUPS   PREP TIME: 5 MINUTES

INGREDIENTS

500ml (2 cups) buttermilk
1 banana, peeled and chopped
240g (1 1/4 cup) fresh or frozen mixed berries
Natural sweetener (honey, maple syrup, or any favorite)
6 ice cubes

STEPS

1. Place the banana and the mixed berries in a blender.

2. Add natural sweetener along with the ice cubes.

3. Blend the mixture until smooth. Serve immediately.

BENEFITS

This smoothie is a refreshing blend that combines the probiotic benefits of buttermilk with the antioxidant-rich mixed berries, offering a delicious way to support gut health and boost immune function. The inclusion of banana not only thickens the smoothie, providing a creamy texture, but also adds potassium, essential for heart health and muscle function. This smoothie is an ideal choice for a nutritious breakfast or a rejuvenating snack, perfectly balancing taste and health benefits in every sip.

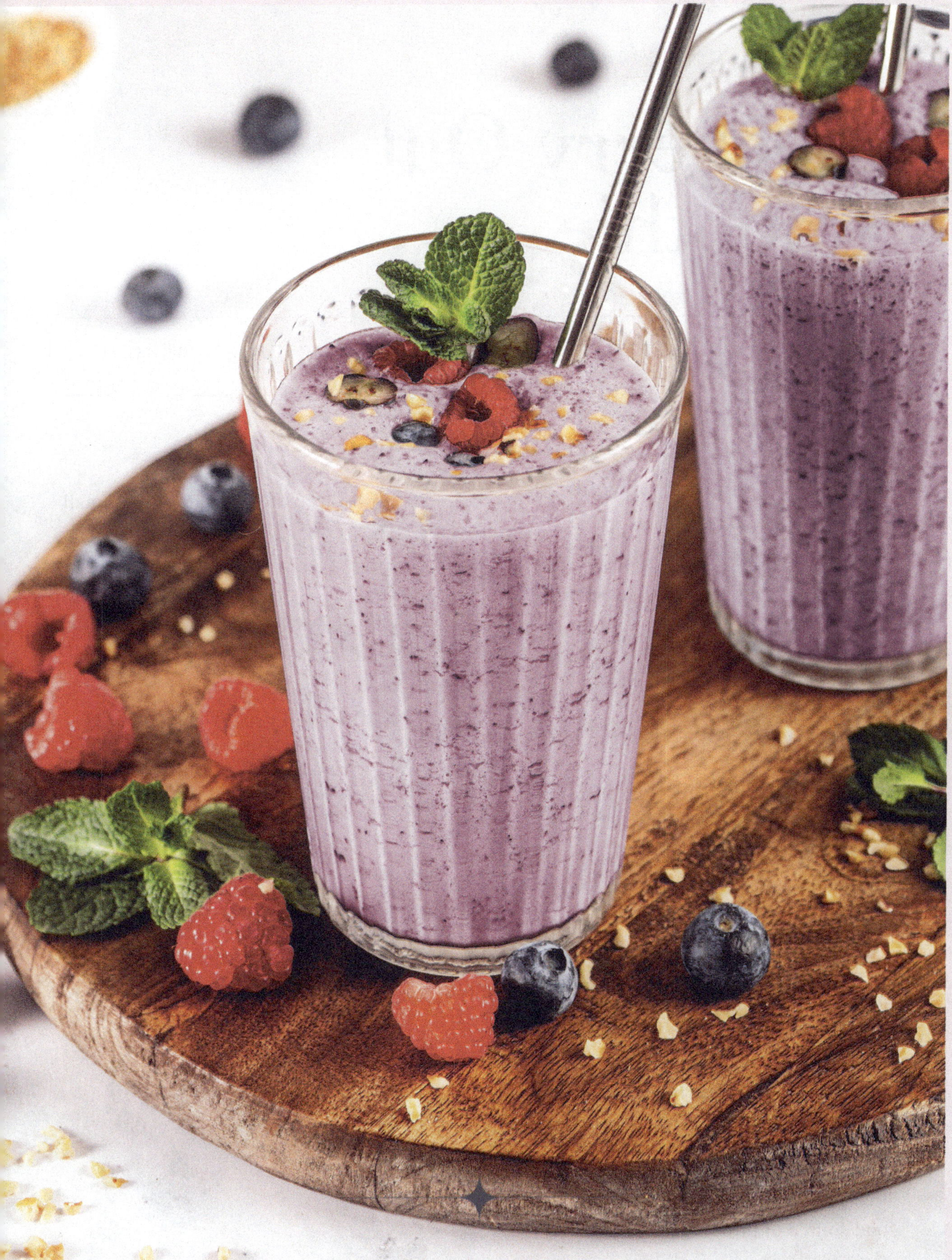

Blueberry Oat Smoothie

| EASY | SERVES: 2 CUPS | PREP TIME: 10 MINUTES |

INGREDIENTS

200 grams (7 oz.) frozen blueberries
35 grams (1/3 cup) rolled oats
2 tablespoons plain greek yogurt
250 milliliters (1 cup) creamy coconut milk
Natural sweetener (honey, maple syrup, or any favorite)
Cold water, if needed

BENEFITS

This is a nutrient-packed beverage that combines the antioxidant-rich qualities of blueberries with the heart-healthy fibers of rolled oats, offering a delicious way to support overall health. Blueberries, known for their high levels of antioxidants, can help combat aging and reduce DNA damage, potentially lowering the risk of chronic diseases. Rolled oats contribute valuable fibers that aid in digestion and have been shown to lower cholesterol levels, promoting heart health. The inclusion of Greek yogurt adds a probiotic boost, enhancing gut health and providing a good source of protein for muscle repair.

STEPS

1. Place the rolled oats in a small pan over medium heat. Toast them for about 6 minutes, stirring occasionally with a wooden spoon until they turn golden brown. Remove from heat and let cool.

2. In a blender, combine the cooled toasted oats, frozen blueberries, Greek yogurt, coconut milk, and sweetener to taste. Blend until the mixture is smooth.

3. If the smoothie is too thick, gradually add water until you reach your preferred consistency. Serve immediately.

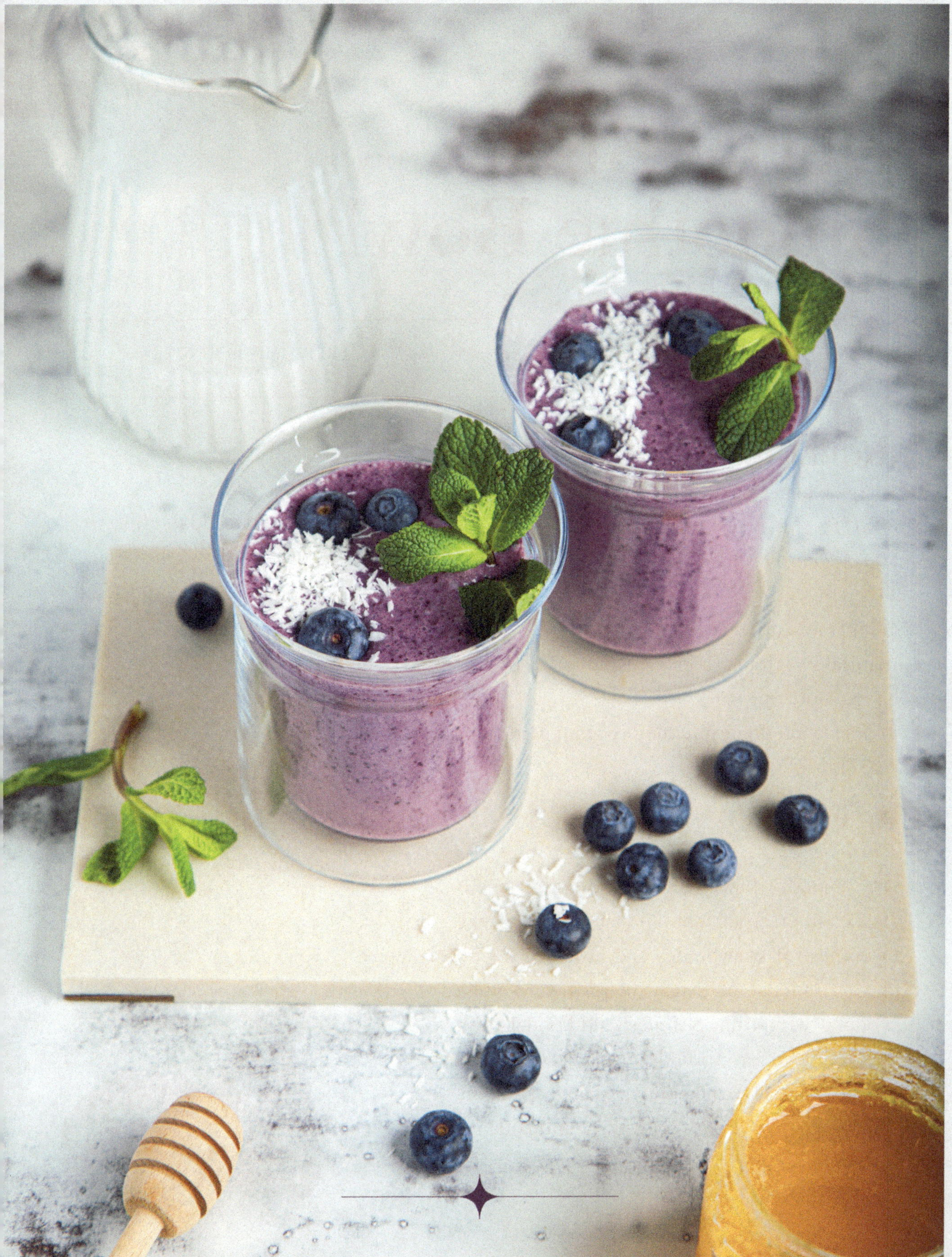

Berry Blast Smoothie Bowl

8

| EASY | SERVES: 1 CUP | PREP TIME: 15 MINUTES |

INGREDIENTS

1 large banana, peeled, sliced, and frozen
80g (1/2 cup) strawberries, hulled and frozen
80g (1/2 cup) raspberries, frozen
110g (1/2 cup) plain yogurt
100ml (1/2 cup) milk
Natural sweetener (honey, maple syrup, or any favorite)
1 tablespoon dried shredded coconut Muesli for serving

BENEFITS

The smoothie bowl is a nutritious and delicious breakfast or snack option that combines the sweetness of strawberries and raspberries with the creaminess of banana, yogurt, and milk. Topped with crunchy muesli, additional fresh berries, and a sprinkle of coconut, this smoothie bowl is not only visually appealing but also packed with vitamins, antioxidants, and fiber.

STEPS

1. In a blender, add the frozen sliced banana, frozen strawberries, and frozen raspberries, yogurt, milk, and sweetener.

2. Blend gradually until smooth and creamy.

3. Pour the smoothie into a bowl and top it with muesli, additional strawberries, raspberries, and shredded coconut. Serve immediately and enjoy with a spoon!

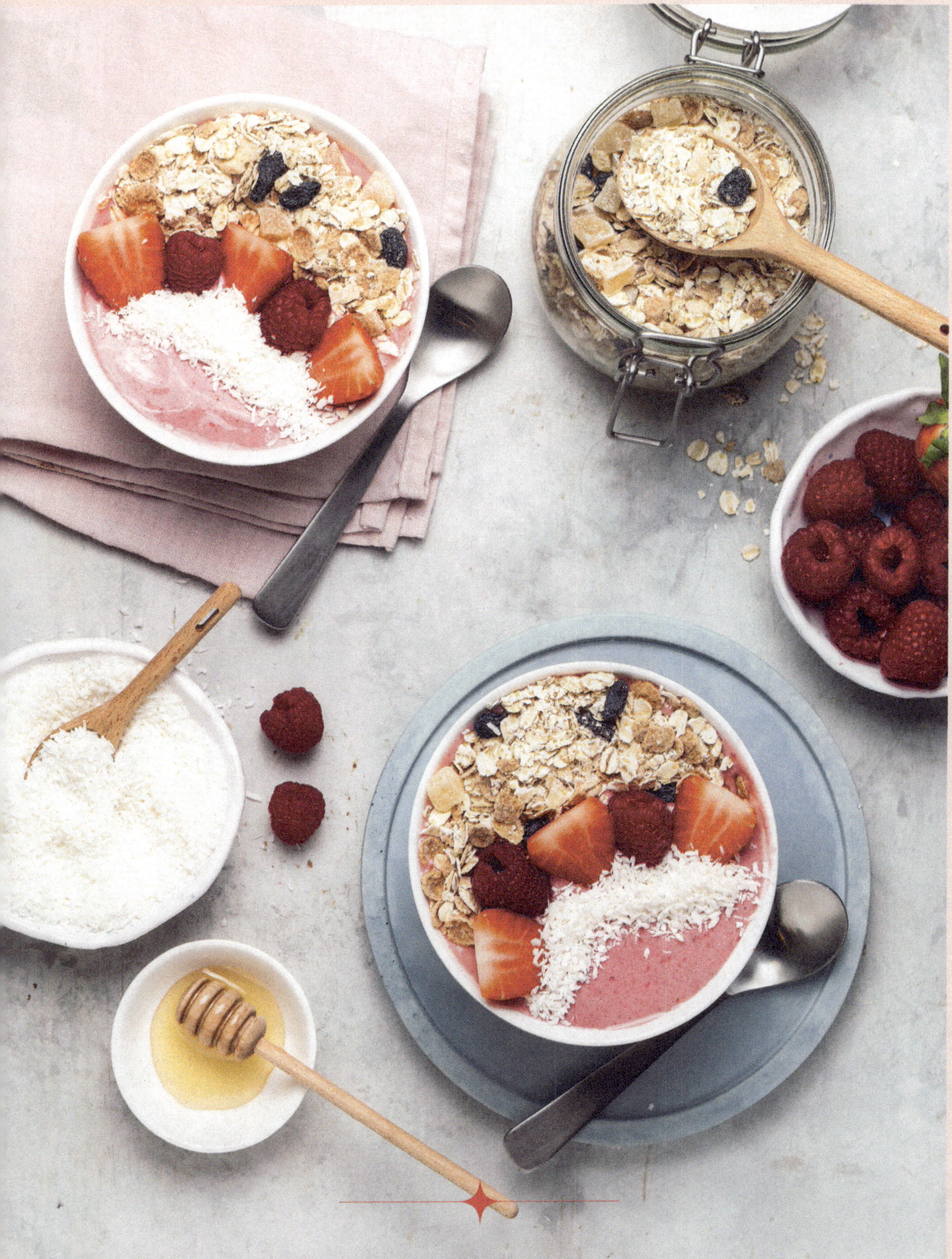

Red Energy Smoothie

| EASY | SERVES: 3 CUPS | PREP TIME: 5 MINUTES |

INGREDIENTS

21 carrot, peeled and roughly chopped
1/2 small red bell pepper, roughly chopped
1/2 banana
1 peach, pitted
1 plum, pitted
2 strawberries 350 ml (about 1 1/2 cups) orange juice
A handful of ice cubes

STEPS

1. In a blender, combine the chopped vegetables, fruit, orange juice, and ice cubes.

2. Blend the mixture until it reaches a smooth consistency.

3. Pour into glasses and serve immediately for the freshest taste.

BENEFITS

The carrot and red bell pepper lay down a foundation rich in vitamins A and C, essential for immune support and skin health, while the assorted fruits contribute antioxidants and fiber, promoting digestion and heart health. The inclusion of orange juice not only adds a refreshing twist but also amplifies the vitamin C content, enhancing absorption of iron from the vegetables. Served chilled with ice, this smoothie is the ultimate energizer.

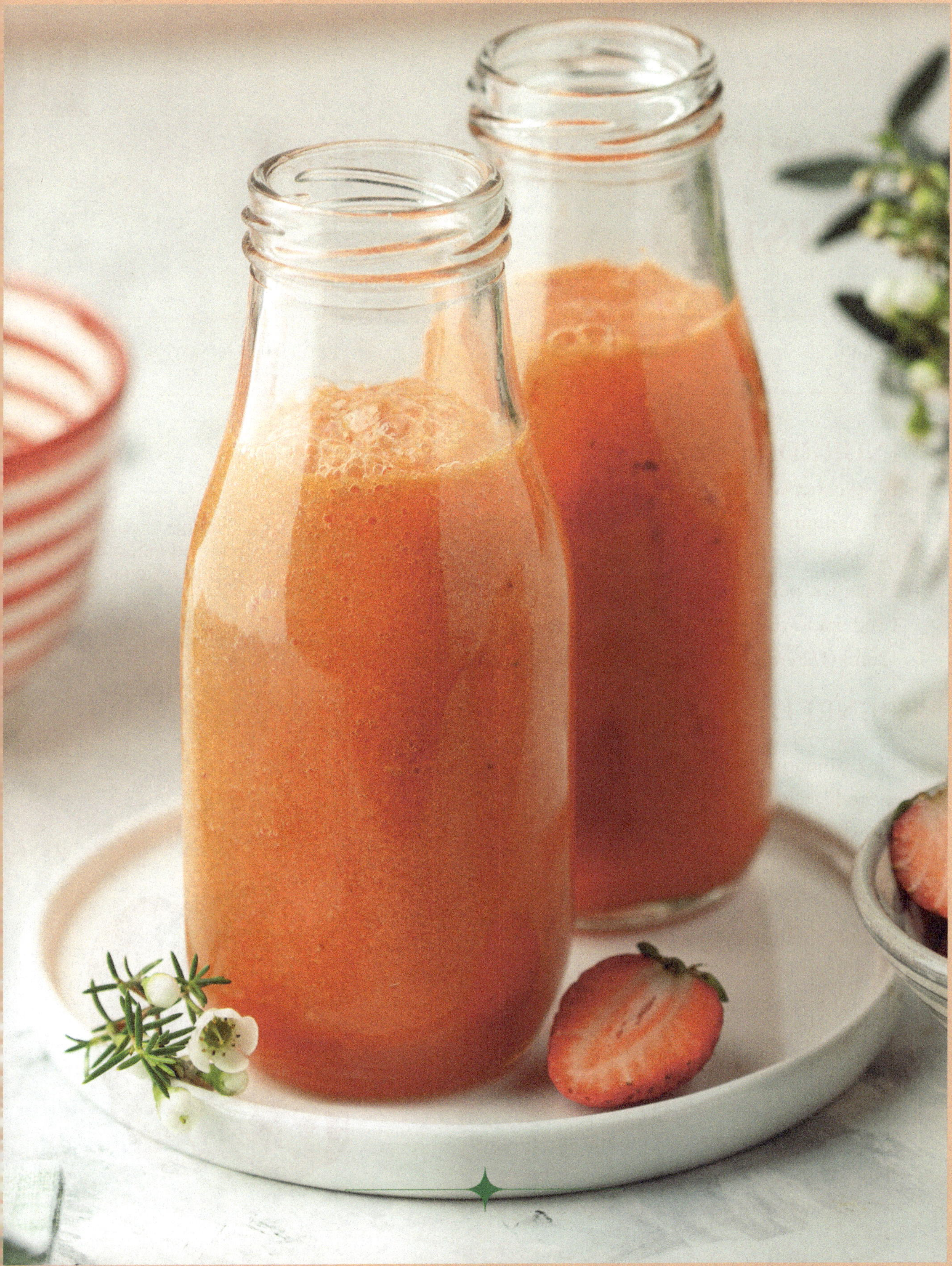

Berry Bell Pepper Fusion

| EASY | SERVES: 2 CUPS | PREP TIME: 5 MINUTES |

INGREDIENTS

10 strawberries, hulled and frozen
1/2 medium red bell pepper, seeded and chopped
2 oranges, peeled and segmented
1 red grapefruit, peeled and segmented
120ml (1/2 cup) water

BENEFITS

This smoothie is a vibrant fusion of fruits packed with vitamins, antioxidants, and refreshing flavors. Frozen strawberries not only provide a cool, satisfying texture but are also rich in vitamin C and antioxidants, which support immune health and fight inflammation. The inclusion of red bell pepper introduces a unique twist, adding vitamin A, vitamin C, and beta-carotene, known for their immune-boosting properties and ability to improve skin health. This smoothie is an excellent way to kickstart your day or replenish your body after a workout, offering a deliciously healthy boost with every sip.

STEPS

1. Combine the frozen strawberries, chopped red bell pepper, orange and grapefruit pieces, water, and ice cubes in a blender.

2. Blend until the mixture achieves a smooth consistency. Serve the smoothie immediately for the freshest taste.

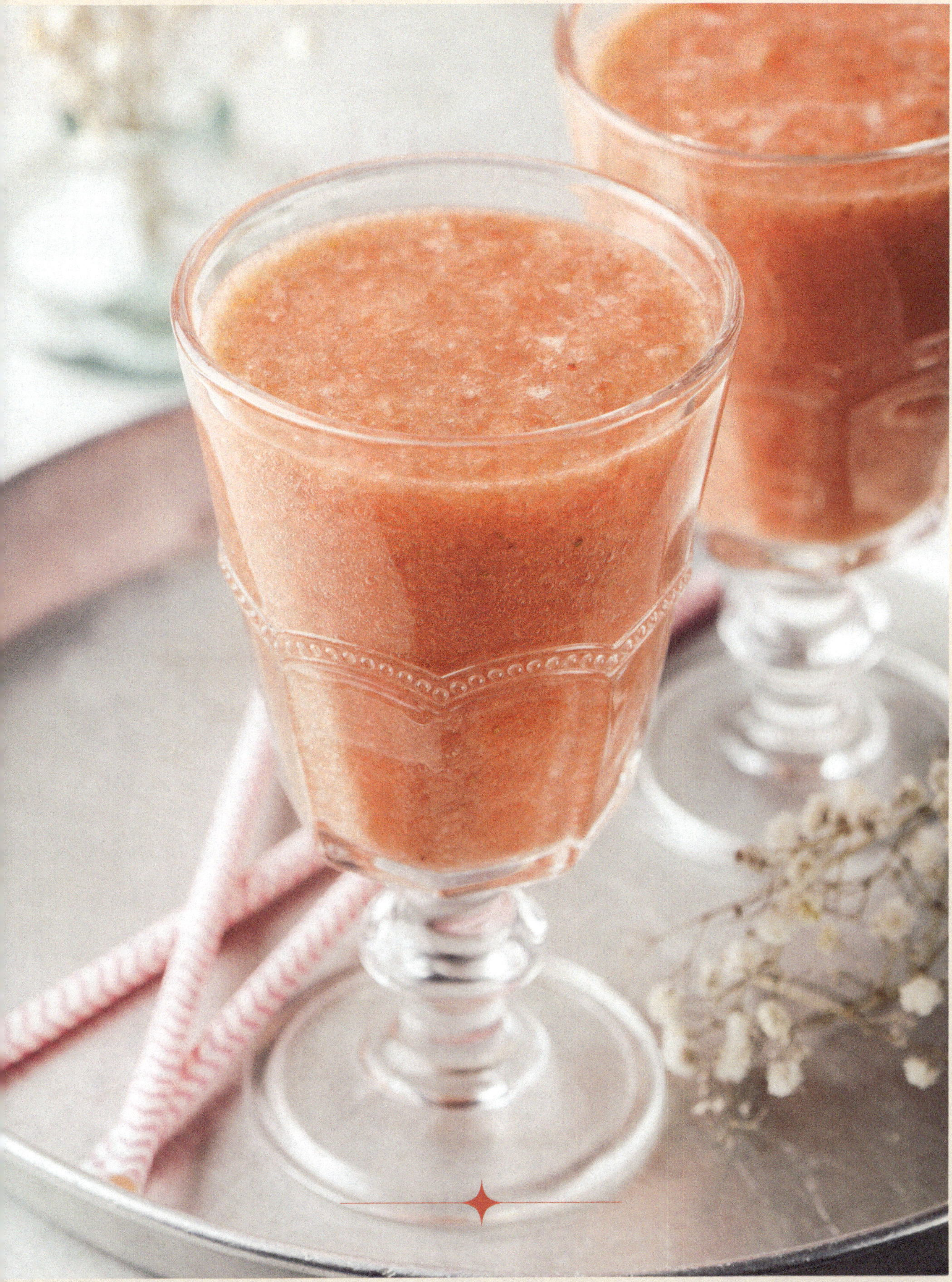

Watermelon Bliss Smoothie

| EASY | SERVES: 4 CUPS | PREP TIME: 10 MINUTES |

INGREDIENTS

2400 grams (14 oz) watermelon, cubed
90 grams (3 oz) strawberries, hulled and sliced
2 oranges, juiced
1/2 banana, sliced
Ice for serving (optional)

BENEFITS

This smoothie is a hydrating and nutrient-rich beverage perfect for boosting hydration and providing a wealth of vitamins and antioxidants. Watermelon, with its high water content, aids in hydration and contains lycopene, a powerful antioxidant known for its heart health and anti-cancer properties. Strawberries add a dose of vitamin C, enhancing immune function and skin health, while the potassium-rich bananas support muscle function and help regulate blood pressure. Orange juice contributes additional vitamin C and flavonoids, promoting further immune support and antioxidant protection.

STEPS

1. Place the cubed watermelon, sliced strawberries, freshly squeezed orange juice, and sliced banana into a blender.

2. Blend all the ingredients until you achieve a smooth, well-combined texture. Serve immediately.

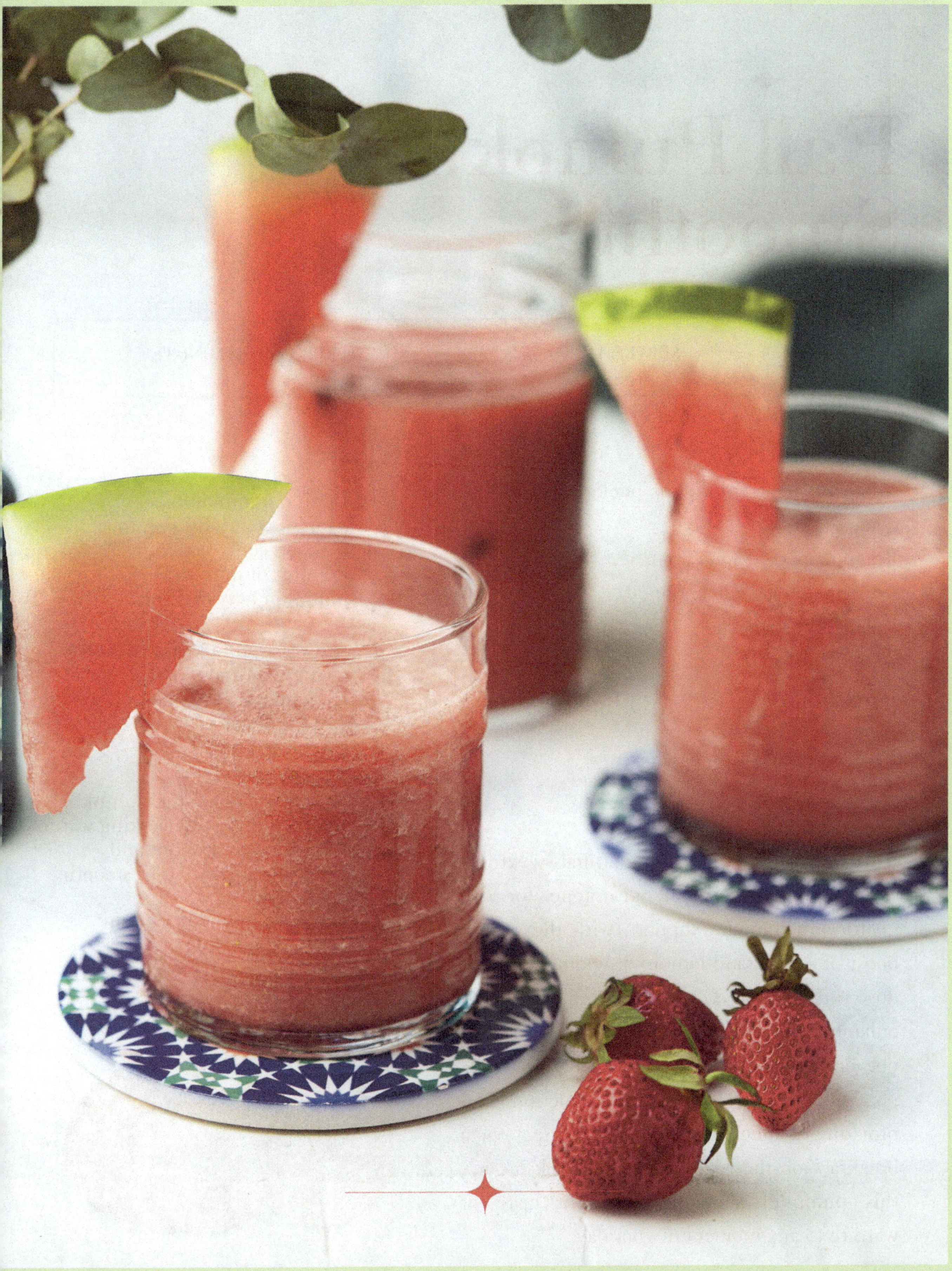

Fall Pumpkin Smoothie

| EASY | SERVES: 4 CUPS | PREP TIME: 15 MINUTES |

INGREDIENTS

350g (13 ounces) pumpkin, peeled and diced
1 orange, peeled and chopped
1 lemon, peeled and chopped
1 banana, peeled and chopped
400ml (1 3/4 cups) water
Natural sweetener (honey, maple syrup, or any favorite)
Ice for serving (optional)

BENEFITS

This smoothie combines the natural sweetness of pumpkin, rich in beta-carotene for eye health and immune support, with the citrusy boost of orange and lemon, providing a potent dose of Vitamin C to fend off colds and enhance skin vitality. The addition of banana not only thickens the texture but also adds potassium, aiding in muscle function and providing a quick energy boost. Perfect for a breakfast on-the-go or a midday pick-me-up, this pumpkin smoothie brings a taste of warmth to any moment of your day.

STEPS

1. Put the pumpkin pieces in a pot of water. Bring it to a boil and cook for about 15 minutes or until the pumpkin becomes soft.

2. After the pumpkin is cooked, strain it and save about 100ml (1/2 cup) of the cooking water. Let the pumpkin cool completely.

3. In a blender, add the pumpkin, fruit, and reserved cooking water, additional cold water, and sweetener. Blend until smooth.

4. Strain the blended mixture. Serve immediately.

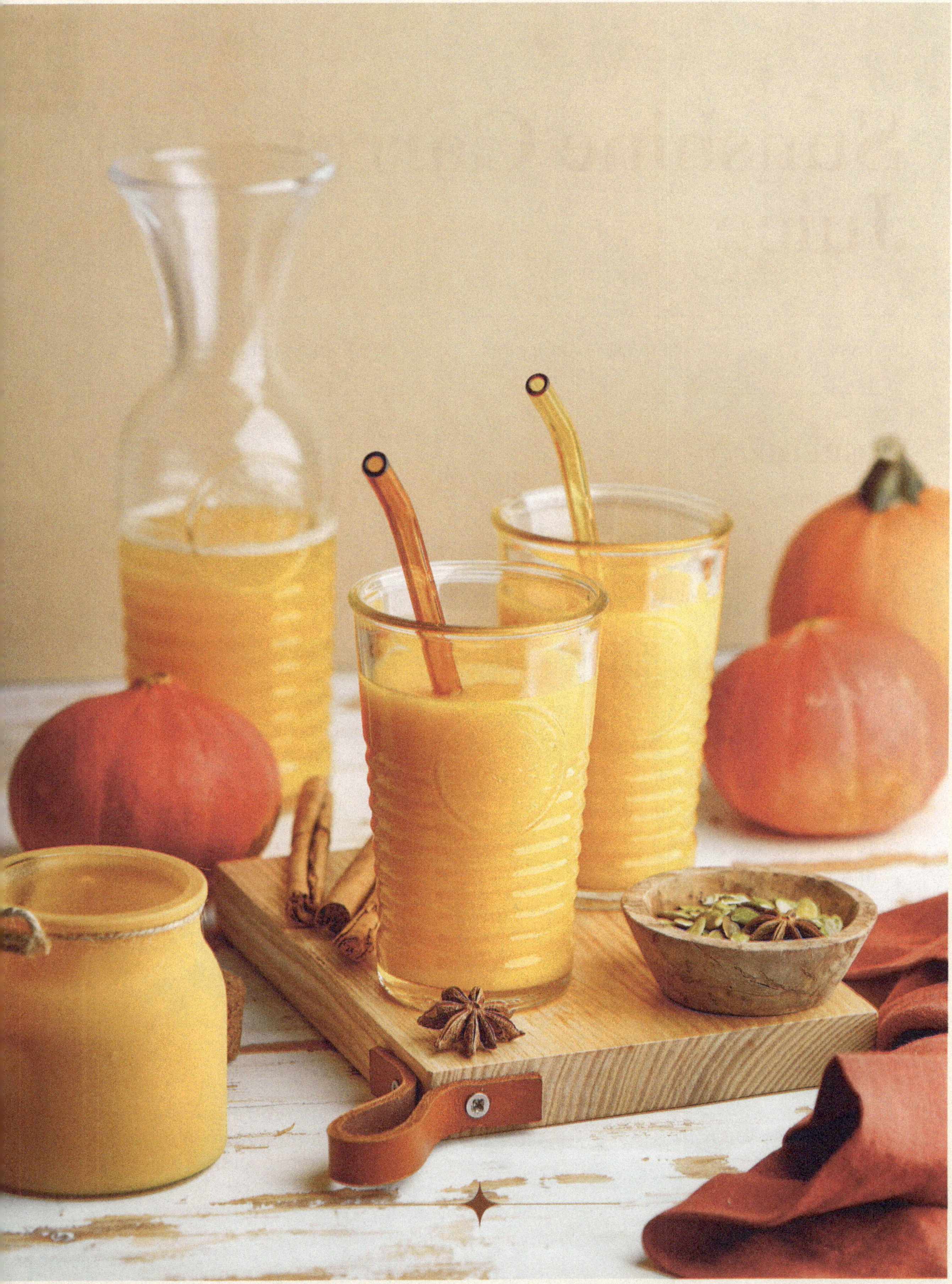

Sunshine Carrot Juice

| EASY | SERVES: 4 LARGE CUPS | PREP TIME: 15 MINUTES |

INGREDIENTS

4 large carrots
500ml (2 cups) water
6 large oranges
Natural sweetener (honey, maple syrup, or any favorite)

BENEFITS

This juice, rich in beta-carotene from carrots and a powerhouse of Vitamin C from oranges, supports eye health and boosts the immune system, making it an ideal start to your day or a refreshing companion to any meal. The addition of orange blossom water introduces a subtle floral note, transforming it into a uniquely Moroccan refreshment.

STEPS

1. Peel and trim both ends of the carrots before chopping them into medium-sized pieces for easier cooking and blending.

2. Cook the carrot pieces in a pot of boiling water over medium heat until they are fork-tender, about 15 minutes.

3. Drain the carrots but reserve the cooking water. Allow both the carrots and the water to cool completely in a heatproof bowl.

4. Halve the oranges and extract the juice using your preferred method.

5. Place the carrots and carrot water in a blender.

6. Add natural sweetener along with freshly squeezed orange juice.

7. Blend the mixture until it's completely smooth, adding more carrot water if necessary to alter the consistency. Serve chilled.

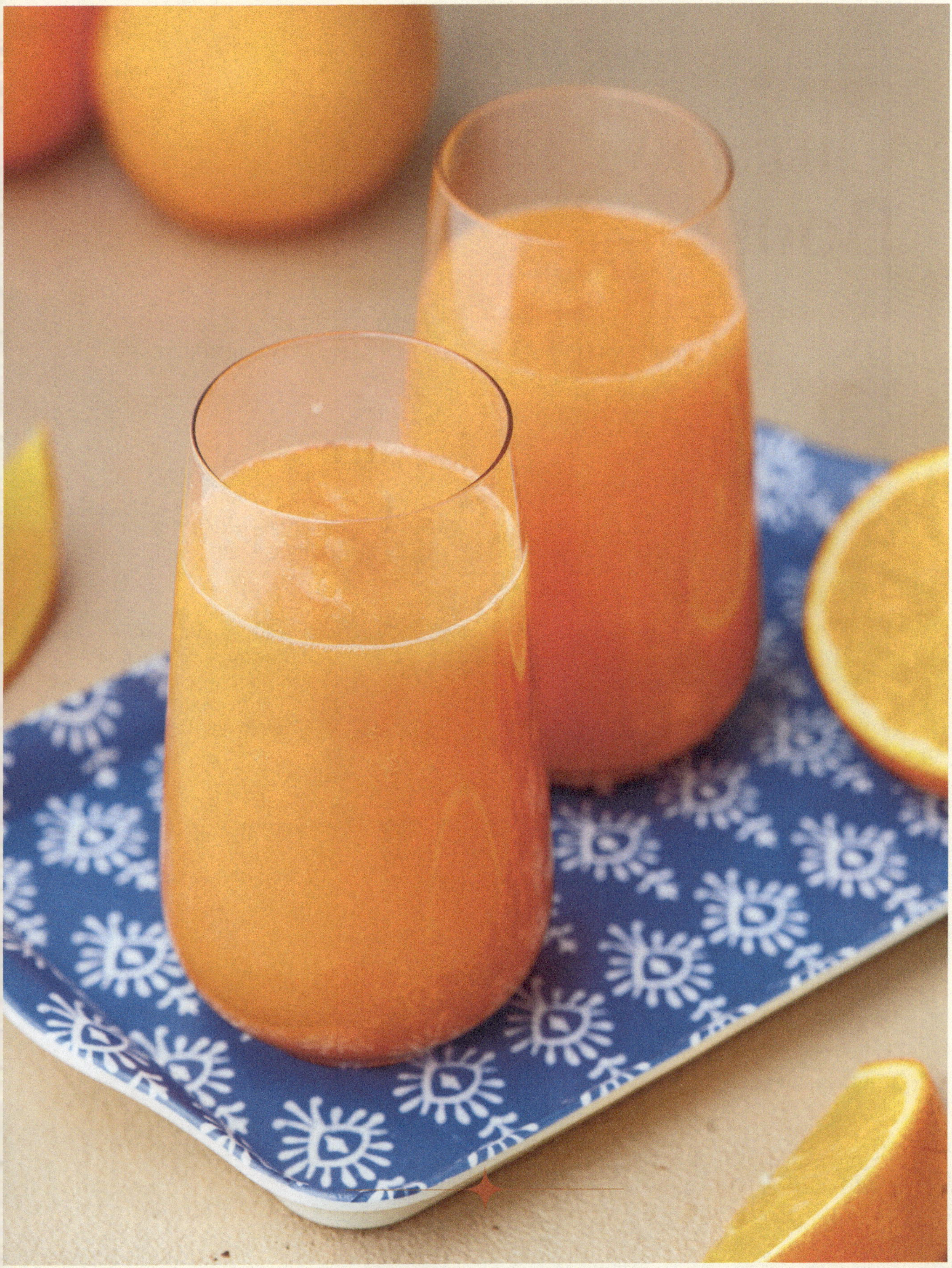

Citrus Carrot Boost

| EASY | SERVES: 4 CUPS | PREP TIME: 10 MINUTES |

INGREDIENTS

5 oranges
2 lemons
4 carrots, peeled and grated
2 teaspoons ground turmeric
A pinch black pepper
3 cm (1 in) fresh ginger, peeled and cut into chunks
Natural sweetener (honey, maple syrup, or any favorite)
Ice for serving (optional)

BENEFITS

This carrot and turmeric juice is as beneficial as it is delicious. The sweetness of carrots and citrus from oranges and lemons provides a high dose of vitamins A and C, supporting eye health and boosting the immune system. Turmeric, with its curcumin content, offers anti-inflammatory properties and aids in digestion, enhanced by black pepper to increase absorption. Fresh ginger adds a zesty kick, further aiding digestion and offering anti-inflammatory benefits.

STEPS

1. Start by juicing the oranges and lemons. Transfer the fresh juice into a blender.

2. Add freshly grated carrots, ground turmeric, a pinch of black pepper, grated fresh ginger, and sweetener to the blender with the citrus juice. Blend Until Smooth.

3. Strain the mixture to remove any chunks, ensuring a smoother juice. Serve immediately.

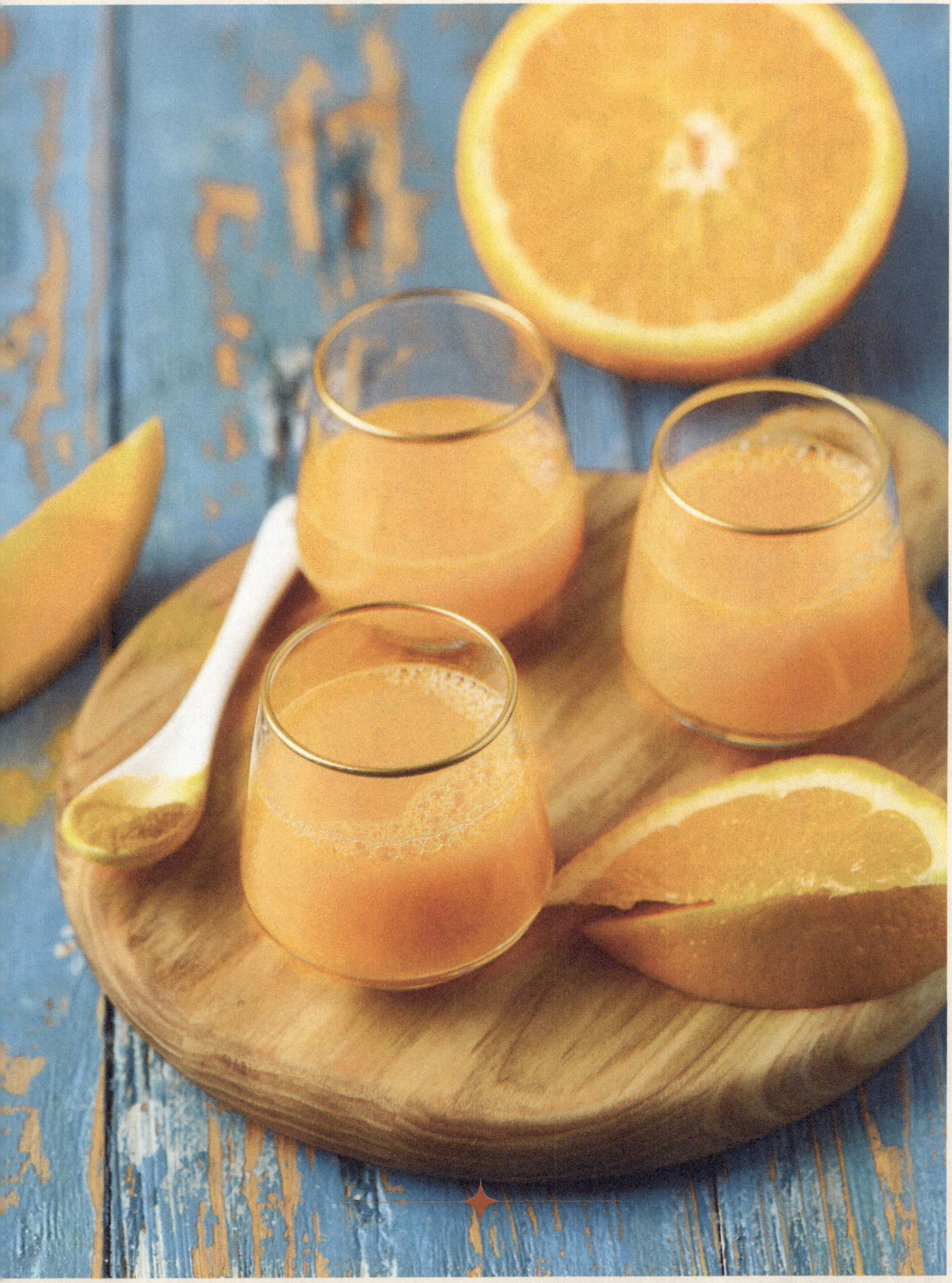

Golden Smoothie

| EASY | SERVES: 3 CUPS | PREP TIME: 10 MINUTES |

INGREDIENTS

470 ml (2 cups) water
1 orange, peeled and cubed
1 cup carrots, peeled and cubed
1 cup pear, cored and cubed
½ cup mango, cubed
½ cup pineapple, cubed 1 teaspoon lemon juice
½ teaspoon turmeric (curcuma)
2 dates, pitted 1 cup ice

STEPS

1. Add all the ingredients into a blender.

2. Blend for 90 seconds or until the mixture is smooth.

3. Serve immediately for the freshest taste.

BENEFITS

This smoothie is a powerhouse of antioxidants from its fruit components, enhancing immune function and providing protective benefits against oxidative stress. The inclusion of carrots adds fiber for digestive health, while the turmeric introduces anti-inflammatory properties, aiding in reducing inflammation and enhancing pain relief. With the natural sweetness and nutritional benefits of dates, this smoothie avoids added sugars, making it a healthy choice for those looking to support their heart health through potassium-rich ingredients and dietary fiber.

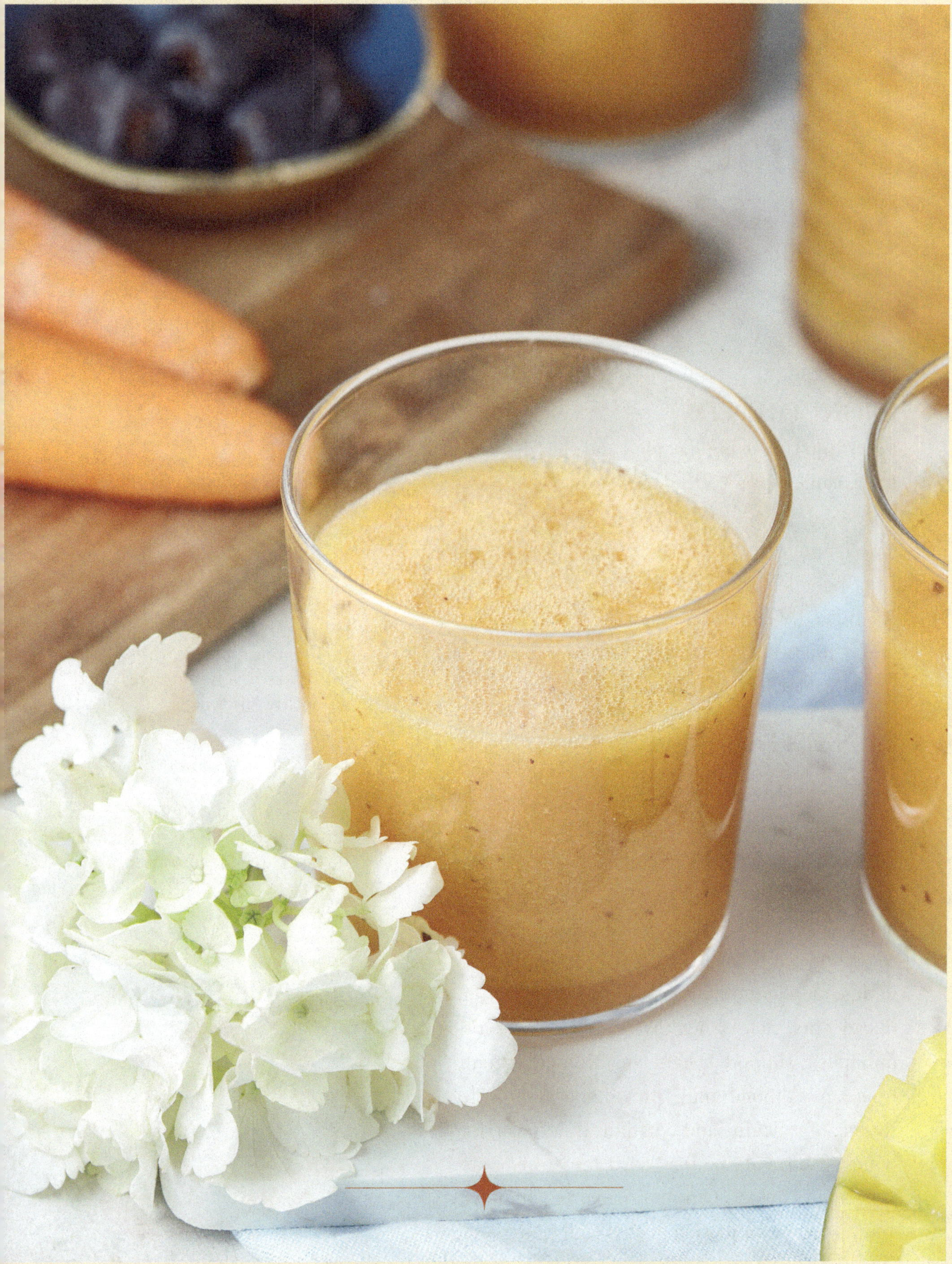

Apricot Sunrise Smoothie

| EASY | SERVES: 2 CUPS | PREP TIME: 10 MINUTES |

INGREDIENTS

1 medium ripe mango, peeled and sliced
1/2 banana, peeled, sliced, and previously frozen
4 dried apricots, chopped
5 pecan nuts
1 teaspoon lemon zest
360 ml (1 1/2 cups) almond milk
Dried goji berries, for garnish
Ice cubes for serving (optional)

BENEFITS

This smoothie is a nutritional delight. Mangoes, packed with vitamins A and C, promote eye health and immune function, while bananas offer potassium and fiber for heart health and digestion. Dried apricots contribute additional fiber and vitamins, aiding in digestion and providing antioxidant benefits. Pecan nuts, rich in healthy fats, vitamins, and minerals, support heart health and brain function. Almond milk provides a dairy-free source of calcium and vitamin D, crucial for bone health. Goji berries, used for garnish, are superfoods loaded with antioxidants, vitamins, and minerals, promoting overall well-being.

STEPS

1. In your blender, combine the ripe mango, frozen banana, dried apricots, pecan nuts, and lemon zest. Blend these ingredients until smooth.

2. Gradually add almond milk to the blender, continuing to blend until you reach your preferred smoothie thickness.

3. Distribute the smoothie evenly among serving glasses. Garnish each glass with goji berries for a burst of color and a nutritional boost. Enjoy Immediately!

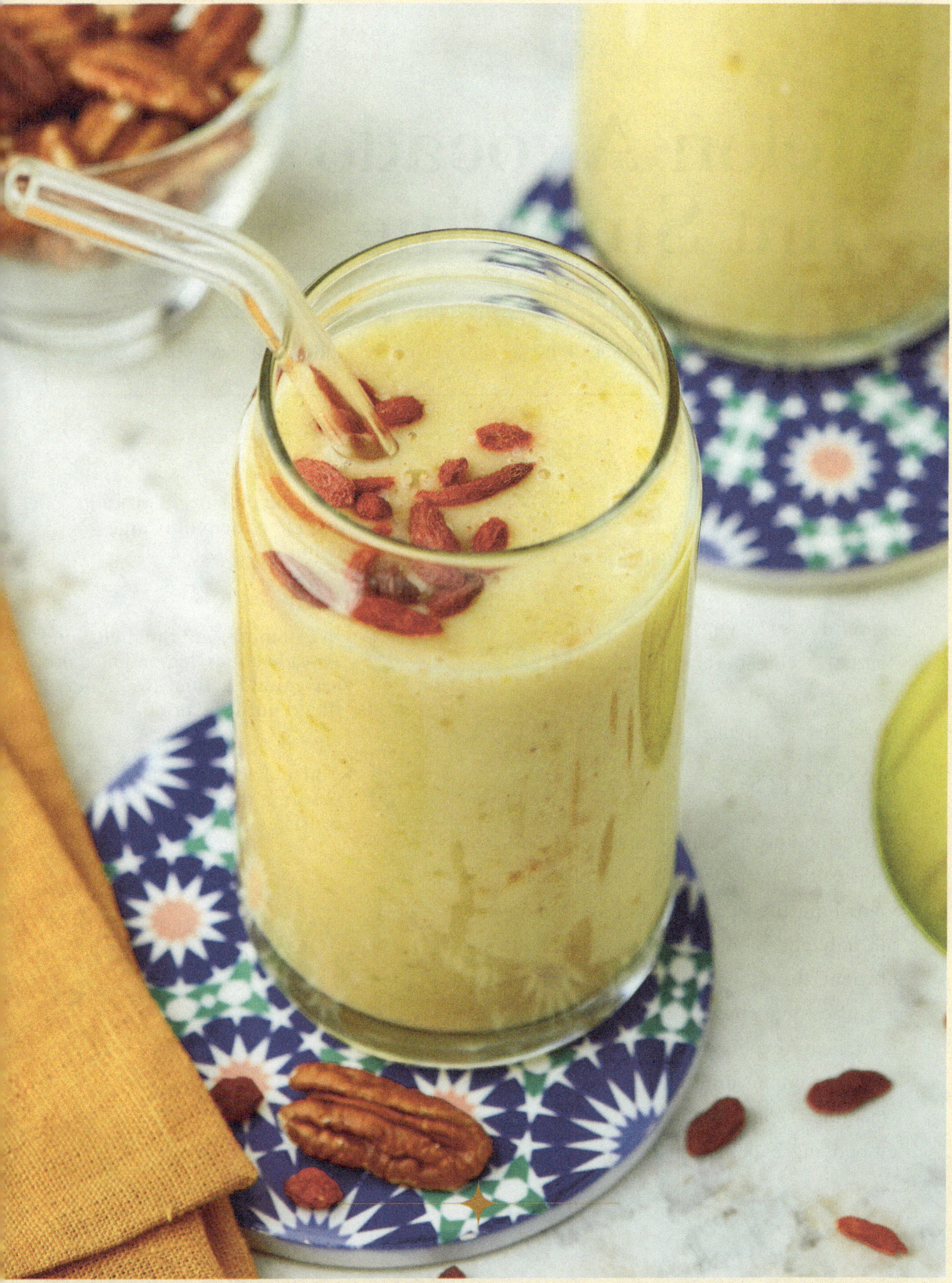

Melon Avocado Mint Smoothie

| EASY | SERVES: 4 CUPS | PREP TIME: 5 MINUTES |

INGREDIENTS

500 grams melon
1 medium avocado
3 to 4 tablespoons lemon juice
3 mint leaves
60 milliliters (1/2 cup) water (optional)
Natural sweetener (honey, maple syrup, or any favorite)
Ice cubes for serving (optional)

BENEFITS

This smoothie is a powerhouse of hydration and healthy fats, ideal for boosting energy and nourishing the skin from within. Lemon juice not only adds a vibrant zest but also enhances nutrient absorption, while mint leaves provide a refreshing burst, making each sip a revitalizing experience. Whether enjoyed as a cooling summer drink or a healthy snack, this smoothie combines taste and wellness, embodying a delightful fusion of flavors and benefits.

STEPS

1. Peel the melon and avocado and cube them into large chunks.

2. In a blender, add the melon and avocado cubes, lemon juice, mint leaves, and natural sweetener. Blend until smooth.

3. Add a little more water if needed to soften the smoothie consistency. Serve immediately.

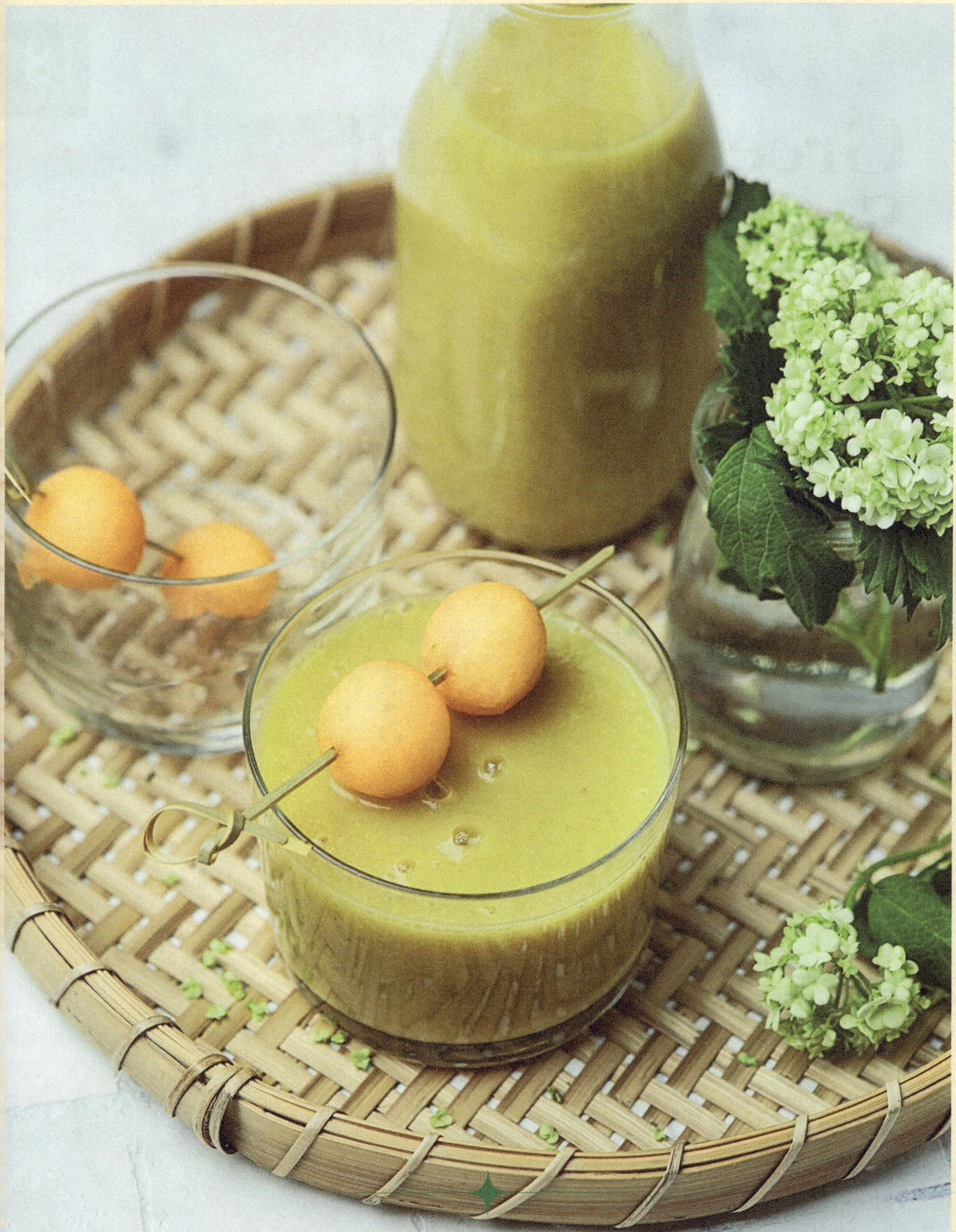

Green Orchard Smoothie

| EASY | SERVES: 4 LARGE CUPS | PREP TIME: 10 MINUTES |

INGREDIENTS

2 lemons
2 medium green apples
1 celery stick
2 kiwis, peeled and cut into slices
2 tablespoons grated fresh ginger
350ml (1 1/2 cups) cold water
Ice for serving (optional)

BENEFITS

This smoothie, enriched with the detoxifying benefits of celery and the vitamin-packed goodness of kiwis, offers a revitalizing boost to your day. Green apples, a rich source of dietary fiber, aid in digestion and help regulate blood sugar levels, while ginger's anti-inflammatory properties can soothe digestion and reduce nausea. The addition of lemons infuses the smoothie with vitamin C, enhancing immune defense and skin health. Serve chilled with ice cubes for a perfect, energizing drink that's as nourishing as it is delicious.

STEPS

1. Start by juicing the lemons and set the juice aside.

2. Rinse and clean the apple and celery. Then, slice them into manageable pieces for easier blending.

3. In a food processor, combine the freshly squeezed lemon juice, sliced apple and celery, kiwi slices, grated fresh ginger, and water. Blend until smooth.

4. Optionally, strain the juice through a fine sieve to refine the texture. Serve immediately.

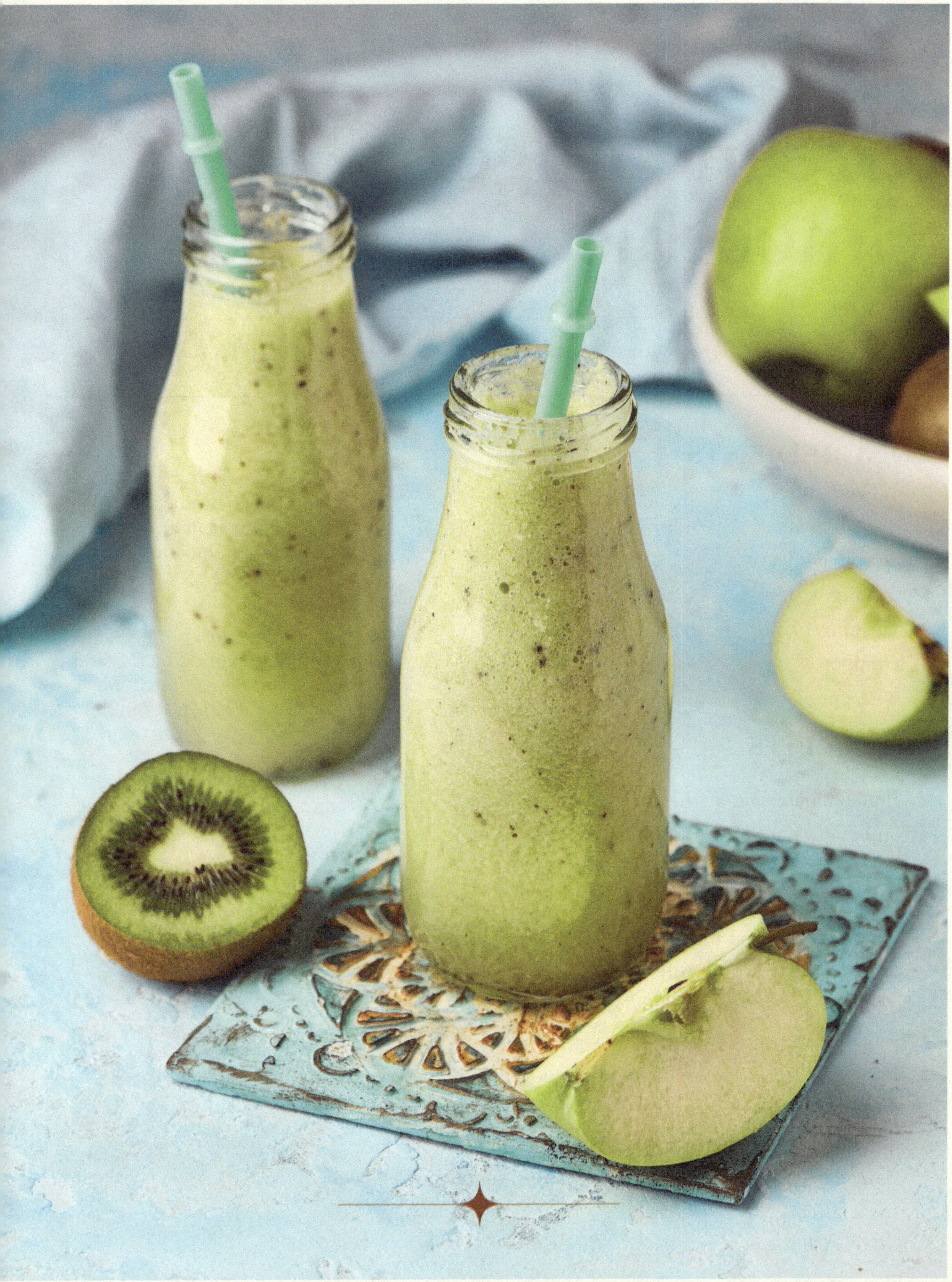

Green Ginger Glow Smoothie

EASY　　　SERVES: 4 CUPS　　　PREP TIME: 15 MINUTES

INGREDIENTS

1/2 cucumber
2 small pears
20 spinach leaves
3 oranges, juiced
15 grams (0.5 oz.) fresh ginger, peeled and chopped
6 ice cubes

BENEFITS

Pomegranates are a fruit that is low in calories and fat, but high in fiber, vitamins, and minerals. They contain antioxidants and polyphenolic compounds, such as punicalagins, anthocyanins, and hydrolyzable tannins, which help protect your cells from free radical damage and may help prevent chronic inflammation associated with disease. Pomegranates have also been observed to have anticancer effects and may slow tumor growth and spread and reduce inflammation, although more research is needed to learn more about these effects .

STEPS

1. Chop the cucumber into large cubes. Half and core the pears, then chop into chunks.

2. Place the spinach leaves, cubed cucumber, cubed pears, freshly squeezed orange juice, fresh ginger, and ice cubes in the blender.

3. Blend until smooth. Serve immediately!

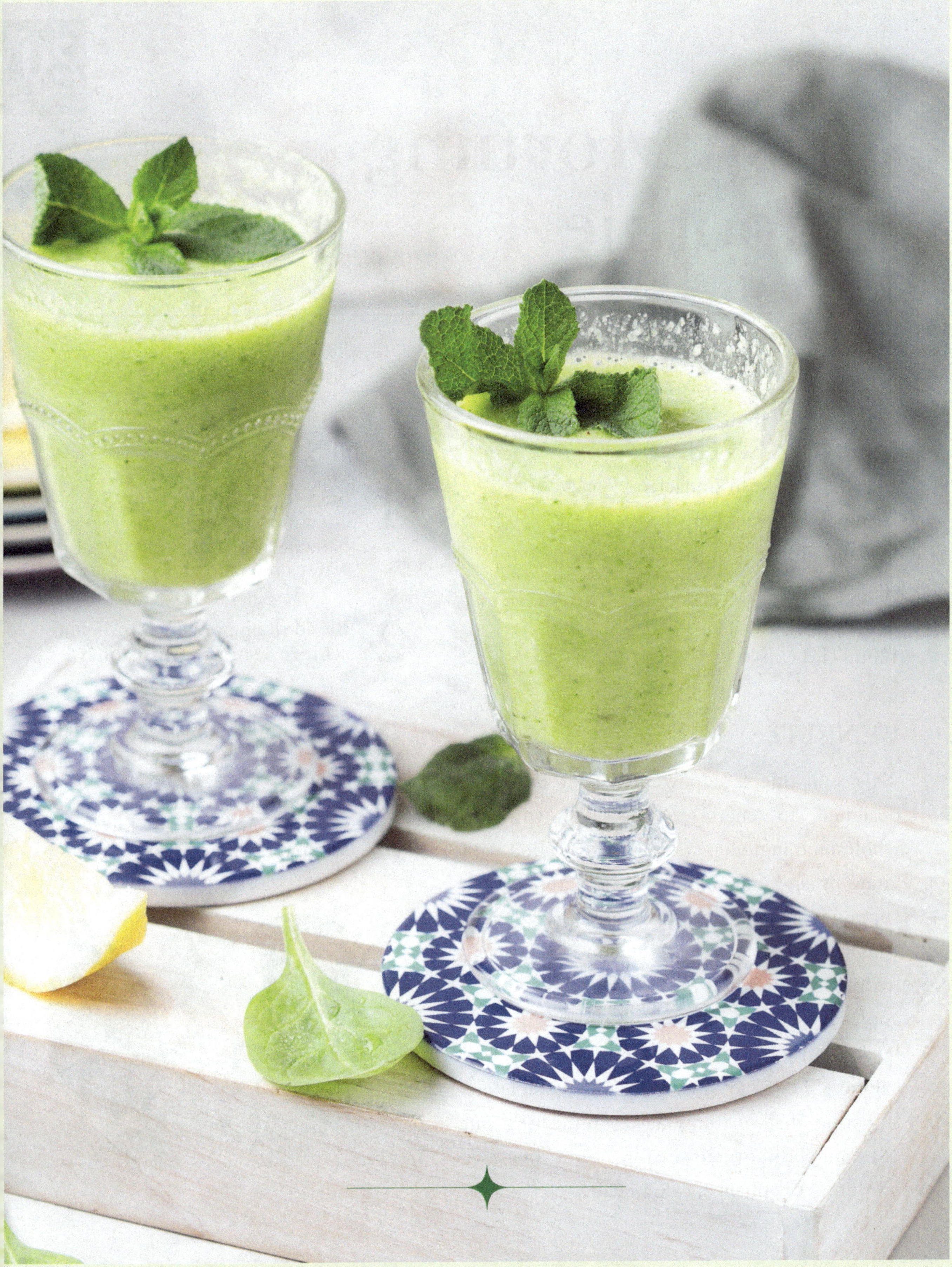

Crisp Morning Smoothie

| EASY | SERVES: 2 CUPS | PREP TIME: 5 MINUTES |

INGREDIENTS

50g (1/4 cup) fresh spinach
1/2 medium cucumber, chopped
1/2 medium green apple, cored and chopped
1/2 medium banana, peeled and sliced
120ml (1/2 cup) water

BENEFITS

This smoothie is a powerhouse of nutrition, designed to energize your day with its wholesome ingredients. Spinach is loaded with vitamins and minerals, including iron, which supports healthy blood flow and energy levels. Cucumbers are high in water content, ensuring hydration and aiding in detoxification. Green apples contribute dietary fiber for digestive health and a subtle sweetness with low calories. Together, these ingredients make a smoothie that not only tastes refreshing but also supports overall health, from boosting immunity to enhancing skin healt.

STEPS

1. Start by adding the spinach, cucumber, green apple, banana, and 60ml (1/4 cup) of water into a blender.

2. Blend the ingredients until you achieve a smooth consistency.

3. For a thinner smoothie, gradually add the remaining water while blending until you reach your desired consistency. Serve the smoothie immediately for optimal freshness and flavor.

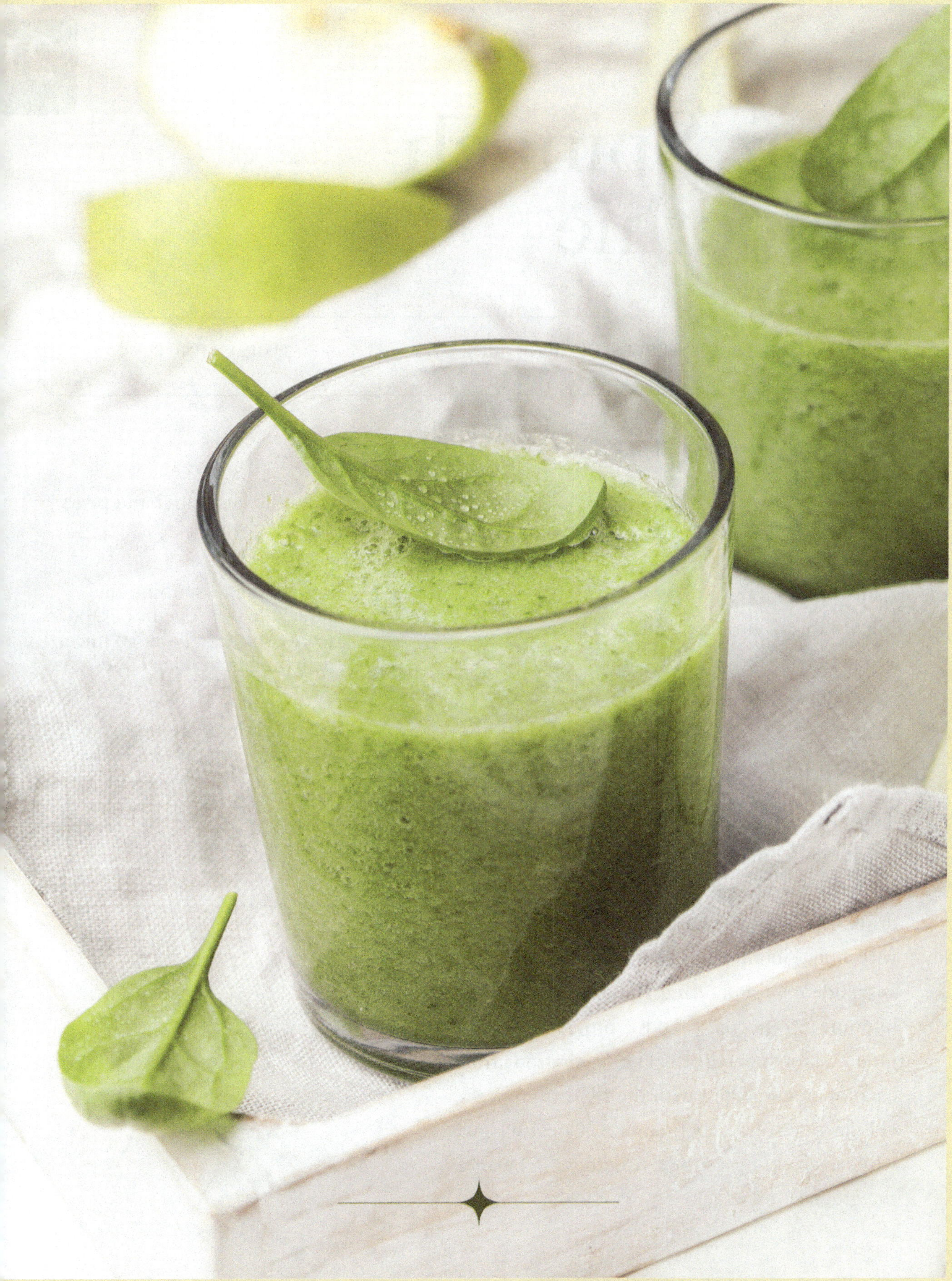

Pear Spinach Smoothie

| EASY | SERVES: 2-3 LARGE CUPS | PREP TIME: 15 MINUTES |

INGREDIENTS

20 spinach leaves
Juice of 3 Navel oranges
1/2 cucumber
2 small pears
15g (1 tablespoon) fresh ginger, peeled and grated
6 ice cubes

BENEFITS

This is a vibrant concoction that packs a nutritional punch, blending the refreshing qualities of its ingredients into a powerhouse drink. Spinach, the base of this juice, is laden with iron, vitamins A, C, and K, and numerous antioxidants, supporting blood health, and immune function, and providing anti-inflammatory benefits. The hydration from cucumber, combined with the fiber from pears, aids in digestion and promotes a healthy gut, while also adding a subtle sweetness to balance the greens.

STEPS

1. Chop the cucumber and pears into large cubes.

2. In a blender, combine the spinach leaves, cucumber, pears, freshly squeezed orange juice, fresh ginger, and ice cubes.

3. Blend all the ingredients until smooth. Serve immediately.

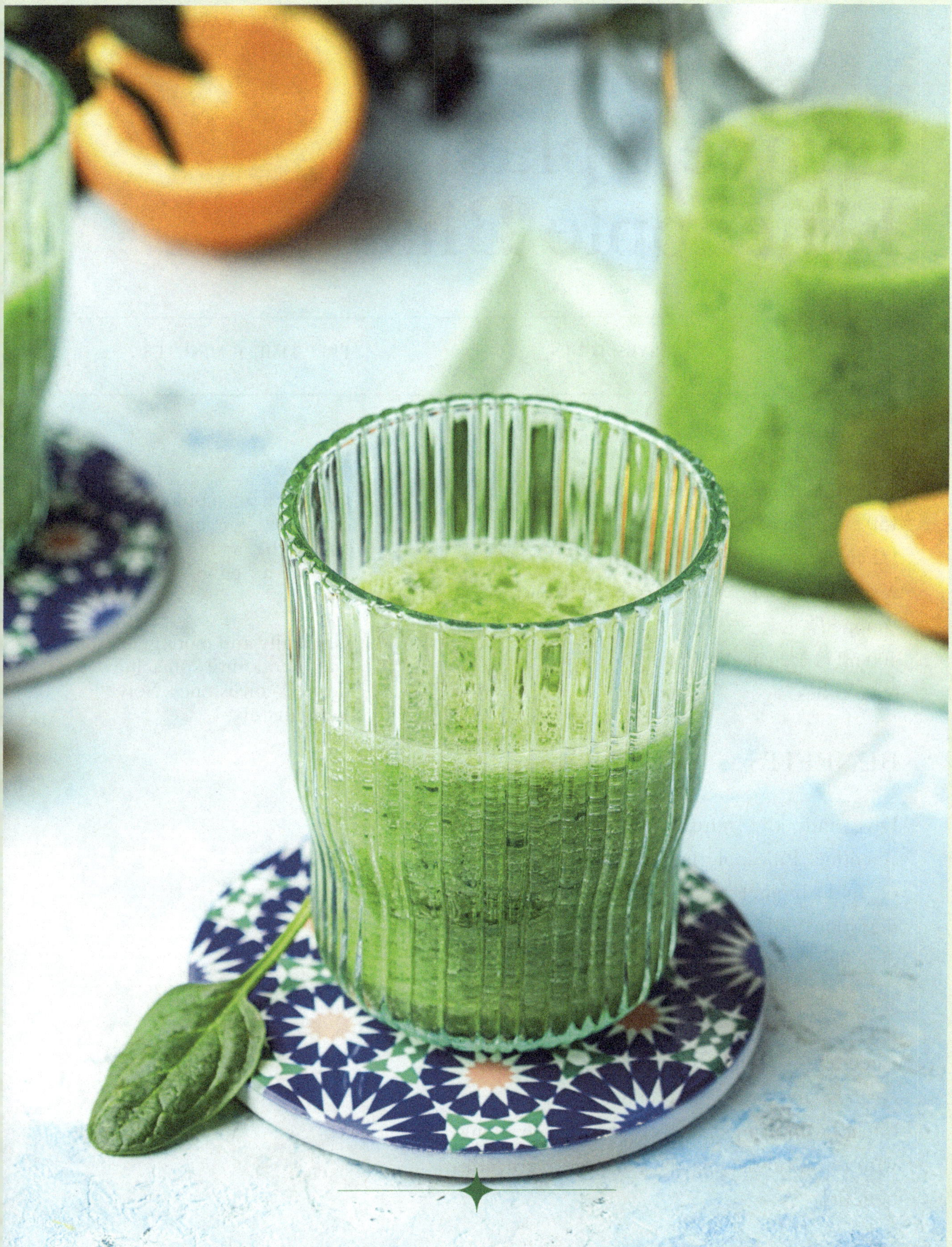

Grape Splash Pineapple Bliss

22

| EASY | SERVES: 4 CUPS | PREP TIME: 10 MINUTES |

INGREDIENTS

1 pineapple, peeled and cubed
150 grams (5 oz) spinach
1/2 cucumber, sliced
A small piece of fresh ginger, peeled and chopped
400 ml (1 1/2 cups) organic grape juice
6 ice cubes

STEPS

1. Combine pineapple, spinach, cucumber, ginger in a blender, half of the organic grape juice, and the ice cubes. Blend until smooth.

2. Gradually add more grape juice and blend until you achieve the desired consistency. Serve immediately.

BENEFITS

Dive into the refreshing embrace of this smoothie. Pineapple brings a burst of vitamin C and bromelain, an enzyme that aids digestion and reduces inflammation. Spinach enriches the drink with iron, magnesium, and vitamins A, C, and K, supporting blood health, bone density, and immune function. Cucumber, being high in water content, ensures hydration and provides a cooling effect, while ginger adds a spicy note along with its anti-inflammatory and digestive health benefits.

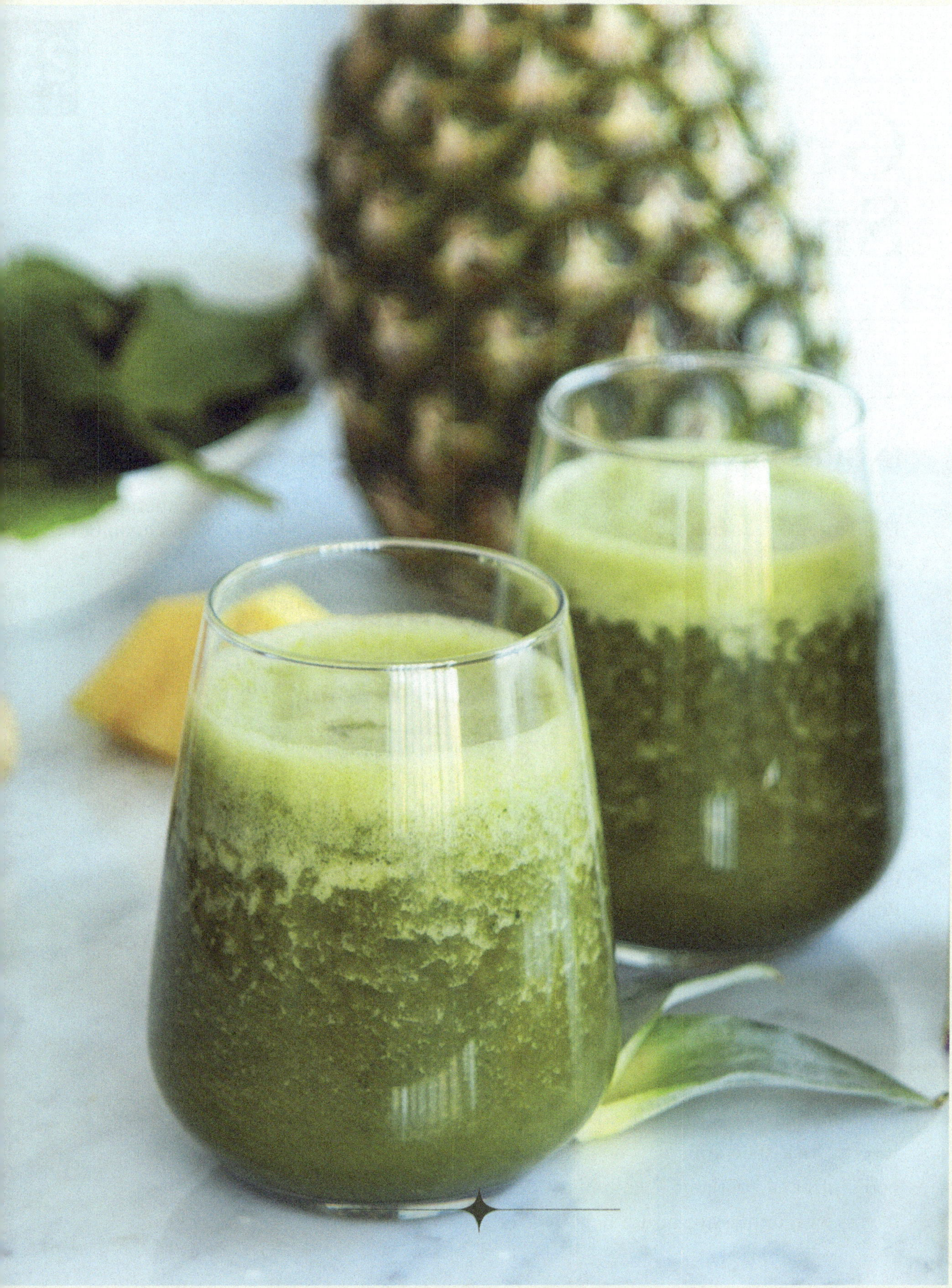

Green Garden Smoothie

| EASY | SERVES: 1 SERVING | PREP TIME: 5 MINUTES |

INGREDIENTS

2 medium pears, cored and chopped
1/2 medium green bell pepper, seeded and chopped
1/2 medium cucumber, chopped
1 celery stick, chopped
150ml (2/3 cup) water
4 ice cubes

BENEFITS

This smoothie is a hydrating and nutrient-rich blend perfect for boosting digestion and providing a wealth of vitamins and minerals. Pears and cucumbers offer hydration and fiber, supporting healthy digestion and promoting skin health. Green bell peppers and celery are low in calories but high in vitamins C and K, antioxidants, and other essential nutrients that can enhance immune function and reduce inflammation. This smoothie is an excellent way to kick-start your day or replenish your body after a workout, combining delicious flavors with impressive health benefits.

STEPS

1. Combine the chopped pear, green bell pepper, cucumber, celery stick, and ice cubes with 100ml of the water in a blender.

2. Blend until the mixture reaches a smooth consistency.

3. Gradually add the remaining water as needed to achieve your preferred consistency. Serve immediately!

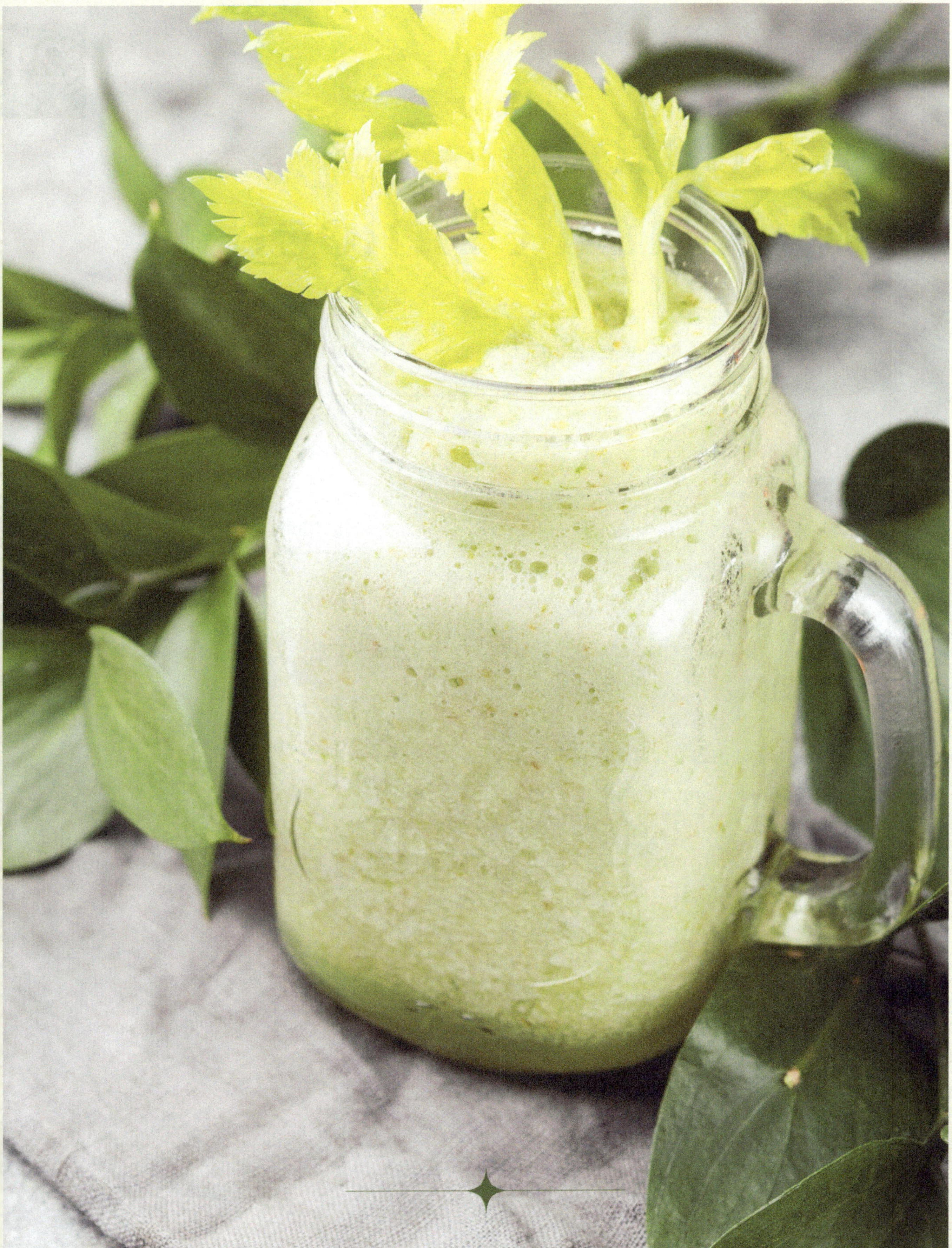

Cucumber Buttermilk Smoothie

| EASY | SERVES: 2 LARGE CUPS | PREP TIME: 10 MINUTES |

INGREDIENTS

2 cucumbers
600ml (2 1/2 cups) cold buttermilk
Natural sweetener (honey, maple syrup, or any favorite)
Ice for serving (optional

BENEFITS

Begin your day with the revitalizing Cucumber and Buttermilk Smoothie blending the hydrating properties of cucumbers with the probiotic benefits of buttermilk. This is a gut-friendly drink that's not only refreshing but also supports digestive health. Its creamy texture and light green hue, combined with a sweet yet slightly tart flavor, make it a delightful morning ritual or a soothing snack.

STEPS

1. Peel the cucumbers, slice in half lengthwise, and scoop out the seeds.

2. Chop the cucumbers into cubes.

3. Add the cucumber cubes, cold buttermilk, and your choice of sweetener to a blender.

4. Blend the mixture on high until it achieves a smooth consistency. Serve immediately.

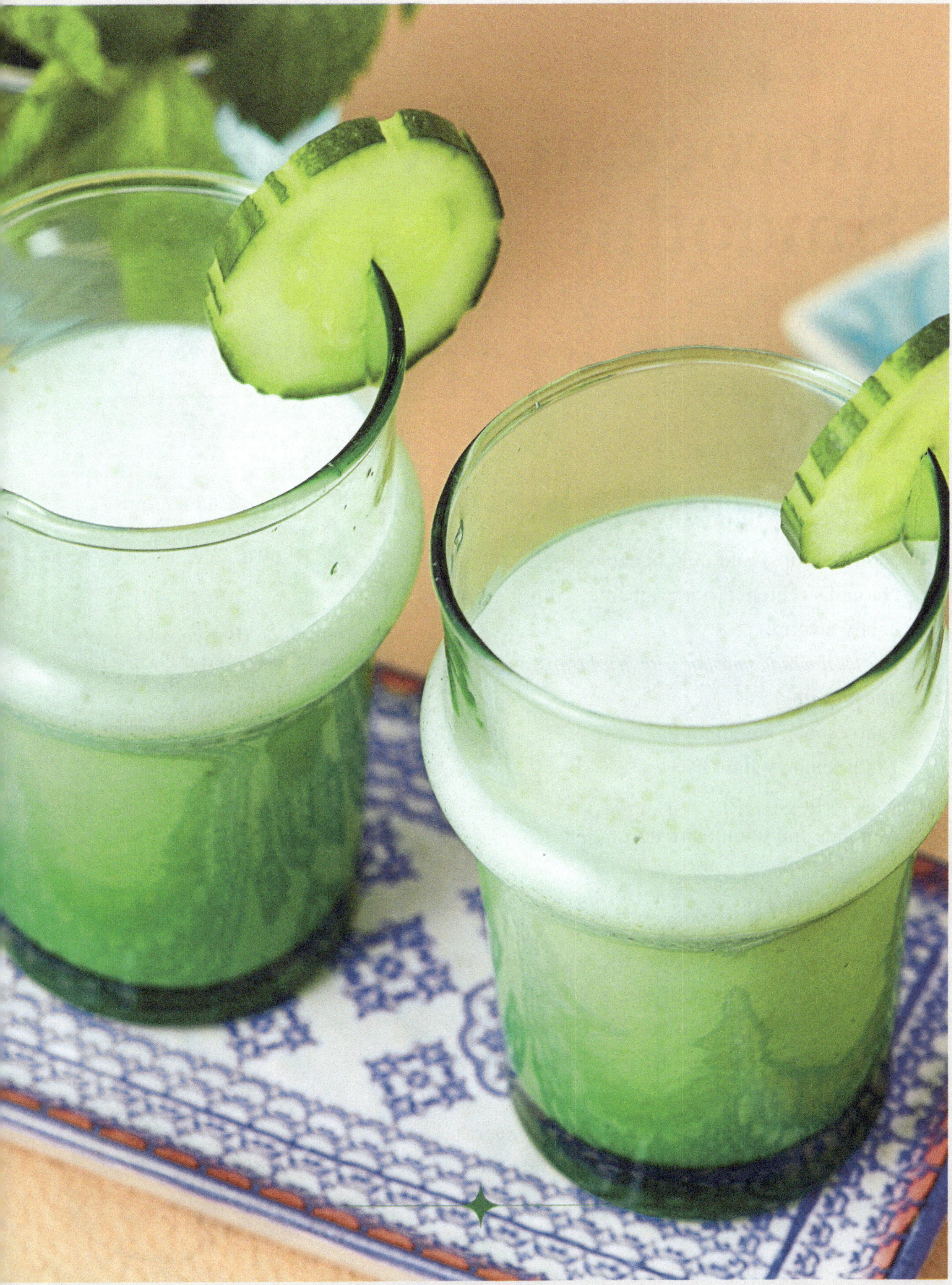

Moroccan Avocado Smoothie

| EASY | SERVES: 2 LARGE CUPS | PREP TIME: 10 MINUTES |

INGREDIENTS

For the classic avocado smoothie

1 large ripe avocado

500ml (2 cups) cold milk of choice

Natural sweetener (honey, maple syrup, or any favorite)

For the avocado smoothie with dried fruits, also prepare

1 tablespoon raw almonds

1 tablespoon walnuts

3 dates, pitted

Almonds and walnuts for decoration

BENEFITS

This smoothie, blending the rich, buttery texture of avocados with the cool freshness of milk, offers a nutrient-dense treat, packed with healthy fats, vitamins E and K, and fiber, promoting heart health and skin vitality. For an enhanced nutritional profile, the Zaazaa version incorporates almonds, walnuts, and dates, adding layers of texture, natural sweetness, and a boost of omega-3 fatty acids, essential for brain health.

STEPS

1. Peel the avocado, remove its core, then chop it into large cubes.

2. Combine the avocado pieces, sweetener, and milk in a blender. Blend until smooth. Serve immediately.

VARIATIONS

Avocado Smoothie with Dried Fruits

Combine the avocado pieces, sweetener, milk in a blender, almonds, walnuts, and pitted dates. Blend until smooth. Serve immediately.

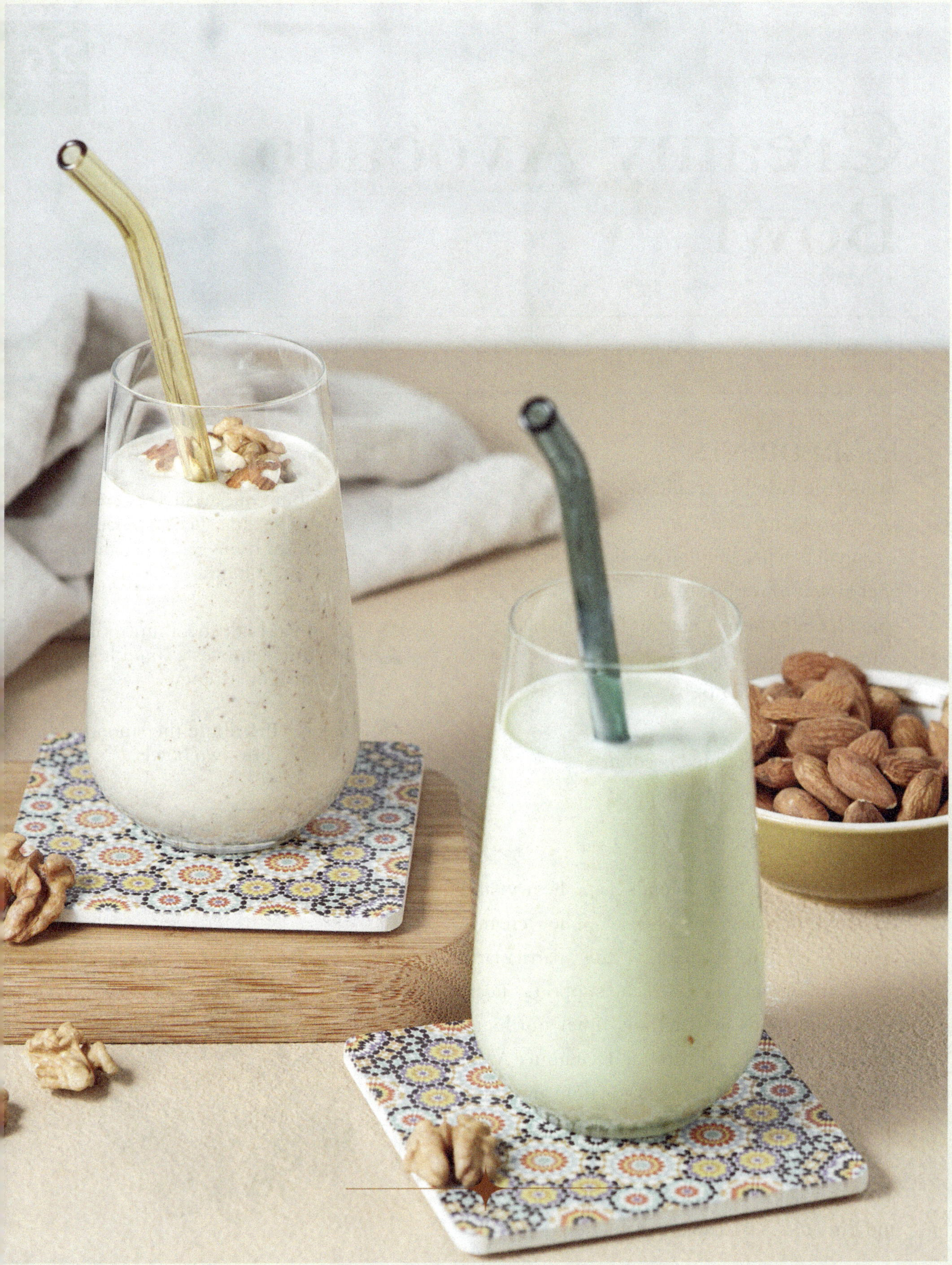

Creamy Avocado Bowl

| EASY | SERVES: 2 CUPS | PREP TIME: 5 MINUTES |

INGREDIENTS

Smoothie Bowl Ingredients:

1/2 avocado, mashed

1/2 small banana, previously sliced and frozen

55gr (1/4 cup) fresh spinach

65gr (1/4 cup) plain yogurt or fromage blanc

180ml (3/4 cup) almond milk

Garnish Ingredients:

Rolled oats

Unsweetened shredded coconut

Raw almonds, roughly chopped

BENEFITS

This smoothie bowl blends is a hearty and healthy breakfast or snack. The creamy avocado is rich in healthy fats, particularly monounsaturated fat, which supports heart health and helps in absorbing other nutrients. Spinach, packed with iron and vitamins A, C, and K, enhances blood oxygenation, immune function, and skin health. The choice of almond milk provides a dairy-free base rich in vitamin E and calcium, supporting bone health and providing antioxidant protection.

STEPS

1. Combine the mashed avocado, frozen banana slices, spinach, yogurt or fromage blanc, and milk in a blender.

2. Blend at high speed until the mixture achieves a smooth, creamy consistency.

3. Evenly distribute the smoothie mixture into two bowls.

4. Garnish each bowl with a generous sprinkle of rolled oats, shredded coconut, and chopped almonds for texture and flavor.

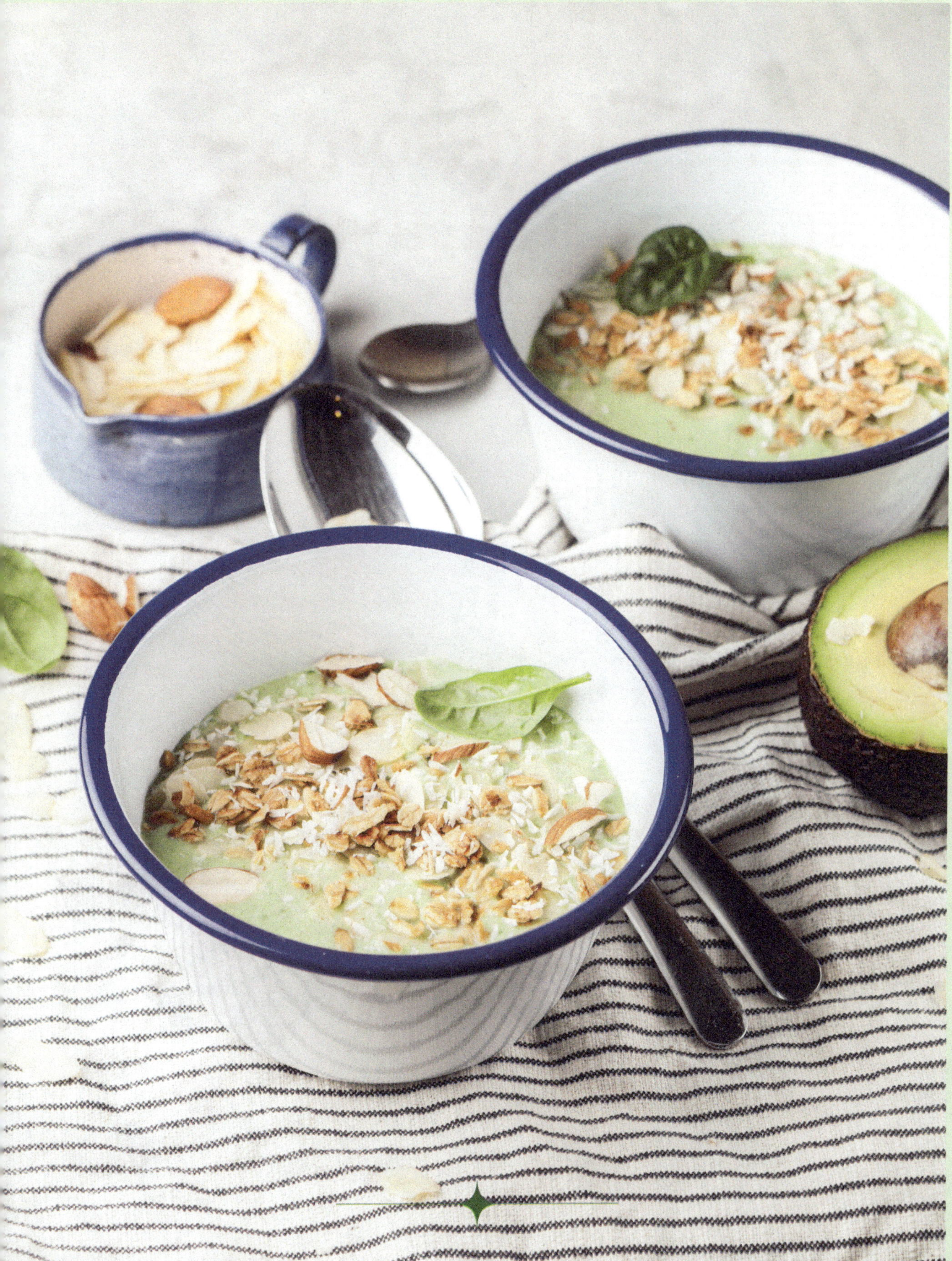

Orange Blossom Cinnamon Lassi

| EASY | SERVES: 4 CUPS | PREP TIME: 5 MINUTES |

INGREDIENTS

440g (2 cups) plain unsweetened yogurt
100ml (1/2 cup) milk
2 tablespoons orange blossom water
Natural sweetener (honey, maple syrup, or any favorite)
1/2 teaspoon ground cinnamon
8 ice cubes

BENEFITS

This lassi not only delights the palate but also offers a myriad of health benefits: the yogurt and milk provide a good dose of probiotics and calcium for digestive health and bone strength, respectively. Orange blossom water is noted for its stress-relieving properties, while cinnamon adds a powerful antioxidant punch, aiding in blood sugar control and possessing anti-inflammatory qualities. Together, these ingredients create a refreshingly aromatic beverage that soothes, nourishes, and energizes, making it a perfect drink for any time of the day.

STEPS

1. Place all the lassi ingredients in a blender, then blend until smooth. Serve immediately and enjoy!

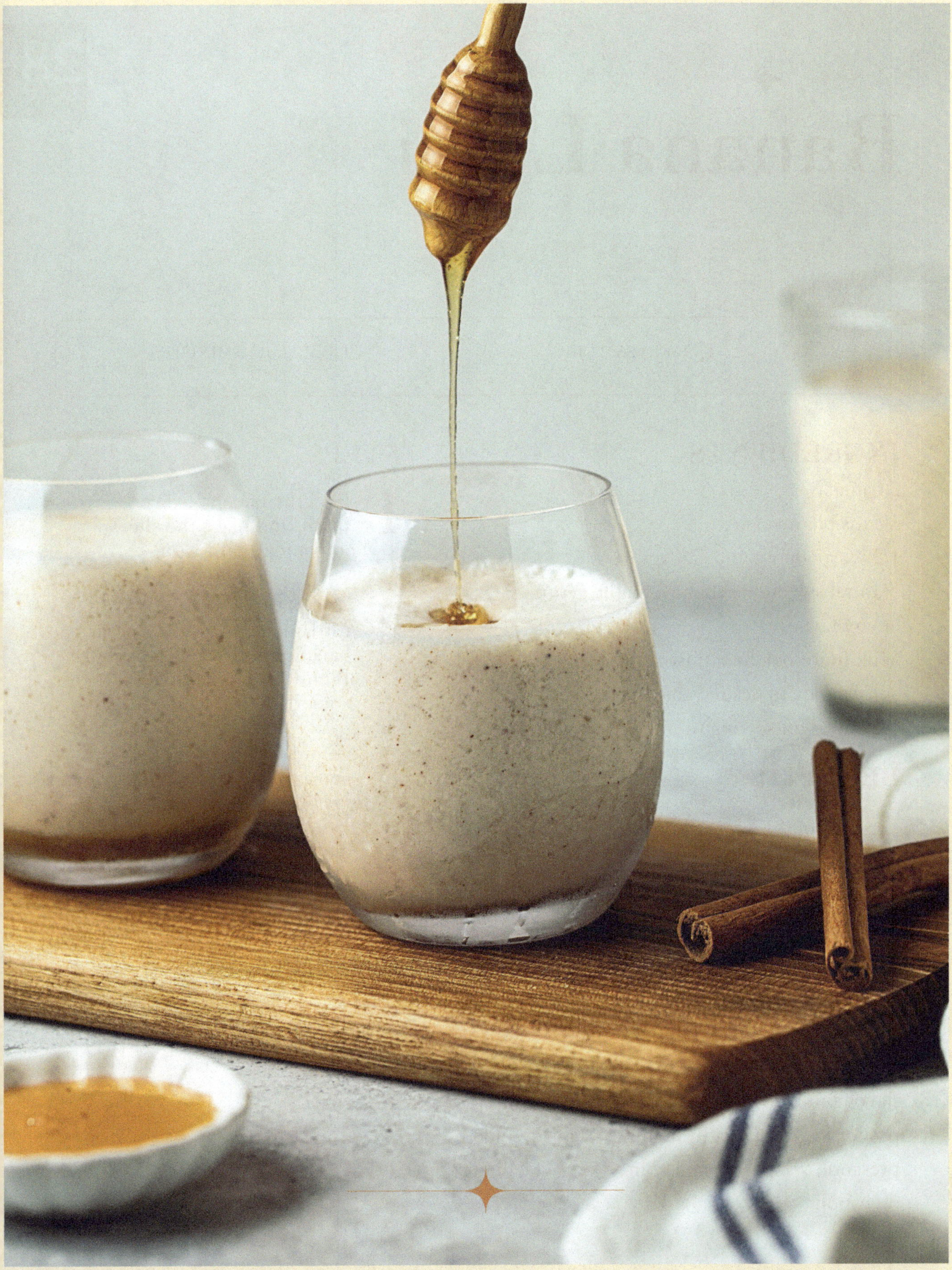

Banana Lassi

28

| EASY | SERVES: 2 CUPS | PREP TIME: 5 MINUTES |

INGREDIENTS

2 bananas
3 cups plain yogurt
1/2 teaspoon ground cardamom
Natural sweetener (honey, maple syrup, or any favorite)
Milk (optional, for adjusting smoothie consistency to desired thickness)
Ice cubes for serving (optional)

BENEFITS

This smoothie is a nutritional powerhouse. Rich in potassium, bananas aid in heart health and muscle function, while the high fiber content supports digestion. The inclusion of yogurt introduces probiotics, calcium, and protein, enhancing digestive health, strengthening bones, and aiding muscle repair. Ground cardamom adds not just a unique flavor but also boasts antioxidant and diuretic properties, potentially helping to lower blood pressure, improve breathing, and facilitate digestion.

STEPS

1. Peel the bananas, slice them, and place the slices into a food processor.

2. Add plain yogurt, ground cardamom, and sweetener to the bananas in the food processor. Blend everything together until smooth.

3. After blending, check the consistency of the banana lassi. If it's too thick for your preference, gradually add milk and blend for another minute until you reach the desired consistency.

4. Pour the banana lassi into glasses, optionally with ice cubes, and enjoy it fresh.

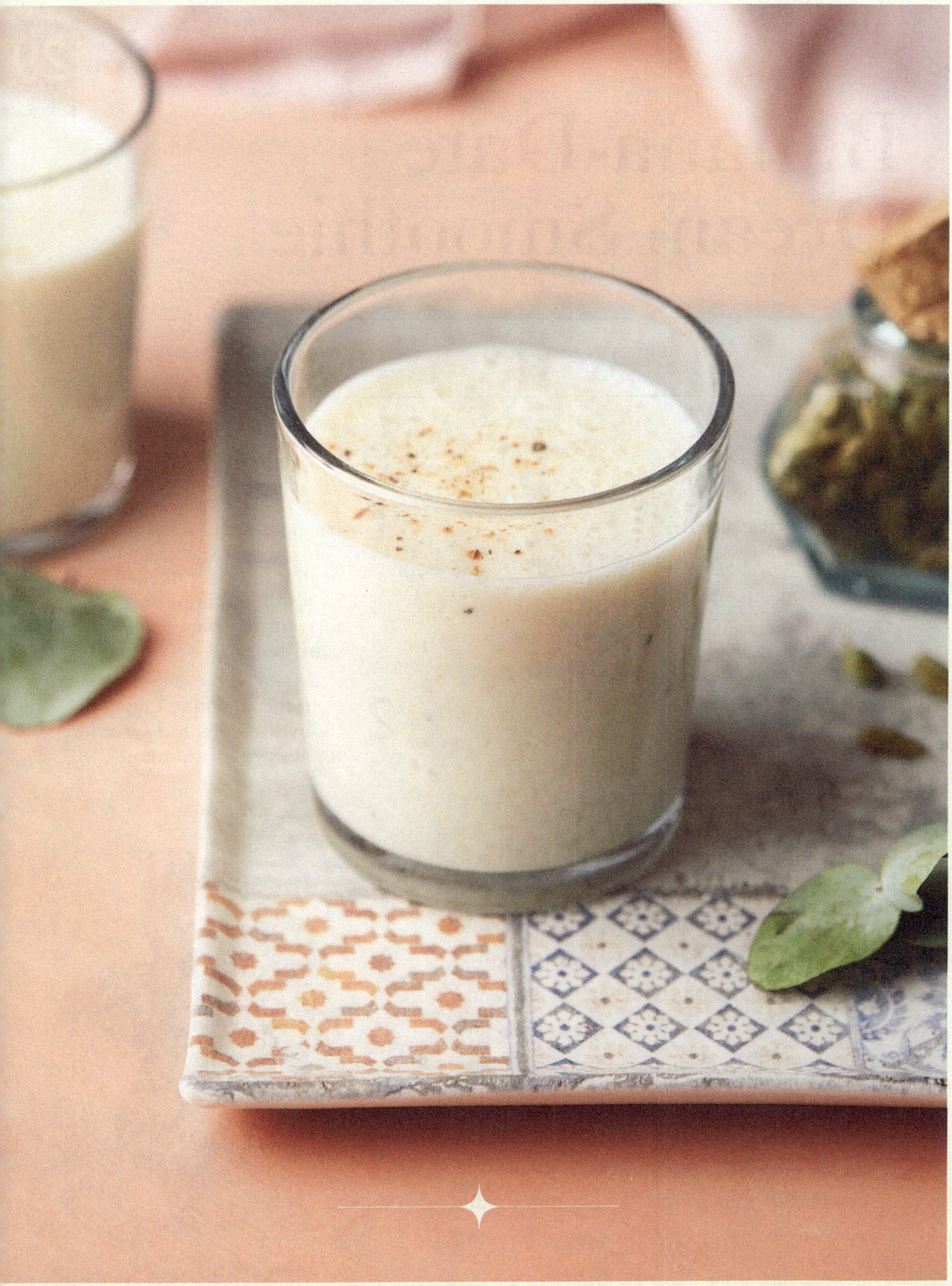

Banana-Date Dream Smoothie

| EASY | SERVES: 2 CUPS | PREP TIME: 5 MINUTES |

INGREDIENTS

2 ripe bananas, peeled and sliced
4 Medjool dates, pitted
A small handful of raw, unsalted walnuts
1 tablespoon chia seeds
2 tablespoons unsweetened, creamy peanut butter
360 ml (1 1/2 cups) cold whole milk
6 ice cubes

BENEFITS

This smoothie is a healthy indulgence, perfect for a filling breakfast or a rejuvenating snack. Bananas offer a quick energy boost and are rich in potassium, supporting heart health and muscle function. Medjool dates provide natural sweetness along with fiber, potassium, and magnesium, contributing to digestive health and energy levels. Walnuts add omega-3 fatty acids, promoting brain health and reducing inflammation. Chia seeds are a great source of fiber, omega-3s, and protein, aiding in digestion and heart health. Peanut butter adds a creamy texture and a healthy dose of protein.

STEPS

1. In a blender, combine the banana slices, Medjool dates, walnuts, chia seeds, peanut butter, milk, and ice cubes. Blend until the mixture achieves a smooth consistency.

2. Pour the smoothie into individual cups and serve for immediate refreshment.

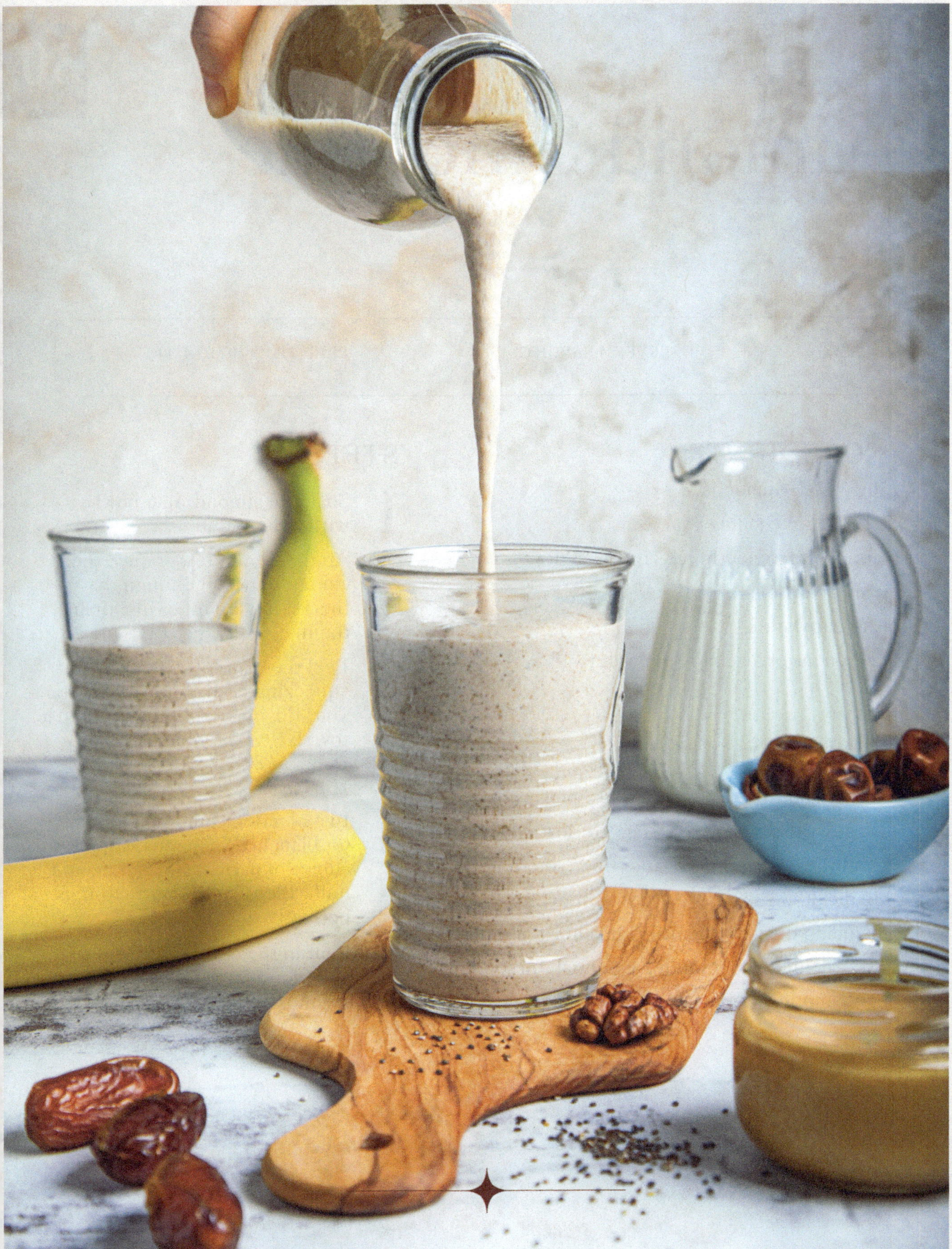

Almond Smoothie

30

EASY | SERVES: 4 LARGE CUPS | PREP TIME: 10 MINUTES

INGREDIENTS

250g (1/2 lb) almonds
1/2L (2 cups) boiling water
Natural sweetener (honey, maple syrup, or any favorite)
1L (4 cups) milk
2 teaspoons orange blossom water

BENEFITS

This smoothie is a nutrient powerhouse. Almonds, the smoothie's star, are loaded with vitamin E, magnesium, and fiber, promoting skin health, supporting muscle function, and enhancing digestive health. The choice of milk adds calcium and protein, essential for bone health and muscle repair.

STEPS

1. Soak the almonds in a bowl with boiling water.

2. After 3-5 minutes, or once the almonds are soft enough that their skins slip off easily, drain them.

3. Peel the skins off by gently squeezing each almond between your fingers or rubbing them in a towel. *Optional: For convenience, start with blanched almonds and skip this step.*

4. In a blender, combine the peeled (or blanched) almonds, your choice of natural sweetener, and milk. Blend until the mixture is perfectly smooth.

5. Pour in the orange blossom water and blend for another 30 seconds. Chill before serving!

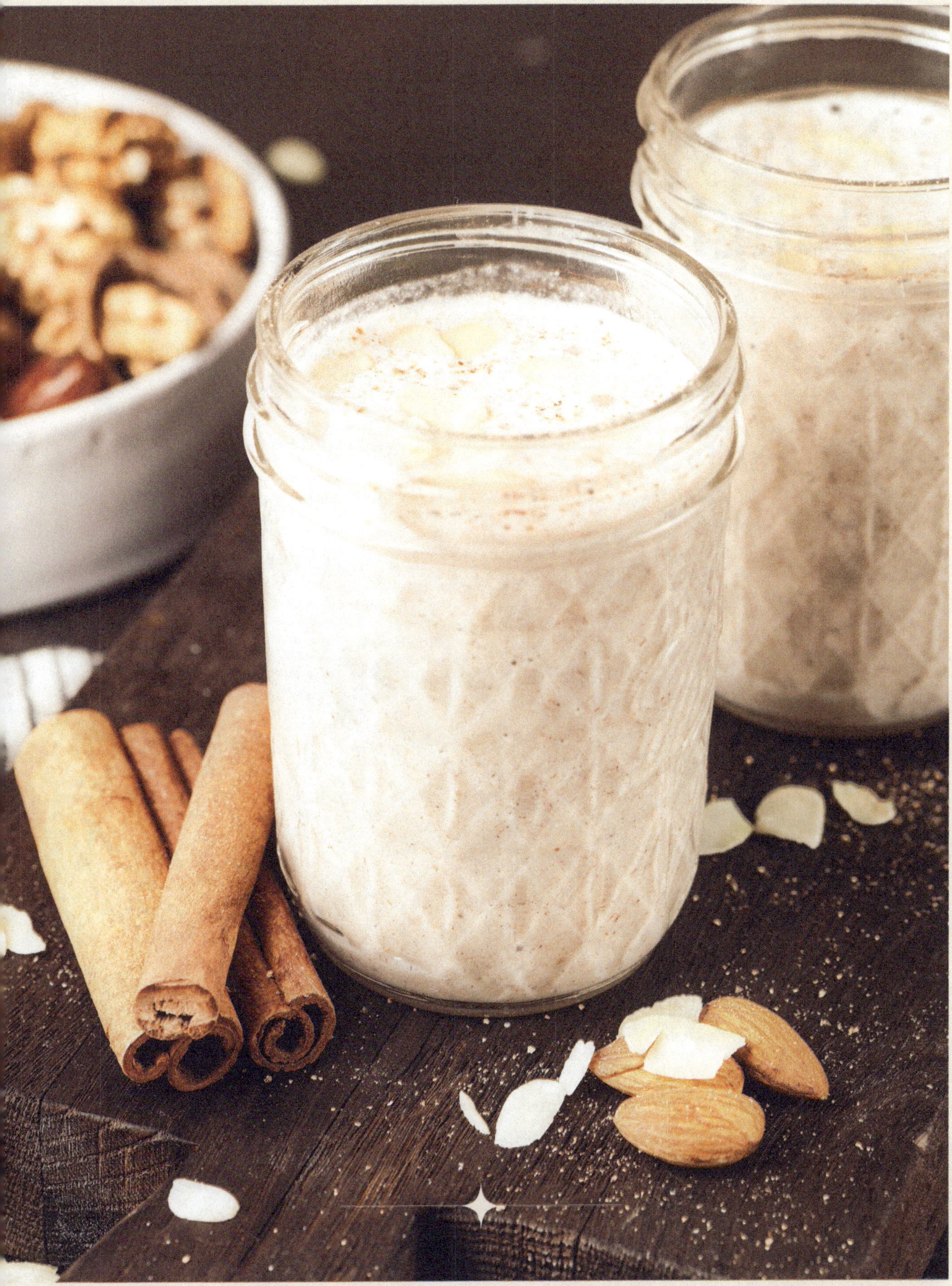

Nutty Sesame Delight Smoothie

| EASY | SERVES: 3 CUPS | PREP TIME: 10 MINUTES |

INGREDIENTS

250ml (1 cup) almond milk
1 tablespoon sesame seeds
7 walnut halves
3 Medjool dates, pitted
1 teaspoon orange blossom water (optional)
1/3 teaspoon ground cinnamon

BENEFITS

The smoothie is a nutrient-dense drink that combines the heart-healthy fats of walnuts and the mineral-rich qualities of sesame seeds into a deliciously smooth beverage. Walnuts are known for their omega-3 fatty acid content, supporting heart health and brain function, while sesame seeds are a great source of calcium and magnesium, essential for bone health and muscle function. The addition of Medjool dates offers natural sweetness along with fiber, helping to promote digestive health. Almond milk, used as the base, offers a dairy-free source of vitamin E and is lighter in calories

STEPS

1. Place the sesame seeds and walnut halves in a pan over medium heat. Toast them for 3 minutes, stirring occasionally to prevent burning. Remove from heat and allow to cool.

2. In a blender, add the cooled sesame seeds, walnuts, dates, orange blossom water, ground cinnamon, and almond milk. Blend until smooth. Serve immediately.

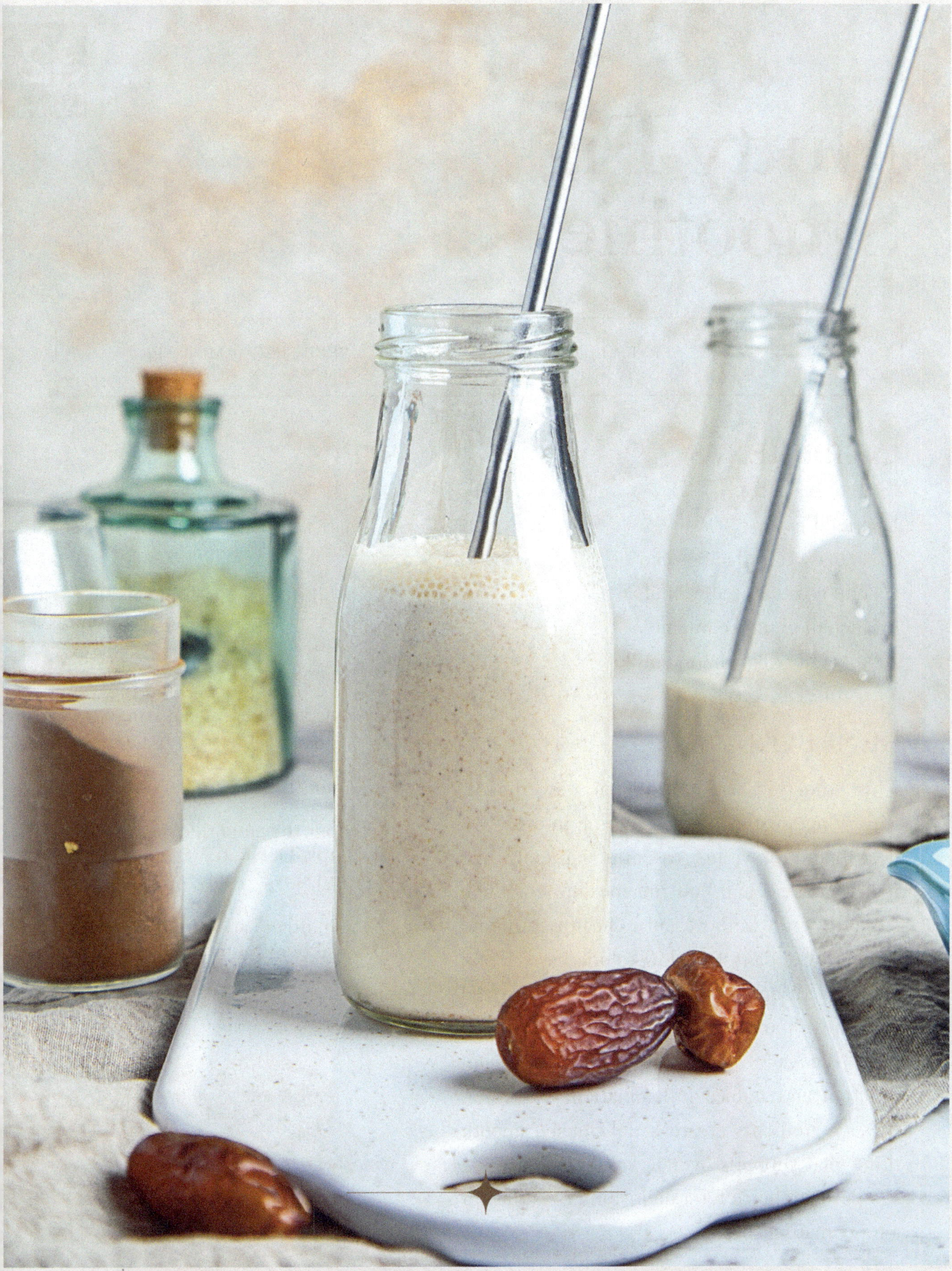

Nutty Fig Smoothie

| EASY | SERVES: 1 LARGE CUP | PREP TIME: 10 MINUTES |

INGREDIENTS

1 bag of black tea
10 dried figs
2 bananas, peeled and sliced
1/4 cup raw unsalted walnuts
A pinch of ground cinnamon
700ml (3 cups) of almond milk
6 ice cubes

BENEFITS

This smoothie is a nutritional powerhouse. Figs bring a wealth of fiber, aiding in digestive health and providing essential minerals like potassium, calcium, and magnesium for bone strength and cardiovascular health. Almond milk offers a dairy-free, low-calorie base rich in vitamins D and E, contributing to improved heart health and skin vitality. Walnuts, packed with omega-3 fatty acids, enhance brain function and reduce inflammation. Together, these ingredients create a deliciously smooth drink that supports overall well-being, making it a perfect choice for a nourishing breakfast or a rejuvenating snack.

STEPS

1. Brew the black tea bag in a large bowl of boiling water for a few minutes.

2. Add the dried figs to the hot tea, letting them soak for 10 minutes until soft.

3. In a blender, combine the softened figs, sliced bananas, walnuts, honey, cinnamon, ice cubes, and hald of the almond milk. Blend until smooth.

4. Pour the smoothie in the serving cups. Decorate with cucumbers and serve.

5. Gradually add almond milk to the blender, blending until you reach your preferred consistency of the smoothie.

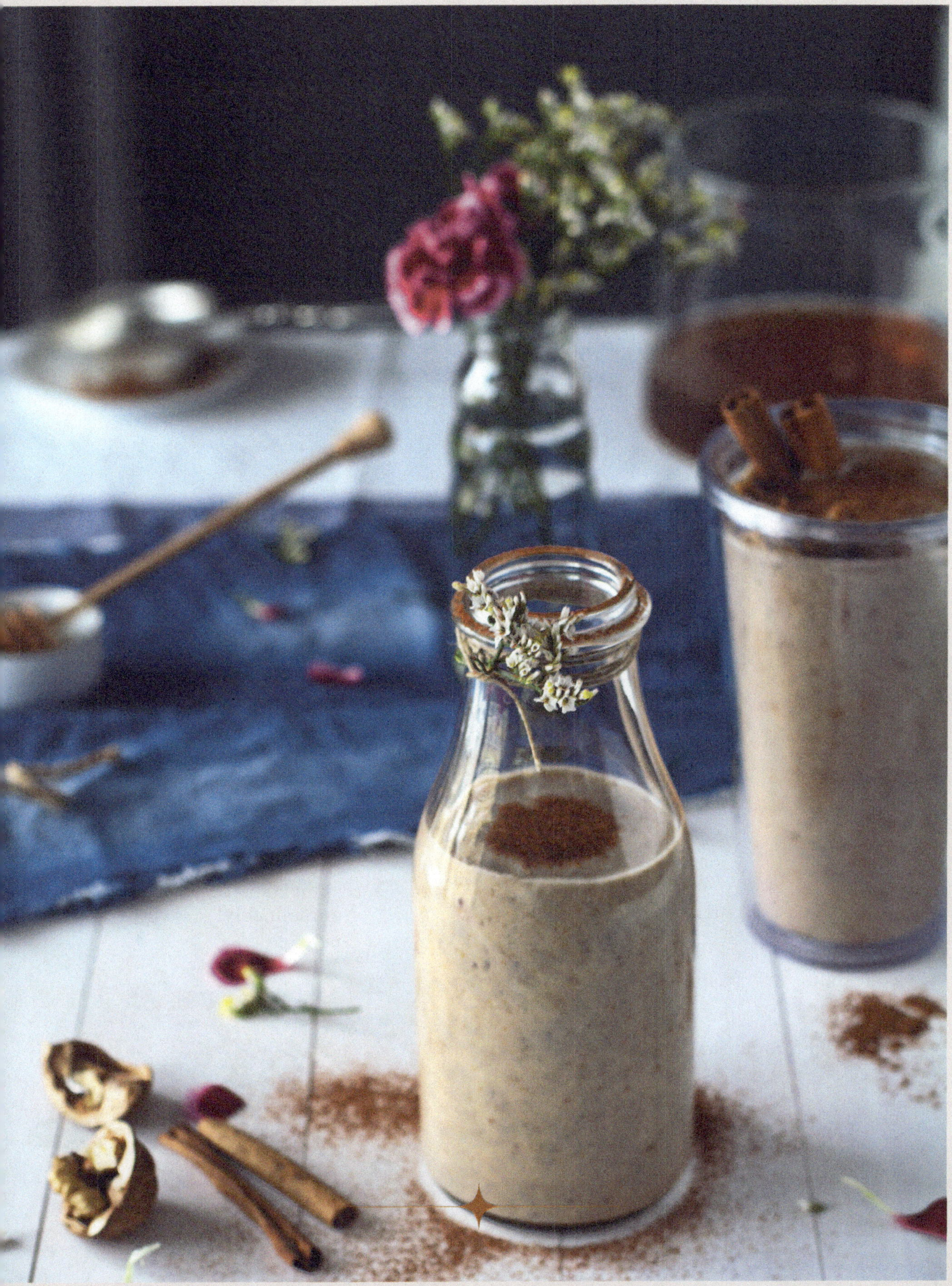

Pomegranate Juice

| EASY | SERVES: 3 CUPS | PREP TIME: 10 MINUTES |

INGREDIENTS

2 large pomegranates
Handful of ice cubes
Natural sweetener (honey, maple syrup, or any favorite)

BENEFITS

This juice is a vibrant and healthful beverage that harnesses the nutritional power of pomegranates, delivering a host of benefits with every sip. Pomegranates are renowned for their high levels of antioxidants, particularly punicalagins and anthocyanins, which help protect the body against oxidative stress and inflammation. Drinking this juice can contribute to heart health by improving cholesterol profiles and protecting LDL cholesterol from oxidative damage. The natural sugars in pomegranates provide a healthy energy boost, while the act of blending the seeds with ice ensures you're getting a good dose of dietary fiber, aiding in digestion and promoting a feeling of fullness.

STEPS

1. Peel the pomegranate, remove all rind and keep only the seeds in a bowl.

2. Rinse and strain the seeds.

3. Place the pomegranates, ice cubes and sweetener in a blender, then blend until smooth.

4. If desired, strain the pomegranate juice. Serve immediately!

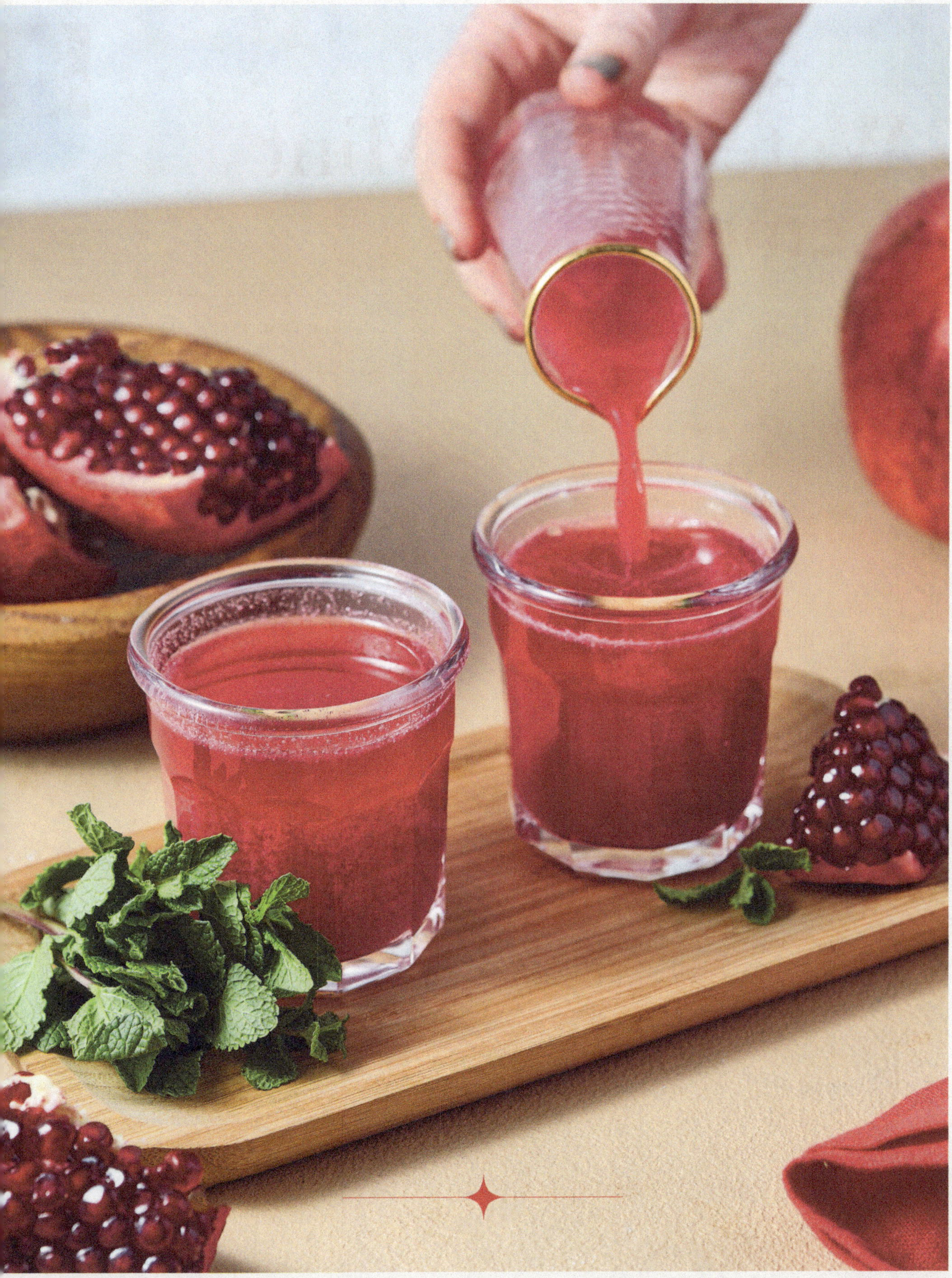

Watermelon Mint Lemonade

| EASY | SERVES: 4 LARGE CUPS | PREP TIME: 15 MINUTES |

INGREDIENTS

For the Mint-Lemon Syrup:

300gr (1.5 cups) light brown sugar

300ml (1 1/4 cups) water

300ml (1 1/4 cups) lemon juice

1 teaspoon lemon zest

15 fresh mint leaves

For the Lemonade:

900 grams (2 pounds) watermelon flesh, roughly chopped

480 ml (2 cups) water

BENEFITS

This refreshing lemonade offers a delightful escape from the heat. Watermelon flesh, rich in water content and lycopene, hydrates the body and provides antioxidant support, potentially reducing the risk of certain diseases. The homemade mint-lemon syrup, featuring lemon juice and zest, infuses the drink with vitamin C, enhancing immune function and skin health. Mint adds a layer of digestive aid and a cooling effect, making this lemonade not just a thirst quencher but a nourishing treat for your digestive system.

STEPS

For the Mint-Lemon Syrup:

1. Combine the light brown sugar and water in a saucepan over medium heat. Bring to a boil and let simmer for 5 minutes.

2. Remove from heat and stir in the lemon zest, lemon juice, and mint leaves. Allow the mixture to cool.

3. Strain the syrup to remove the solids, then transfer it to a bottle and refrigerate until cold.

For the Lemonade:

1. Puree 800 grams of watermelon in a blender until smooth.

2. In a large pitcher, mix together 240ml (1 cup) of the mint-lemon syrup with 480ml (2 cups) of water and 1L (4 cups) of watermelon juice.

3. Strain the lemonade through a sieve to remove any remaining pulp or seeds. Chill thoroughly and serve cold for a refreshing drink.

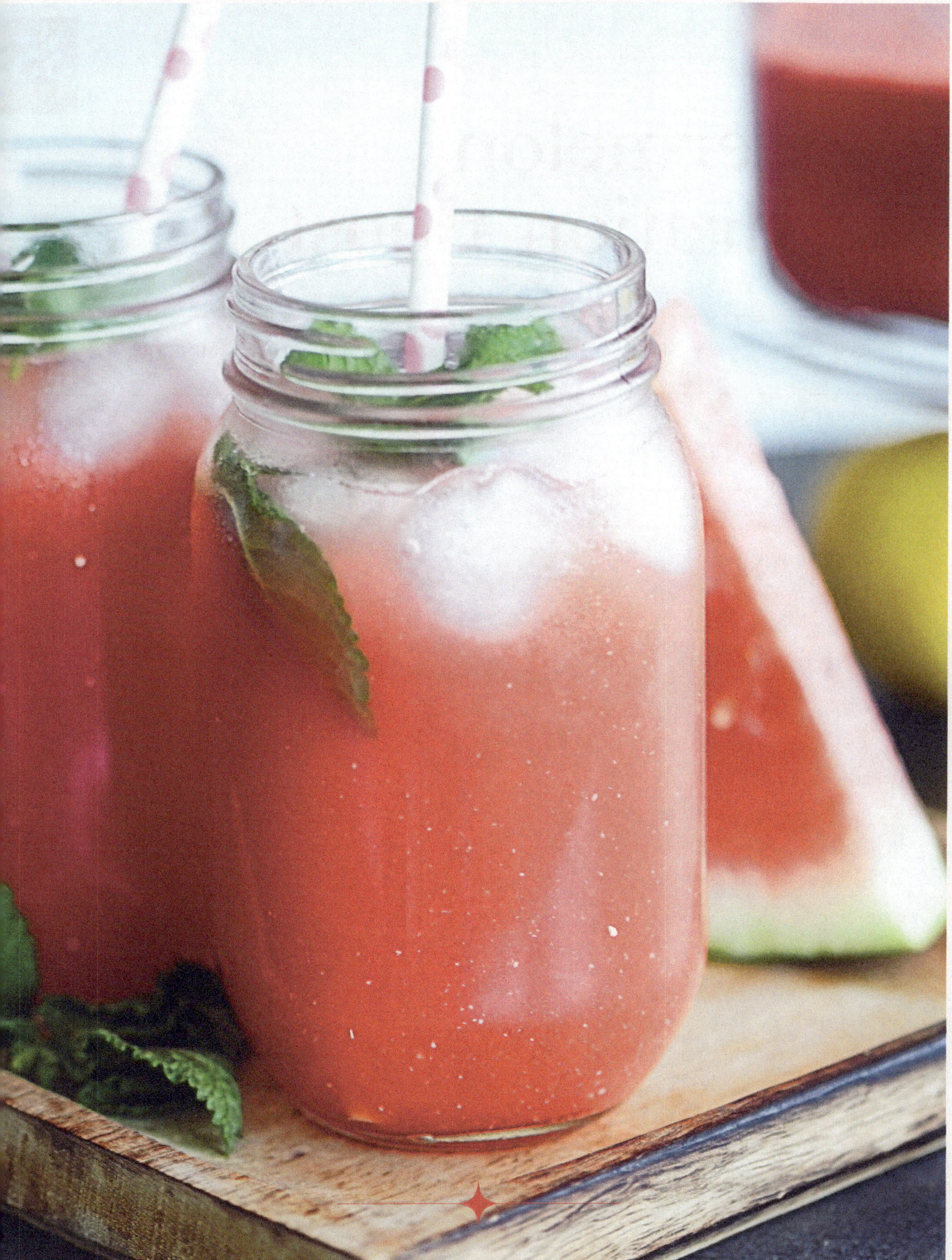

Watermelon Hydration Boost

| EASY | SERVES: 4 LARGE CUPS | PREP TIME: 15 MINUTES |

INGREDIENTS

400 grams (0.8 pounds) watermelon flesh, cubed
10 fresh mint leaves
1 liter (4 cups) water

BENEFITS

This drink offers a refreshing and healthful way to stay hydrated, particularly during warm weather. Watermelon, rich in vitamins A and C, antioxidants, and amino acids, aids in hydration and can help reduce muscle soreness after exercise. Its high water content, combined with the soothing properties of mint, makes this drink not only invigorating but also beneficial for digestion and promoting a sense of well-being. Mint leaves add a cooling effect and can help improve digestion and reduce inflammation. This simple yet powerful combination supports overall hydration, which is crucial for maintaining energy levels, supporting kidney function, and enhancing skin health.

STEPS

1. Place the cubed watermelon and mint leaves into a liter-sized jar or bottle.

2. Fill the container with water, then cover it.

3. Chill in the refrigerator for at least 1 hour to allow the flavors to infuse. Serve cold

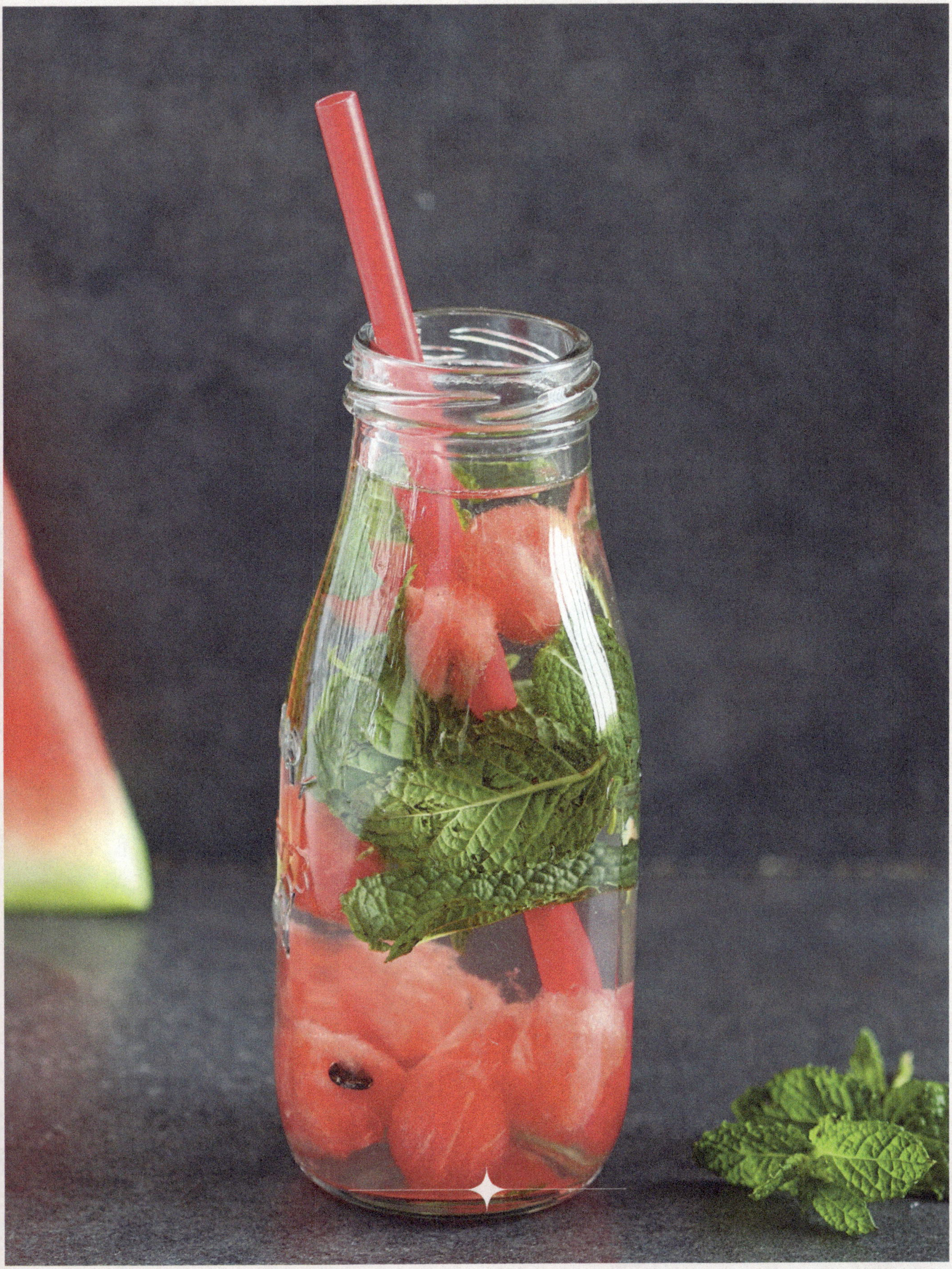

Zesty Ginger Lemonade

| EASY | SERVES: 3 CUPS | PREP TIME: 10 MINUTES |

INGREDIENTS

6 large ripe lemons
60g (2 ounces) fresh ginger
Natural sweetener (honey, maple syrup, or any favorite)
1L (4 cups) water 500ml (2 cups) ice cold water (or to taste)

BENEFITS

The lemon and ginger juice not only promises to refresh and hydrate on the warmest of days but also brings a wealth of health benefits. Lemons, bursting with Vitamin C, enhance immune function and skin health, while ginger, known for its anti-inflammatory properties, aids digestion and soothes sore throats.

STEPS

1 Peel lemons to remove all white pith, minimizing bitterness.

2 Slice the lemons into rounds and remove the seeds.

3 Peel the ginger and chop into medium-sized pieces.

4 Combine lemon rounds and ginger in a blender.

5 Add sweetener and 1L of water; blend until the mixture is smooth.

6 Strain the blend into a large bowl or pitcher, discarding the solids.

7 Stir in the rest of the cold water. Serve chilled.

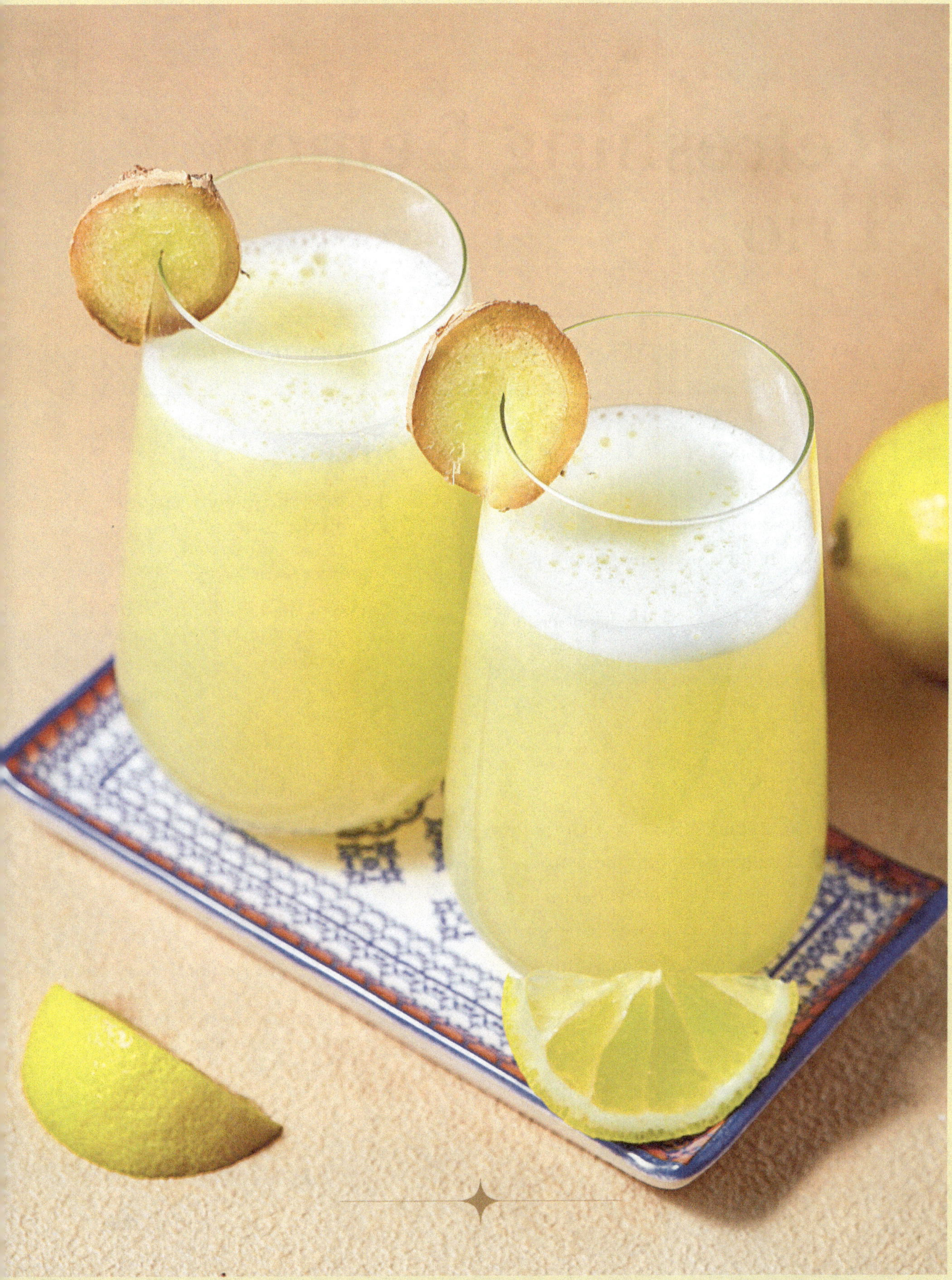

Refreshing Lemon Trio

| EASY | SERVES: 3 CUPS | PREP TIME: 10 MINUTES |

INGREDIENTS

2 Lemons

750ml (3 cups) cold water

Natural sweetener (honey, maple syrup, or any favorite)

Option 1 - Mint and lemon juice: Handful of mint leaves

Option 2 - Banana and lemon juice: 2 bananas, peeled, chopped, and frozen

BENEFITS

This classic blend offers a rich source of Vitamin C, enhancing immune support and skin health, while the mint variation not only refreshes but also promotes digestion and mental clarity. The banana-infused juice stands out as a nourishing option, packed with potassium and energy.

STEPS

1. Peel the lemons, ensuring all the white pith is removed to avoid bitterness.

2. Cut the lemons into rounds, meticulously removing any seeds.

3. In a blender, place the lemon pieces, water, and your choice of natural sweetener. Process until the mixture is completely smooth.

4. Strain the blended mixture to ensure a smooth juice.

VARIATIONS

1. Mint and Lemon Juice Variation: Add fresh mint leaves to the blender with the prepared lemon juice base. Blend and serve chilled.

2. Banana and Lemon Juice Variation: Combine frozen chopped bananas with the prepared lemon juice base in a blender. Blend until smooth. Serve immediately.

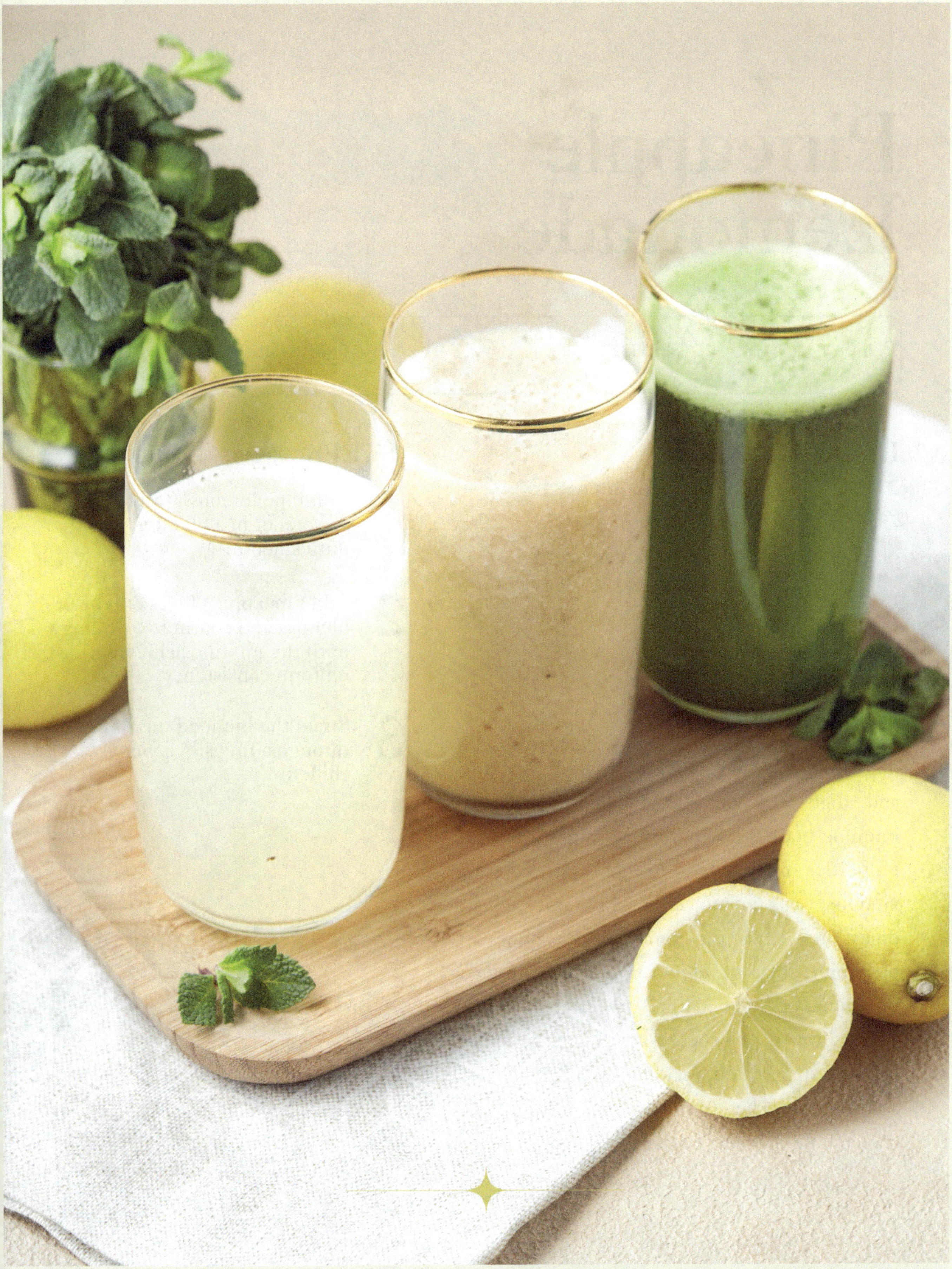

Pineapple Lemonade

EASY   SERVES: 4 CUPS   PREP TIME: 10 MINUTES

INGREDIENTS

2 lemons, chopped and seeds removed
750ml (3 cups) cold water
Natural sweetener (honey, maple syrup, or any favorite)
1/2 pineapple, peeled and diced
Ice cubes for serving (optional)

BENEFITS

This refreshing juice combines the detoxifying and digestive benefits of lemon with the immune-boosting and anti-inflammatory properties of pineapple. Lemons, packed with vitamin C, promote clear skin and aid in digestion, while the bromelain enzyme in pineapple supports digestion and may reduce inflammation. The natural sweeteners add a healthy touch of sweetness without the spike in blood sugar levels, making this drink not just a thirst-quencher but also a nutrient-rich choice for enhancing overall well-being.

STEPS

1. Combine lemons, water, and sweetener in a blender. Blend until smooth.

2. Add pineapple chunks to the blender and continue blending until the mixture achieves a uniform consistency.

3. Strain the blended mixture through a fine sieve. Serve chilled.

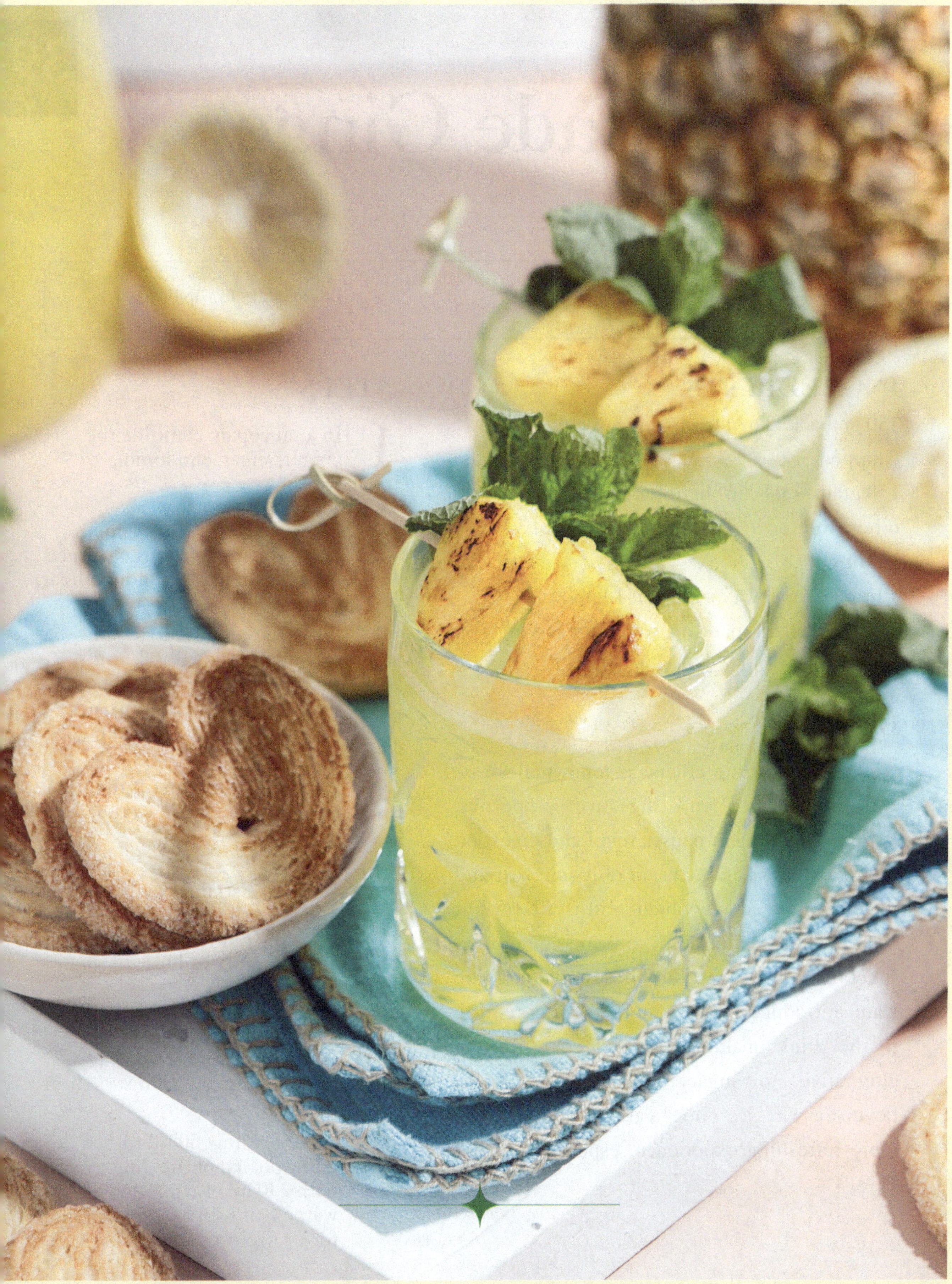

Homemade Ginger Ale

| EASY | SERVES: 10 CUPS | PREP TIME: 15 MINUTES |

INGREDIENTS

150 grams (5.2 oz.) fresh ginger, peeled and chopped
150 grams (3/4 cup) light brown sugar or other sweetener of your choice Zests of 3 lemons
1 litre (4 cups) water Juice of 1 lemon
2 litres (8 cups) sparkling water, for serving
Ice cubes for serving (optional)

BENEFITS

Ginger, the star ingredient, is renowned for its anti-inflammatory and digestive properties, potentially aiding in nausea relief and digestion improvement. The inclusion of lemon zest and juice not only adds a vibrant, citrusy flavor but also contributes vitamin C, enhancing immune function and skin health. The use of sparkling water introduces a fizzy, more exciting texture to the drink, making it a perfect, refreshing alternative to sugary sodas. Serving this beverage with ice cubes can provide an even more refreshing experience, especially on hot days.

STEPS

1. In a saucepan, combine the ginger, sugar, and lemon zest.

2. Pour in the water and lemon juice, stirring to combine. Place the saucepan over medium heat.

3. Bring the mixture to a boil, stirring occasionally. Let it simmer uncovered for about 10 minutes, or until the mixture reaches a syrupy consistency.

4. Take the saucepan off the heat and allow the syrup to cool for 10 minutes.

5. Position a strainer over a bowl and pour the syrup through it, straining out the ginger pieces and lemon zest. Discard the solids.

6. Allow the syrup to cool completely. Once cooled, transfer it to a jar and store it in the refrigerator.

7. To enjoy, mix 50 ml (3 tablespoons) of the ginger syrup with 240 ml (1 cup) of sparkling water. Stir well and serve chilled for a refreshing drink.

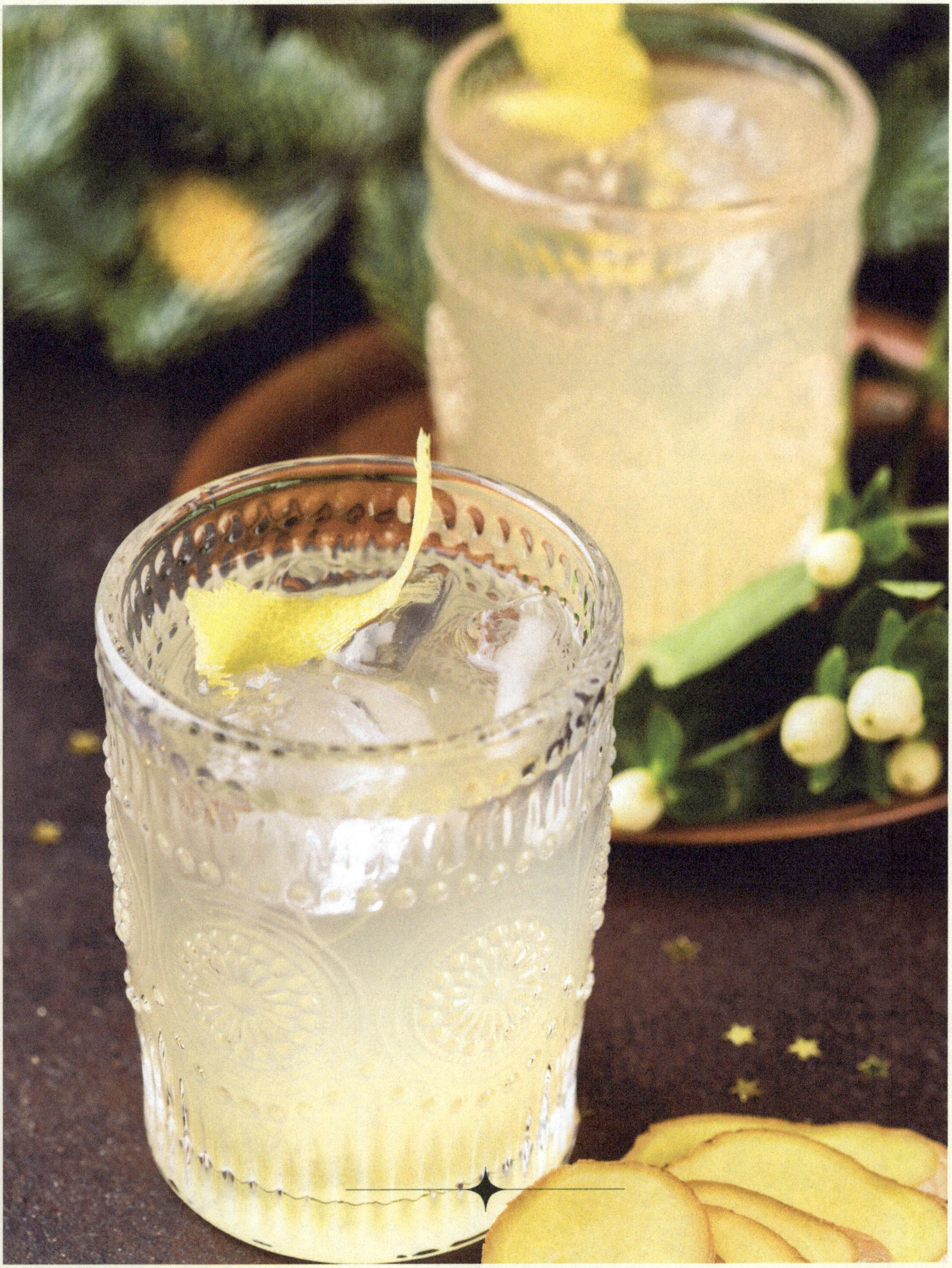

Citrus Cinnamon Infusion

| EASY | SERVES: 8 CUPS | PREP TIME: 10 MINUTES |

INGREDIENTS

1 liter (4 cups) water
2 tablespoons lemon juice
3 tablespoons natural sweetener (honey, maple syrup, or any favorite)
2 cinnamon sticks
500ml (2 cups) orange juice
250ml (1 cup) pineapple juice
1 medium navel orange, sliced
Ice cubes for serving

BENEFITS

This infusion is rich in vitamin C from the lemon, orange, and pineapple juices, boosting the immune system and promoting skin health. The natural sweeteners like honey or maple syrup provide a healthier alternative to refined sugars, adding antioxidants that fight inflammation and supporting overall wellness. Cinnamon sticks, steeped in the infusion, offer anti-inflammatory properties and can help regulate blood sugar levels. This drink is not only hydrating but also aids in digestion, thanks to the digestive enzymes present in pineapple juice.

STEPS

1. In a saucepan, combine the water, lemon juice, natural sweetener, and cinnamon sticks. Stir well to mix.

2. Heat the mixture over medium heat, bringing it to a boil and stirring until the sweetener is completely dissolved.

3. Remove the saucepan from the heat. Stir in the orange and pineapple juices.

4. Allow the mixture to cool down completely. Once cooled, add the slices of navel orange.

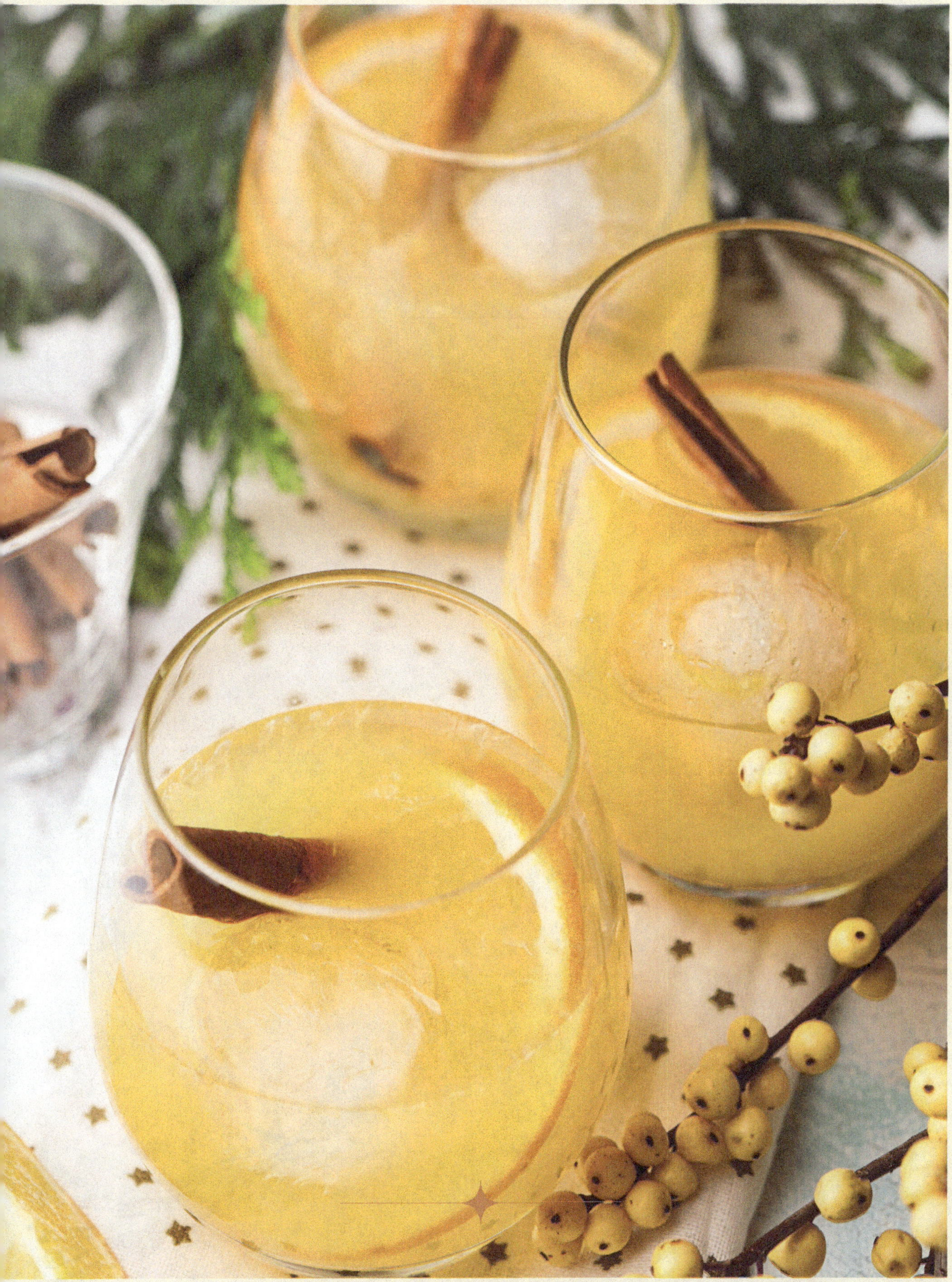

Grapefruit Thyme Sparkler

| EASY | SERVES: 4 CUPS | PREP TIME: 10 MINUTES |

INGREDIENTS

1 liter unsweetened sparkling water
2 medium grapefruits, halved
6 sprigs of fresh thyme
Ice for serving (optional)

BENEFITS

The Grapefruit-Thyme Sparkler is a refreshing beverage that combines the detoxifying and immune-boosting properties of grapefruit with the soothing and digestive aid of thyme. Grapefruit, rich in vitamin C and antioxidants, supports the immune system, aids in weight loss, and helps lower cholesterol levels. Thyme, known for its antiseptic and anti-inflammatory properties, can improve digestion and promote respiratory health. This drink, infused with unsweetened sparkling water, offers a hydrating and low-calorie alternative to sugary beverages, making it an excellent choice for maintaining hydration and overall well-being.

STEPS

1. Juice one grapefruit and set aside.

2. Rinse the second grapefruit, then slice it.

3. In a large pitcher, combine the grapefruit slices, thyme sprigs, and the freshly squeezed grapefruit juice.

4. Pour sparkling water into the pitcher. Add ice cubes to the pitcher and serve immediately!

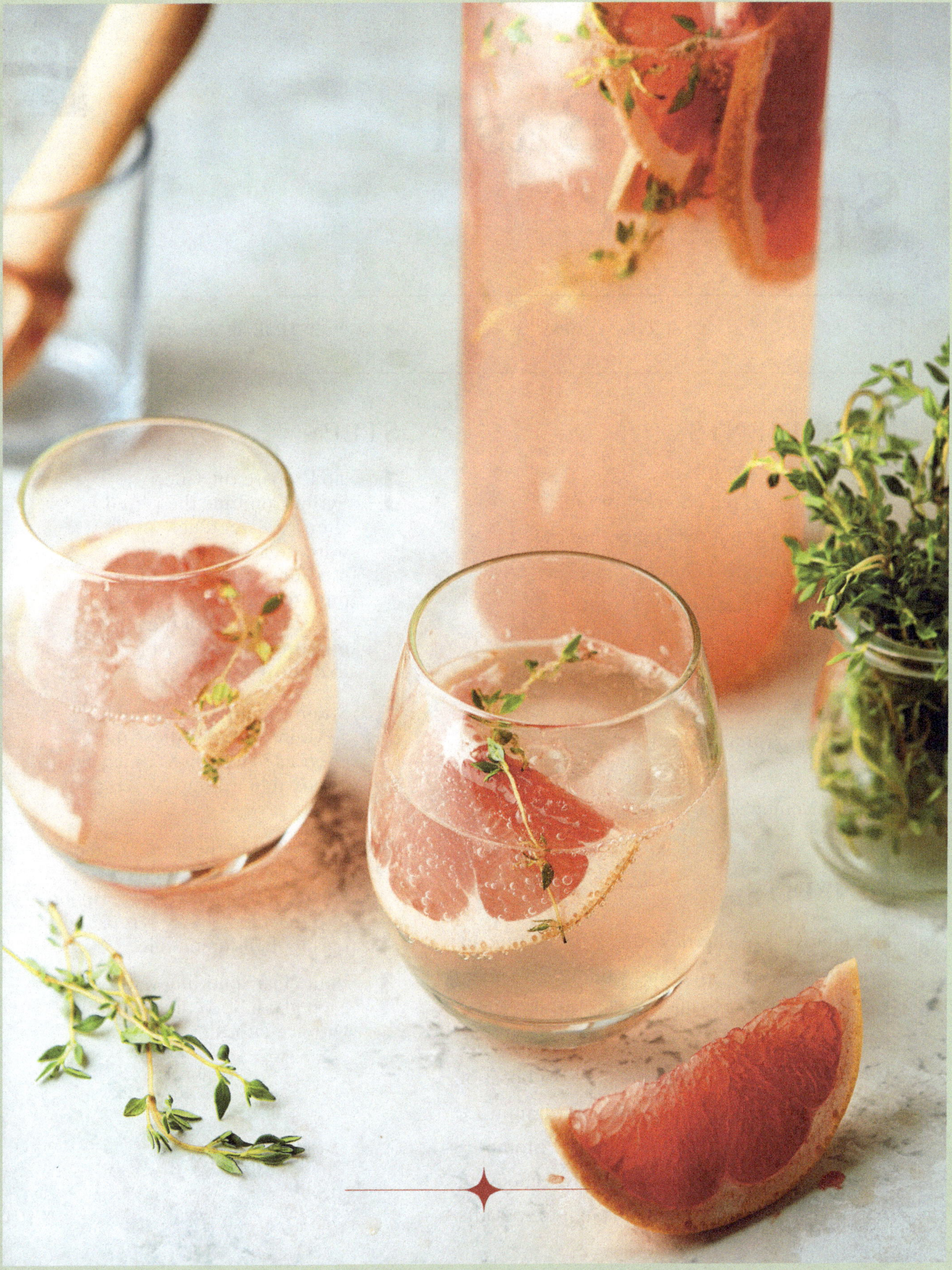

Cherry Basil Sparkler

| EASY | SERVES: 4 CUPS | PREP TIME: 10 MINUTES |

INGREDIENTS

For the Cherry Syrup:
70 grams (2.4 oz) red cherries, pitted
1 tablsepoon natural sweetener (honey, maple syrup, or any favorite)
3 tablespoons water For the Drink:
1 liter (4 cups) clear sparkling water
10 red cherries, pitted and halved
12 fresh basil leaves
Cherry syrup (prepared earlier)
Juice of
1 lemon Lemon slices for garnish
Ice cubes

BENEFITS

The inclusion of cherries adds a rich source of antioxidants and vitamins, aiding in heart health and sleep quality to this drink, while basil offers its own range of anti-inflammatory and antibacterial benefits, along with a boost of antioxidants. Lemon juice, rich in vitamin C, not only adds a zestful twist but also promotes skin health and hydration. By choosing sparkling water as the base, this mojito remains a light.

STEPS

1. To Prepare the Cherry Syrup Combine the pitted cherries, sweetener, and water in a saucepan over medium heat. Cook for 5 minutes, stirring occasionally, until the mixture thickens to a jam-like consistency.

2. Strain the mixture through a sieve into a bowl, pressing the cherries to extract as much syrup as possible. Allow the syrup to cool.

3. To assemble the drink, into each serving glass, add 5 cherry halves, 3 basil leaves, 1 teaspoon of the cooled cherry syrup, and 1 teaspoon of lemon juice."

4. Pour clear sparkling water into each glass. Serve immediately with ice cubes!

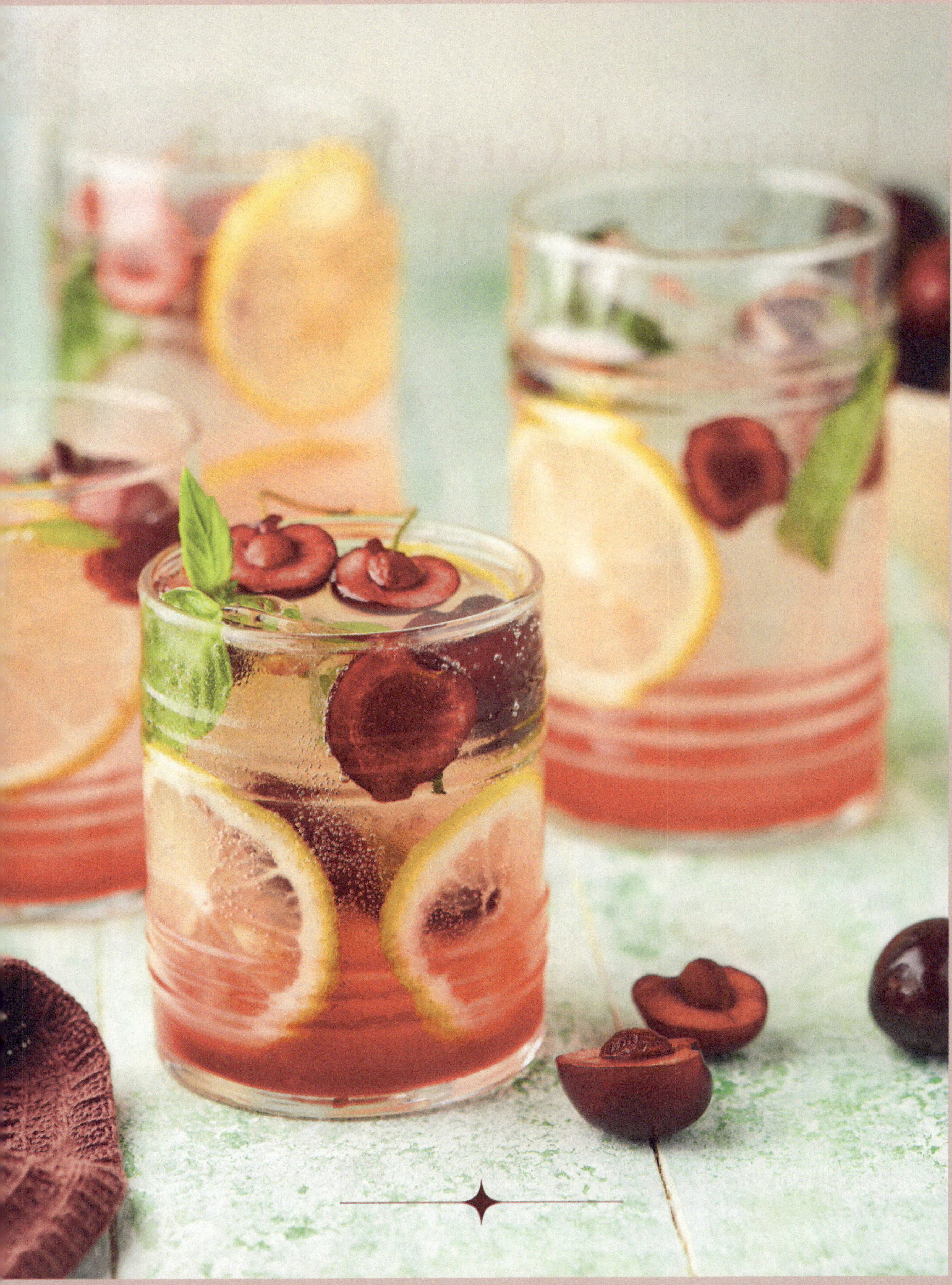

Tropical Grapefruit Refreshment

| EASY | SERVES: 3 CUPS | PREP TIME: 15 MINUTES |

INGREDIENTS

240 ml (1 cup) grapefruit juice
1/2 pineapple, peeled and cubed
5 strawberries
240 ml (1 cup) cold water
Ice cubes for serving

BENEFITS

This refreshing drink is an excellent source of vitamin C, vital for boosting the immune system, enhancing skin health, and promoting collagen production. Pineapple brings a bounty of bromelain, an enzyme that aids digestion and reduces inflammation, making this drink not only delicious but also beneficial for gut health. The addition of strawberries introduces antioxidants and additional vitamins, further supporting heart health and blood sugar control. Served with ice, this beverage is perfect for hydration, offering a natural and healthful way to stay refreshed and energized throughout the day.

STEPS

1. In a blender, combine the grapefruit juice, cubed pineapple, strawberries, and cold water.

2. If desired, strain the mixture to remove any pulp, ensuring a smooth texture. Serve immediately with ice cubes.

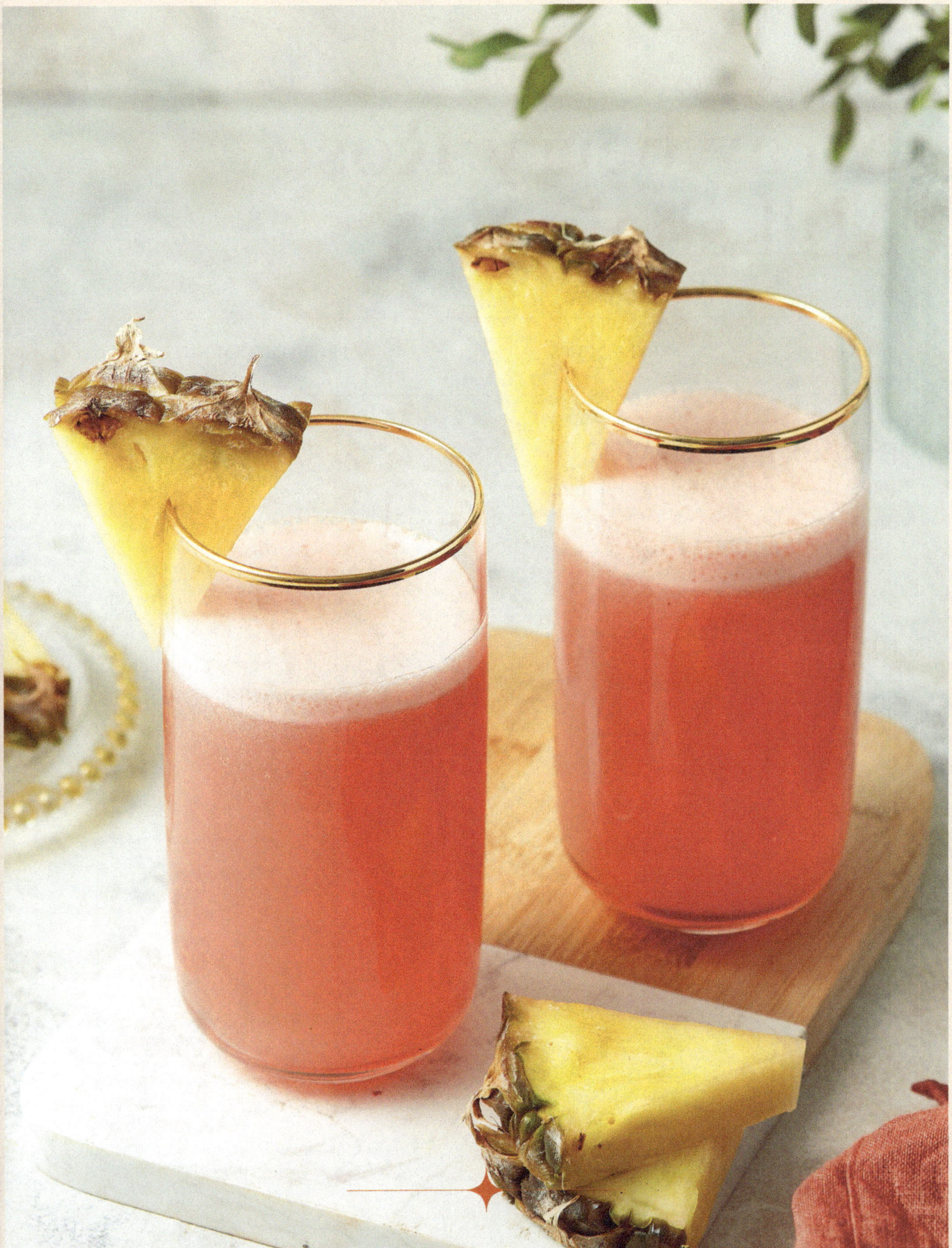

Strawberry Rose Milkshake

| EASY | SERVES: 2 CUPS | PREP TIME: 5 MINUTES |

INGREDIENTS

400g (14 oz.) low-calorie, high-protein vanilla ice cream
180g fresh (6 oz.) strawberries, hulled
3 tablespoons rose water

BENEFITS

For those looking to indulge without compromising on their calorie intake, the Strawberry Rose Bliss Milkshake presents an ideal option. Blending low-calorie, high-protein vanilla ice cream with the natural sweetness of fresh strawberries and the aromatic essence of rose water, this milkshake allows you to enjoy a decadent treat while keeping calories in check.

STEPS

1. 1- In a blender, combine vanilla ice cream, fresh strawberries, and rose water. Blend until the mixture achieves a smooth consistency.

2. Distribute the milkshake evenly among serving cups. Serve immediately.

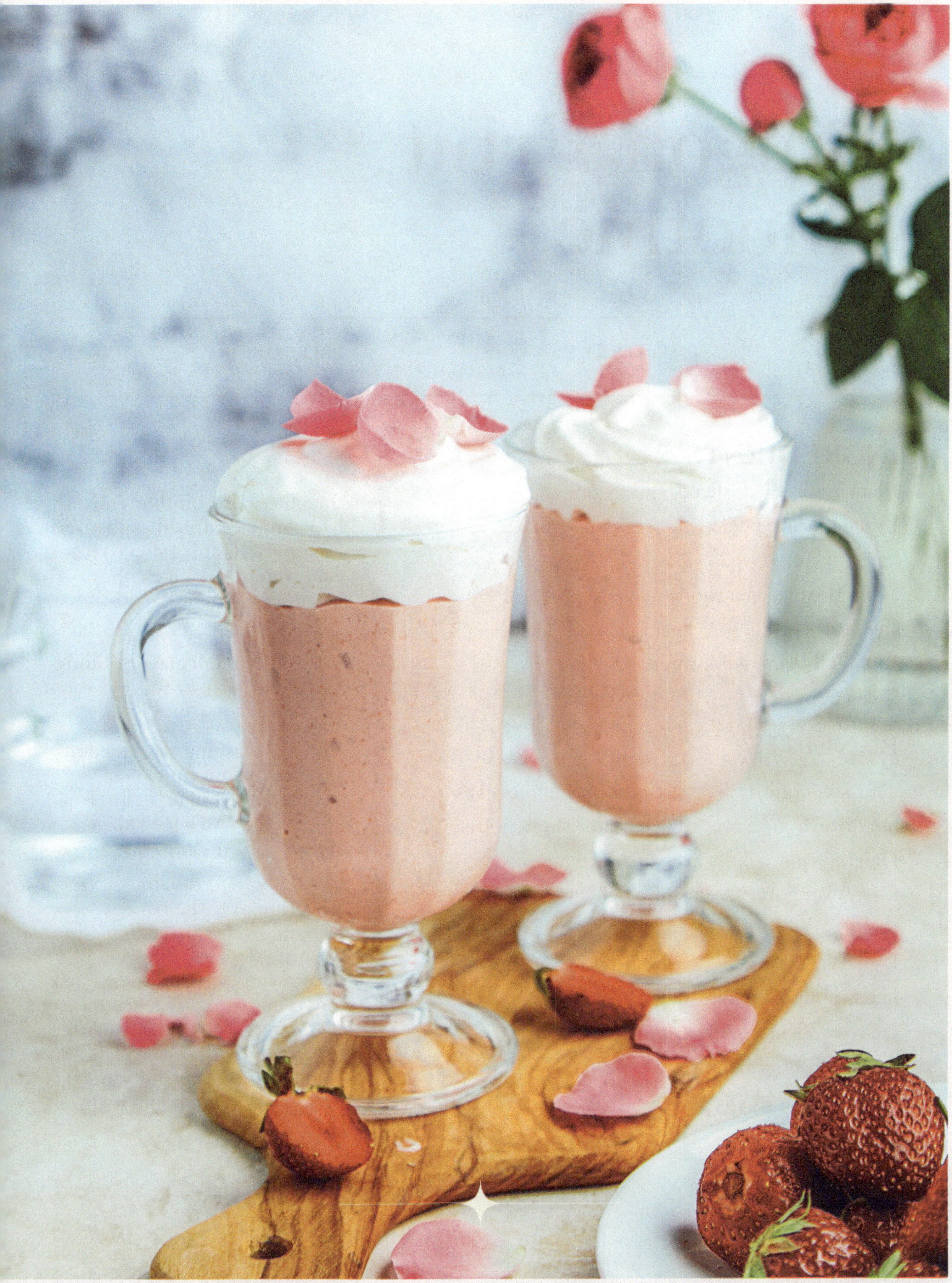

Dragon Fruit Smoothie

| EASY | SERVES: 2 LARGE CUPS | PREP TIME: 10 MINUTES |

INGREDIENTS

1 banana, peeled, sliced, and frozen
1 dragon fruit, peeled and chopped Juice of 1 lime
Natural sweetener (honey, maple syrup, or any favorite)
120ml (1/2 cup) cold water
6 ice cubes

BENEFITS

The smoothie is not just a feast for the eyes but also a treasure trove of health benefits. Dragon fruit, rich in antioxidants, vitamins, and fiber, supports a healthy gut, boosts the immune system, and maintains healthy skin. Bananas, loaded with potassium and magnesium, promote heart health and muscle recovery. Lime adds a refreshing twist while contributing vitamin C, enhancing immune defense and skin health.

STEPS

1. In a blender, combine frozen banana slices, freshly squeezed lime juice, 60ml (1/4 cup) ice-cold water, and 3 ice cubes. Blend until smooth.

2. Pour this banana smoothie mixture into tall glasses, filling each only halfway to leave room for the dragon fruit blend.

3. Without washing the blender, add the dragon fruit slices, sweetener, 60ml (1/4 cup) ice-cold water, and 3 ice cubes. Blend until smooth.

4. Carefully pour the dragon fruit smoothie over the banana mixture in the glasses, creating a beautiful layered effect.

5. Serve immediately, encouraging your guests to stir the smoothie before enjoying it to watch the colors blend beautifully and enjoy the phenomenal texture.

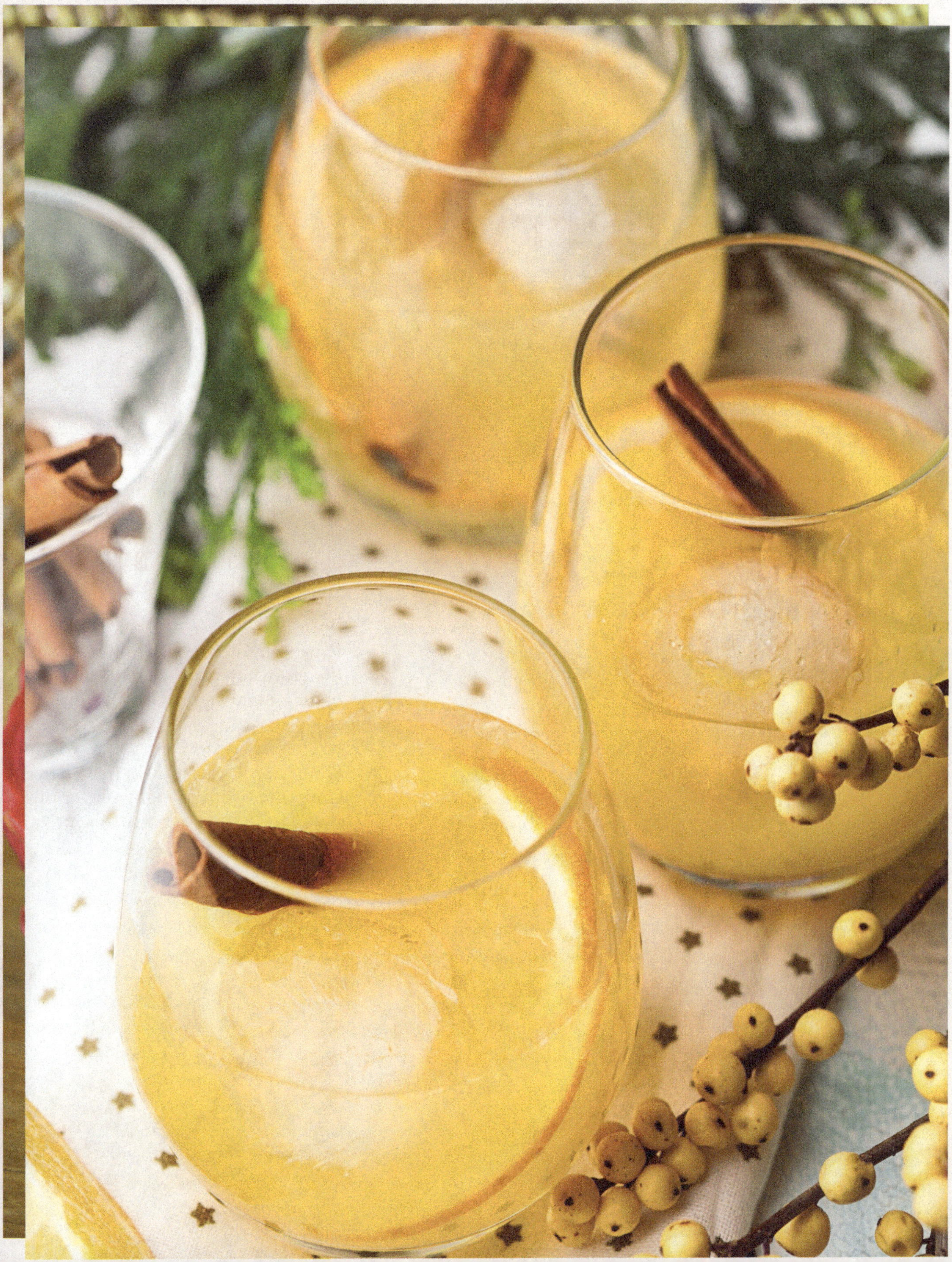

Sunset Mango-Strawberry Smoothie

EASY   SERVES: 2 TALL CUPS   PREP TIME: 10 MINUTES

INGREDIENTS

For the Mango Smoothie:
1 large mangoes, peeled and cut into chunks
120ml (1/2 cup) freshly squeezed orange juice
4 ice cubes

For the Strawberry Layer:
6 strawberries, hulled
60ml (1/4 cup) freshly squeezed orange juice
4 ice cubes

BENEFITS

This smoothie offers a delightful blend of vitamins, minerals, and antioxidants. Mangoes, rich in vitamin C and beta-carotene, support immune function and promote healthy skin, while strawberries add additional vitamin C and manganese, aiding in antioxidant protection and overall wellness. The inclusion of orange juice not only enhances the smoothie's vitamin content but also provides a citrusy zest that boosts absorption of iron from the mango and strawberries.

STEPS

1. For the mango smoothie layer, blend the mango chunks with the orange juice and ice cubes until smooth. Pour this mixture halfway into two tall glasses and set aside.

2. Rinse the blender, then blend the strawberry pieces with the orange juice and ice cubes until smooth.

3. Gently pour the strawberry smoothie over the mango layer in the glasses to create a two-layer effect.

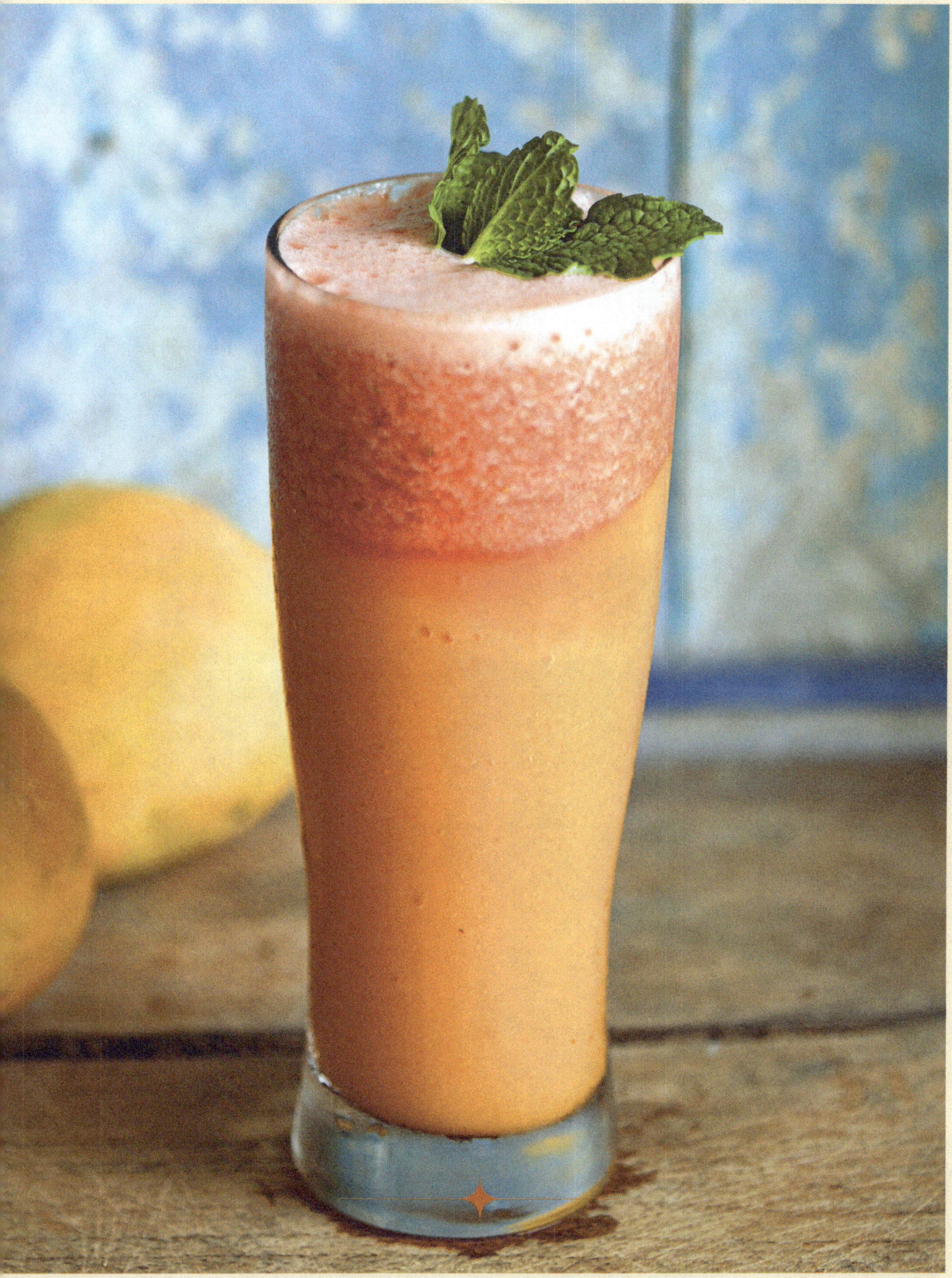

Frozen Colorful Smoothie

| EASY | SERVES: 2-3 LARGE CUPS | PREP TIME: 10 MINUTES |

INGREDIENTS

Purple layer: 1 cup blueberries, frozen 3 tablespoons of water

Orange layer: Half a banana (peeled, sliced and frozen), half an orange (peeled, sliced and frozen), 3 frozen raspberries, 3 tablespoons of water

Green layer: 2 kiwis (peeled, sliced and frozen), 3 tablespoons of water

Yellow layer: 1 cup pineapple (peeled, sliced, and frozen), 3 tablespoons water

Red layer: 1/2 cup frozen raspberries, 1/2 cup frozen strawberries, 3 tablespoons of water

STEPS

1. Blend each layer individually in a food processor and save in 5 medium bowls.

2. Create different colors like a rainbow by stacking the smoothies in tall cups.

3. Put back in the freezer for an additional 10 minutes and serve immediately.

BENEFITS

The frozen colorful smoothie artfully stacks vibrant fruits into a nutritious rainbow, each layer packed with specific benefits: blueberries for antioxidants, banana and orange for vitamin C and potassium, kiwis for vitamin K, pineapple for bromelain to reduce inflammation, and raspberries and strawberries for heart health.

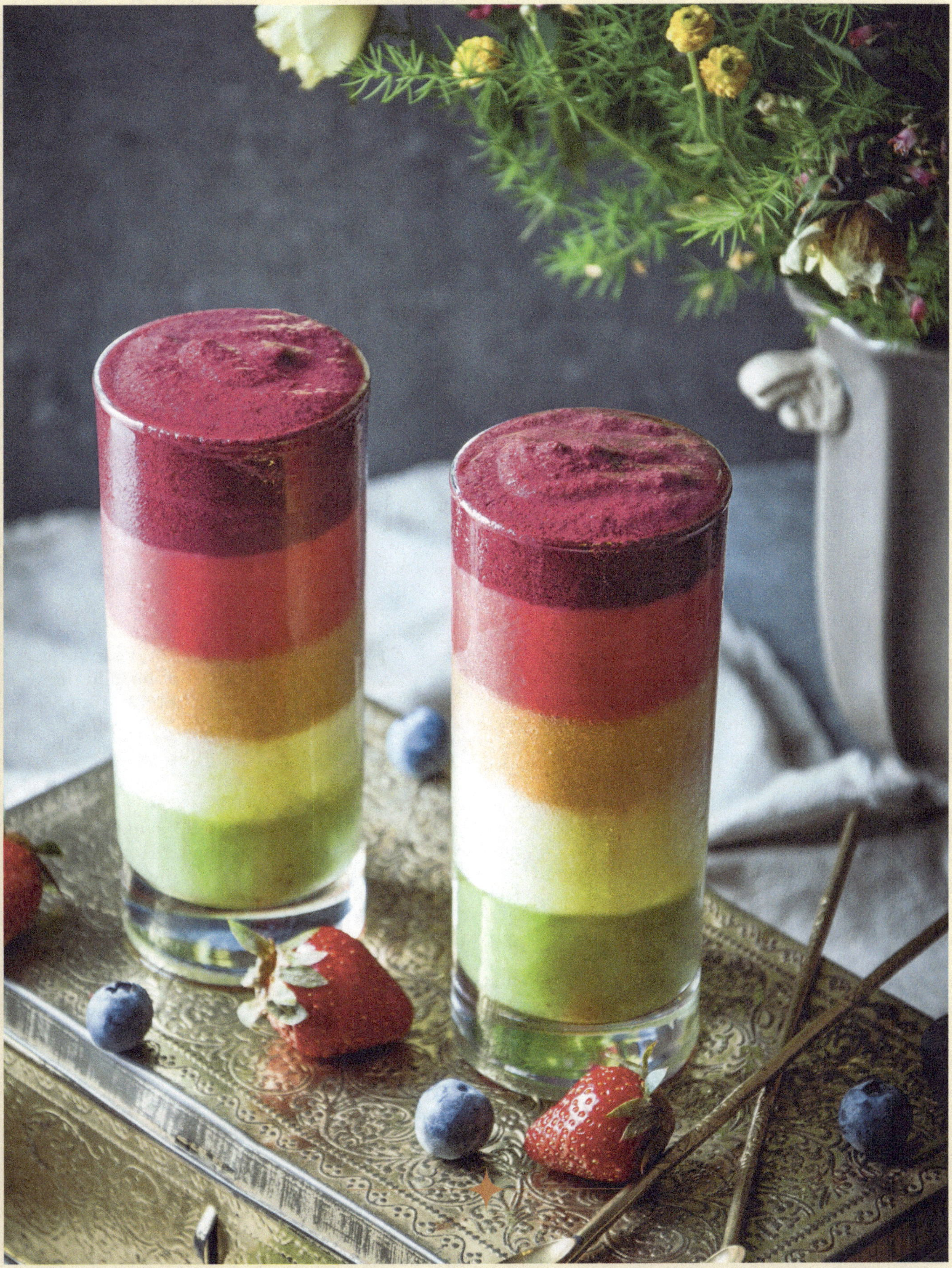

Peanut Butter and Oatmeal Smoothie

| EASY | SERVES: 2 CUPS | PREP TIME: 5 MINUTES |

INGREDIENTS

200ml oat milk
1 tablespoon peanut butter
2 medium bananas, peeled and chopped
Natural sweetener (honey, maple syrup, or any favorite)
1/4 teaspoon cinnamon
Ice cubes for serving (optional)
Option 1: Chocolate and Peanut Butter Smoothie 1 tablespoon unsweetened cocoa powder
Option 2: Berry and Peanut Butter Smoothie 1/4 cup mixed frozen berries

BENEFITS

This smoothie offers a rich source of protein and healthy fats from peanut butter, enhancing muscle repair and providing long-lasting energy. Oat milk contributes beneficial fibers for digestive health, while bananas supply potassium, vital for muscle function and recovery. Cinnamon adds anti-inflammatory properties, and honey introduces antioxidants.

STEPS

1. Combine oat milk, peanut butter, bananas, sweetener, cinnamon, and ice cubes in a blender. Blend until smooth.

2. For the Chocolate and Peanut Butter Smoothie option, add the unsweetened cocoa powder to the mix and blend for another minute. Serve immediately.

3. For the Berry and Peanut Butter Smoothie, add the mixed frozen berries (instead of the unsweetened cocoa powder) and blend for another minute. Serve immediately.

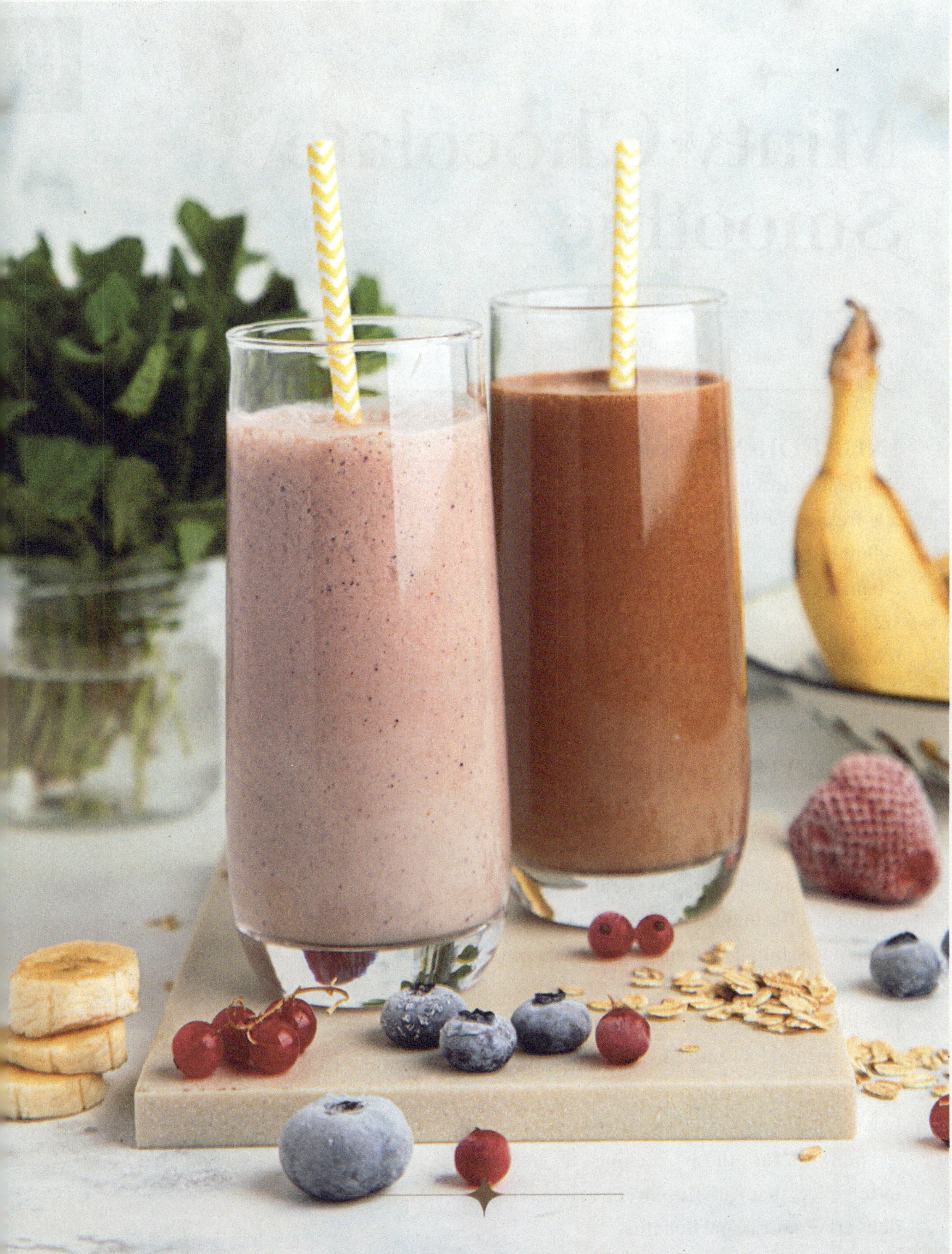

Minty Chocolate Smoothie

| EASY | SERVES: 4 CUPS | PREP TIME: 10 MINUTES |

INGREDIENTS

50g fresh spinach
50g fresh mint leaves
500ml milk
2 bananas, sliced
1/2 avocado, peeled and sliced
6 Medjool dates, pitted
2 tablespoons unsweetened cocoa powder
6 ice cubes

STEPS

1. Place the spinach, mint leaves, and milk in an electric blender. Mix until smooth.

2. Add the banana slices, avocado slices, dates, cocoa powder, and ice cubes. Continue blending until the mixture is completely smooth. Serve immediately!

BENEFITS

Spinach and mint leaves are rich in vitamins A and C, iron, and antioxidants, promoting immune function and eye health, while also adding a refreshing zest. Bananas and avocados bring potassium, fiber, and healthy fats into the mix, aiding in heart health, digestion, and providing sustained energy. Medjool dates offer natural sweetness along with fiber, vitamins, and minerals, contributing to a balanced and nutritious sweetness. This recipe is perfect for those seeking a healthful indulgence that satisfies sweet cravings while delivering nutritional benefits.

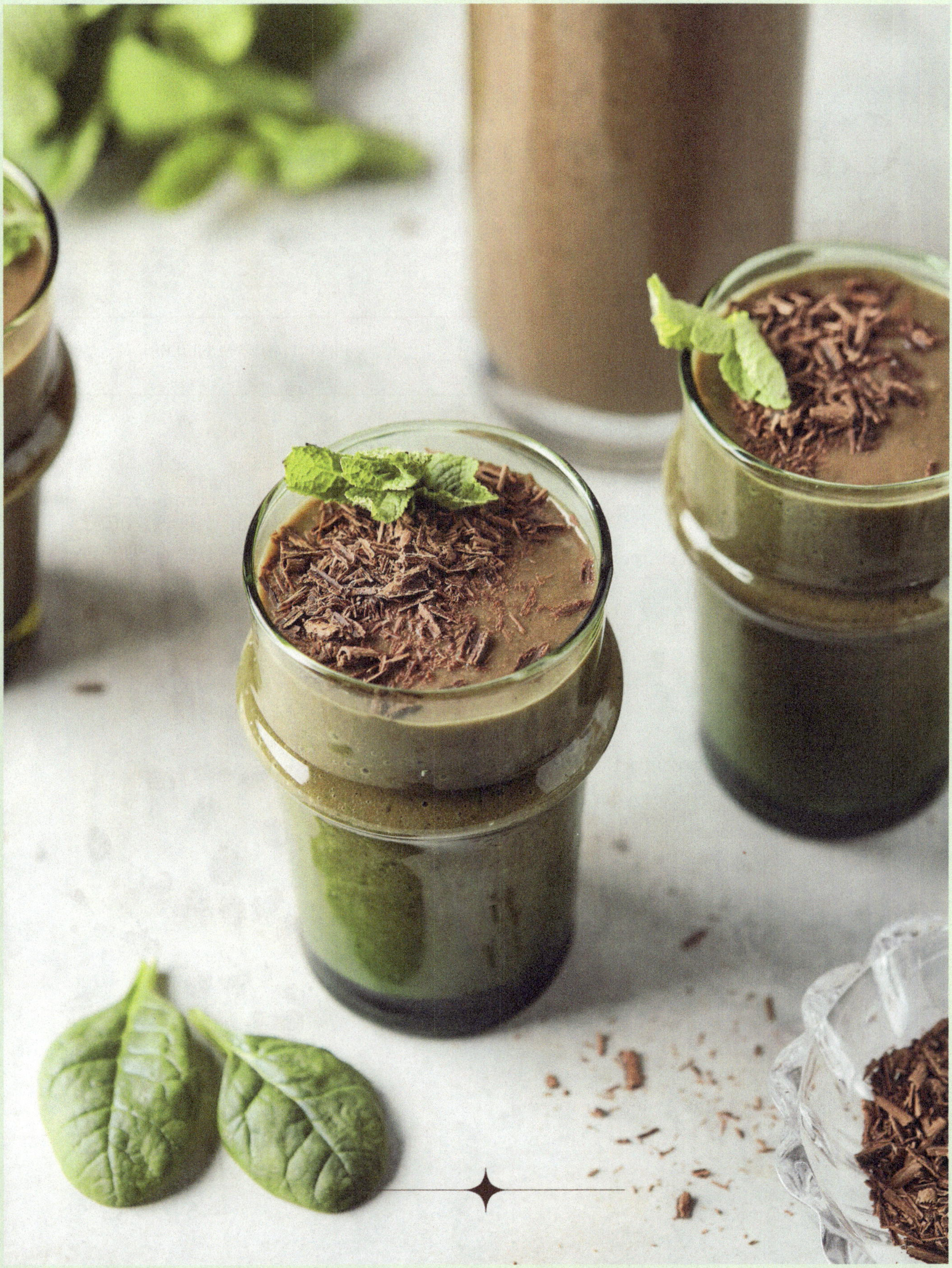

Café Mocha Power Smoothie

| EASY | SERVES: 4 CUPS | PREP TIME: 5 MINUTES |

INGREDIENTS

3 bananas, peeled, chopped and frozen
4 medjool dates, pitted
120ml (1/2 cup) brewed coffee
2 teaspoons instant coffee
4 tablespoons unsweetened cocoa powder
Ice cubes

BENEFITS

This is an energizing concoction designed to kick-start your day or boost your energy levels anytime. This smoothie combines the natural sweetness and nutritional richness of bananas and Medjool dates with the invigorating qualities of coffee, offering a healthy alternative to traditional caffeinated beverages. Bananas provide a good source of potassium, vitamin C, and dietary fiber, supporting heart health and digestion. The brewed and instant coffee offer caffeine, which can enhance mental alertness and physical performance

STEPS

1. In a blender, combine the frozen bananas, dates, coffee, instant coffee, cocoa powder, and ice cubes. Blend until smooth.

2. Serve the smoothie right away to savor its energizing flavors and benefits.

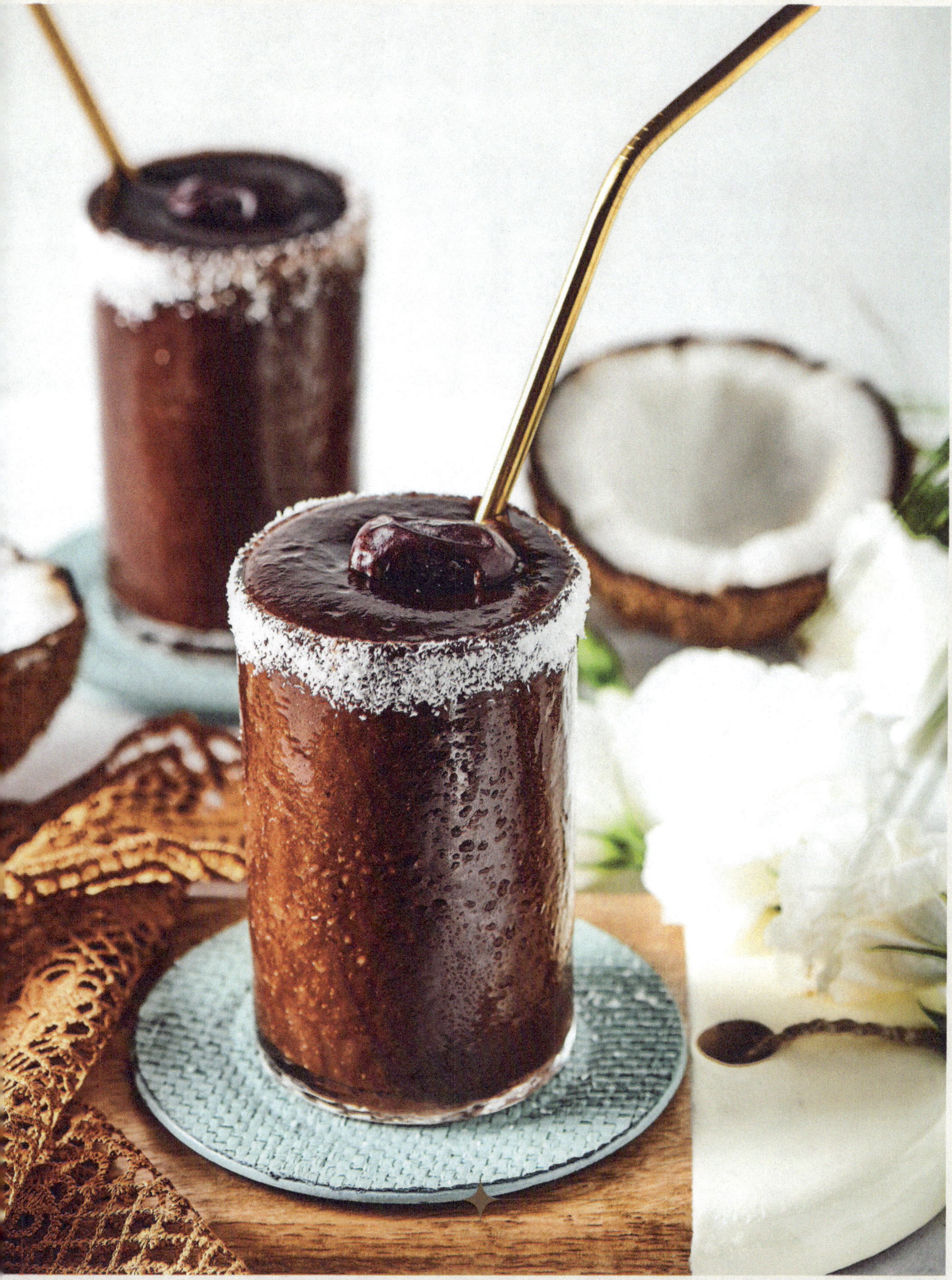

Thanks

Made in the USA
Las Vegas, NV
30 March 2025